KEY PLAYERS IN AA HISTORY

by bob k

Copyright

Key Players in AA History

Copyright 2015 by bob k

All rights reserved. No part of this book may be used or reproduced by any means, graphic, electronic, or mechanical, including photocopying, recording, taping or by any information storage retrieval system without the written permission of the publisher except in the case of brief quotations embodied in critical articles and reviews.

Library and Archives Canada Cataloguing in Publication

K., Bob, 1949-, author
    Key players in AA history / by Bob K.

Issued in print and electronic formats.
ISBN 978-0-9917174-9-1 (pbk.).--ISBN 978-0-9940162-0-1 (epub)

    1. Alcoholics Anonymous--Biography. 2. Alcoholics Anonymous--History. I. Title.

HV5278.K2 2015	362.292'860922	C2015-900066-1
		C2015-900067-X

Published in Canada by AA Agnostica

Interior layout and eBook version formatted by Chris G.

Table of Contents

Introduction...1
SECTION I THE FOUNDERS..3
    Chapter 1 Bill Wilson's Vermont Roots (Prequel to a prequel)...............4
    Chapter 2 Young Bill Wilson (Prequel to BILL'S STORY)......................9
    Chapter 3 The LSD Experiments..18
    Chapter 4 Bill and Rumors of Other Women..25
    Chapter 5 Doctor Bob - Part One (1879-1935).....................................33
    Chapter 6 Doctor Bob - Part Two (1935-1950).....................................41
SECTION II PRE-HISTORY...50
    Chapter 7 Dr. Benjamin Rush...51
    Chapter 8 The Washingtonian Society..58
    Chapter 9 What is "New Thought"?...66
    Chapter 10 Jerry McAuley and The Water Street Mission....................74
    Chapter 11 20th Century Influences on AA...80
    Chapter 12 Charles Towns...91
    Chapter 13 Frank Buchman and The Oxford Group..............................98
    Chapter 14 Sam Shoemaker...106
SECTION III THE PROFESSIONALS...112
    Chapter 15 William James..113
    Chapter 16 Carl Jung..120
    Chapter 17 William D. Silkworth..128
SECTION IV NOTABLE DRUNKS...135
    Chapter 18 Rowland Hazard...136
    Chapter 19 Ebby Thacher..144
    Chapter 20 Henry Parkhurst...151
    Chapter 21 Clarence Snyder...159
    Chapter 22 Jim Burwell..166
    Chapter 23 Richmond Walker...173
SECTION V WOMEN PIONEERS...179
    Chapter 24 Lois Wilson..180
    Chapter 25 Anne Ripley Smith...188
    Chapter 26 Florence R..194
    Chapter 27 Sylvia K...197
    Chapter 28 Marty Mann and the Early Women of AA..........................203
    Chapter 29 Henrietta Seiberling...211
SECTION VI Publicity..217
    Chapter 30 Willard Richardson and the Rockefellers..........................218
    Chapter 31 Selling AA - Early Publicity..224
    Chapter 32 Anonymity in the 21st Century..231

Dedication

In late April 1961, my father, Moe, came home late one night to find his bags packed and a chain lock on the front door. He passed out on the sun porch and contacted AA the next day. He had no idea that he would never drink again; he was just trying to "take the heat off". After some of the initial struggles that so many of us experience, he came to love AA and the whole sober lifestyle.

While never achieving the serenity found by some, he was very real. His was truly a spirituality of imperfection. Frequently, I am approached by what are now oldtimers who tell me of being helped by Moe. He helped a lot of people. In 2006, with his health in rapid decline, he LOVED the two times a week that I would take him to AA meetings. In August, he came with a cane, in September a walker, and by October a wheelchair. In November, he could come no longer.

This book was originally dedicated to Moe K. alone, but the unhappy news of the passing of Ernie Kurtz on January 19, 2015 has prompted me to add his name as a second honoree. You will find quotations from the works of this legendary historian in almost every chapter of my book, but he had a personal humility that would have rendered him self-conscious about being called "legendary".

Nonetheless, he was ubiquitously regarded as the foremost name in the chronicling of AA history. My father also was no great seeker of the limelight. Although touched that I honor his memory, he would likely have offered to step aside to make room for Ernie.

There is no need.

Foreword

Story and storytelling lie at the very heart of Alcoholics Anonymous. AA's basic text and voices within AA meetings across the globe "disclose in a general way what we used to be like, what happened, and what we are like now." From the catalytic meeting between two desperate men in the mid-1930s to today's growing varieties of AA experience, the history of AA is a story about stories and the healing power of mutual storytelling. Anyone wishing to truly understand AA must look first, not to ideas, techniques, or studies, but to stories.

As historians of AA and other recovery mutual aid societies, we have been particularly drawn to the stories of those who played critical roles in the birth and early history of AA, for it is in those stories that we find what distinguishes AA from recovery mutual aid societies that went before but failed to thrive and what distinguishes AA from newer groups that have followed in the wake of AA's worldwide growth. Also of interest to us is why the stories of these early AA figures continue to hold such attraction among rank and file AA members. We suspect such fascination comes from a powerful sense of continued identification - that the stories of AA's founding generation continue to be mirrored in the lives of contemporary AA members. Such interest surely also emanates from a powerful sense of gratitude for a fellowship that so many continue to find life-saving and live-transforming.

Interest is growing in the early history of AA, as evidenced by the growing number of recent biographies of those who played important roles within this history - from multiple biographies of AA co-founder Bill Wilson to biographies of early AA members (e.g., Marty Mann, Clarence Snyder) and non-alcoholics who played critical roles in the early development of AA (e.g., Dr. William Silkworth, Sister Ignatia Gavin, Lois Wilson). We expect this insatiable fascination with AA history to continue unabated far into the future.

In spite of the growing body of literature on AA history, lacking to date has been a collection of brief profiles of these important figures within a single text. That void is now filled by *Key Players in AA History* by Bob K., which offers an engaging window into the lives and times of AA predecessors, AA founders, early AA members (including women pioneers within AA), and the professionals who stood with AA in its early years. Here again is the essence of AA conveyed, as it so often is, in story.

The profiles crafted by Bob K. are drawn from multiple sources and presented in an engaging manner accessible to all those interested in the history of AA. So let the stories begin.

Ernest Kurtz, Author, *Not-God: A History of Alcoholics Anonymous*
William White, Author, *Slaying the Dragon: The History of Addiction Treatment and Recovery in America*

Introduction

This book attempts to tell the story of the "key players" in AA history. Some were alcoholics and some weren't. Some were members of Alcoholics Anonymous, while others were deceased long before AA even existed. It is a fascinating cast of characters.

The most important of these, and possibly the most compelling, is Bill Wilson, of whom a great deal has been written. "Co-founder" may be an overstatement of Dr. Bob Smith's role, but I have endeavored to tell his story in detail, drawing on the limited resources available. With Bill, it is assumed that the reader will be familiar with the basics of the tale, and I have tried to focus on lesser known elements of the Wilson narrative. The book's most controversial essay, "Bill and Rumors of Other Women," is simply a report on what has been written by others, as are all of the other chapters in the book.

With the bulk of the "lesser" players, there are snippets to be found in a variety of places in the existing literature, and on the Internet. I have tried to gather these to present biographies of "key" AA members such as Jim Burwell, Hank Parkhurst, Clarence Snyder, and Richmond Walker. The "Women Pioneers" section provides accounts of the struggles of the earliest female alcoholics to find seats at the recovery banquet, particularly in the Marty Mann essay. Florence R. is the only woman member whose story appeared in the First Edition. Marty and Florence are joined in this section by Henrietta Seiberling, spouses Anne Smith and Lois Wilson, and Chicago's iconic Sylvia K.

The names of William James and Carl Jung are known to virtually all members of Alcoholics Anonymous, yet there is little in our literature about these two intriguing men of academia. Granting the limitations of space, the background of these AA influencers is explored.

The Oxford Group, the Washingtonians, the Emmanuel Movement, and New Thought are commonly cited for their impact on AA thinking and procedures, and a summary of each of these is offered herein. As with the biographies of individuals, the names of these groups, to most, may be far more familiar than their philosophies and practices. Other well-known names are Sam Shoemaker, Frank Buchman, Charles Towns, William Silkworth and Benjamin Rush. These men have engrossing histories, short forms of which are set forth in this book.

There are also less commonly recognized names such as Jerry McAuley, Courtenay Baylor, Frank Jacoby, Elwood Worcester, John Gough, William Mitchell, and others. All of these were involved with movements affecting Alcoholics Anonymous.

I confess to having a perverse fascination with the stories of drunks bringing shame to their wealthy, aristocratic families, and we have such a "rogues' gallery" with Rowland Hazard, Richard Peabody, and class president, Ebby Thacher.

There is a piece on early publicity, and another on the pursuit of Rockefeller sponsorship. "Anonymity in the 21st Century" reviews the history of the anonymity breaches in the 1940s, and examines some "new thinking" on the issue in our new millennium.

I hope you enjoy the book. The history of the fellowship has enthralled many of us - it's an alluring subject. Among the poorest sources of AA history, unfortunately, are AA meetings. As with the "telephone game", much seems to get garbled in the re-transmissions. My astute friend from Pittsburgh is wont to say, "Just assume that anything you hear about AA history in a meeting is wrong".

bob k

SECTION I THE FOUNDERS

Chapter 1 Bill Wilson's Vermont Roots (Prequel to a prequel)

> "War fever ran high in the New England town to which we new, young officers from Plattsburg were assigned, and we were flattered when the first citizens took us to their homes, making us feel heroic. Here was love, applause, war; moments sublime with intervals hilarious. I was part of life at last, and in the midst of the excitement I discovered liquor. I forgot the strong warnings and the prejudices of my people concerning drink. In time we sailed for "Over There". I was very lonely and again turned to alcohol."

Thus begins the book - the "big" book - that has affected the lives of millions of people. From a writer's perspective, it is a strong opening. As a frightened twenty-one year old soldier faces the most uncertain of futures, "Bill's Story" begins with the discovery of alcohol, and its mystical power to transform. In fact, Bill's story starts some twenty years earlier, and in a very real sense, a good deal earlier than that.

Nineteenth Century America

The events described in this essay take place in the nineteenth century, amid circumstances that were stupendously different from the world as we experience it today. Bill Wilson was born in 1895. The main means of transportation were the horse and the railroad. The Wright brothers were mere bicycle shop proprietors, five years away from their very first testing of gliders. The earliest automobiles were seen broken down on the sides of roads, and mocked by those passing in carriages drawn by trusty steeds. The rambunctious Teddy Roosevelt was not yet a "Roughrider", and five years away from becoming America's youngest ever President at forty-two. The sitting President was Grover Cleveland.

The world of 1895 was a dangerous place. Minor infections often spread through the body unchecked - a cut on the hand could lead to a crudely executed amputation, or even a fatality. This America of the late nineteenth century was particularly harsh for women, thousands dying in childbirth, and a distressingly large number of children failed to reach adulthood.

Bill Wilson's parents were born only five years after the end of the American Civil War, and eleven years prior to the Earp brothers' legendary gunfight at the OK Corral. Bill's grandparents, the males only, of course, may have voted for (or against) Abraham Lincoln. Emily Griffith Wilson, Bill's mother, was a highly intelligent woman who became a medical doctor, an osteopath, but she got to vote in no Presidential elections until she was fifty years of age.

The volume of alcoholic beverage consumption had risen explosively earlier in the century, as had the consequences. The forces of temperance were vocal, and in ascension. Drinkers of the time were shamed, much as are cigarette smokers in current times. Dr. Bob's recollection of the same era was that "men who had liquor shipped in from Boston or New York by express were looked upon with great distrust and disfavor by most of the good townspeople". (Doctor Bob's Nightmare, p. 171) National Prohibition was as yet some time away, but the "anti-alcohol" forces were moving forward with a growing momentum.

Divorce was almost unheard of and carried a ferocious stigma, especially in America's heartland. Young Bill Wilson would be teased relentlessly by other children for having no parents; his father had fled across the continent when Bill was nine, and within a year, his mother had abandoned him to her parents' care in order for her to attend school in Boston. Some people suffer the misfortune of having one parent dreadfully unsuited to the role. The adolescent Vermonter seems to have had two.

The Vermont "Ethos"

> *The Green Mountains of Vermont ... were the cradle of the taciturn New England virtues - thrift, honesty, industry. Of course, an undercurrent of New England vices thrived there as well - tobacco, homemade cider, illegal whiskey from Canada, and hotheadedness often legitimized by the euphemism "rugged individualism". Ethan Allen, from a Dorsett family, was the leader of the Green Mountain Boys during the Revolution. A young man who might in another state and another time be classified as a juvenile delinquent, Allen used his hatred of authority and his willingness to take insane risks, to become a great American hero and the epitome of Vermont values. (My Name is Bill, Susan Cheever, p. 9)*

Vermont was a "dry state" when Bill Wilson was growing up, "a state where self-righteousness about not drinking lived side by side with self-righteousness about drinking anyway". (Cheever, p. 13) In the late nineteenth century, the Temperance Movement in America was strong.

Dorset and East Dorset

Even today, Dorset is a very small town with a population of about 2,000. Mount Aeolus divides the town into three distinct hamlets. Bill's sister Dorothy recalled the East Dorset of her youth as "a small village of about twenty homes on two main streets... There were two general stores, two marble mills, a cheese factory, a blacksmith shop, and a cobbler shop; also a public school and two churches". (Pass It On, p. 18) "East Dorset... was a gritty, blue-collar town. The marble quarry owners lived in Dorsett, the workers in East Dorset." (My First Forty Years, Bill Wilson, p. vii)

The East Dorset of the twenty-first century is extremely rural, ethnically homogenous, and possessed of a strange mixture of conservatism and rebelliousness. Quarrying was the main industry in the Dorset area, eventually slowing at the turn of the twentieth century, and nearly extinct by 1920. The marble mined in the East Dorset area was considered among the world's finest, and the local industry was booming around the turn of the century, fuelled by contracts to supply major projects such as the New York Public Library.

Cool Wind and Blinding Light

Bill's paternal grandfather, William C. Wilson, a quarryman, and the son of a quarryman, in 1865 "married Helen Barrows, one of whose ancestors had built the largest house in East Dorset, a great rambling structure... For years this house had been run as an inn called the Old Barrows House, but soon after the wedding William discovered that, along with working in the marble quarries, he enjoyed managing the inn and the name was changed to Wilson House". (Bill W., Robert Thomsen, p. 14) The property was directly across the street from the railroad station, which had opened in East Dorset in 1851.

Grandfather Wilson, enthusiastic innkeeper, had had his good friend, alcohol, turn against him. "One Sunday morning in despair he climbed to the top of Mount Aeolus and beseeched God to help him. He saw a blinding light and felt a great wind, and rushed down to interrupt the service at the Congregational Church. Demanding that the minister leave the pulpit, Wilson described his experience to the congregation... Emily loved this story about her husband's father, and she told it to her son and husband as often as they would listen. In the eight years that he lived after that experience, the elder Wilson never had another drink." (Cheever, p. 17)

Fifty-seven years later, the extremely desperate future AA founder was a very frightened patient at Towns Hospital. It was his fourth visit. Perhaps the oft told tale of his grandfather came to mind. Bill's 1934 "spiritual experience" was remarkably similar to that of the old innkeeper near the summit of a windy mountain in 1877. Perhaps a nurse inadvertently contributed to the grand event by leaving a window open.

Gilman and Family

Following the death of her husband in 1885, Helen Wilson was assisted in the day-to-day business of innkeeping by her two teenaged sons, one of whom was Bill's father, Gilman, called "Gilly" by some, and "Jolly" by others. William C. Wilson's son, Gilman Barrows Wilson followed his father's footsteps into three family enterprises - quarry work, hotel management, and drinking. Gilman "was an immensely likable man, known as an excellent storyteller with a fine voice that got even better with a few drinks... He managed a marble quarry near East Dorset, and he was so highly regarded as a leader that later, when he went off to work in British Columbia, a number of old East Dorset quarrymen pulled up stakes to follow him". (Pass It On, p. 14)

"Gilly" may have been, what some would term today, a "functioning alcoholic". For this or other reasons, throughout his life Bill remained reluctant to brand his father an alcoholic, all the while acknowledging a history of alcohol abuse among the Wilsons.

"Emily taught school before she married... She had intelligence, determination, ambition and immense courage. She would later become successful in a profession, long before most career fields were open to women." (Pass It On, p. 15) One may wonder what the gregarious Gilly saw in the bookish and reserved Emily Griffith? "Emily was a tall, extremely handsome young woman with masses of dark chestnut hair and deep-set thoughtful eyes." (Thomsen, p. 15) Physical attraction and a lack of other options in the tiny village may have driven their decision to marry. At twenty-four, Emily may have felt some social pressure to stave off "spinsterhood".

As with Griffith before her, Emily was a proud woman, but also high-strung and hard. She did not have a forgiving nature, and she rapidly tired of her husband's unrelenting recalcitrance. Early on, it was evident that "these two were of extremely dissimilar temperaments". (Thomsen, p. 13) Of course, as is often the case, "Emily had hoped that marriage would turn him into a responsible man". (Cheever, p. 7)

"Emily found herself in love with a fellow she never truly understood. If, during their brief engagement, certain things troubled her, she was quite able to rationalize them... And whatever worries might have presented themselves, they were all ignored in the beautiful spring of 1894... and in September they were married in the white Congregational church." (Thomsen, pp. 15-16) Marriage failed to tame the gregarious quarryman. The thought that fatherhood would render "Jolly" Wilson more domesticated probably crossed Emily's mind, and she became pregnant early in 1895.

A Difficult Birth

It was the night before Thanksgiving, when the pains of child labor drove Emily Griffiths Wilson from preparations for the next day's meal. "Emily's pains drove her from out of the kitchen into the north parlor. She lay on a couch there, trying to breathe, doubling over as the contractions wracked her body... In and out of consciousness, she screamed and cried out as midnight passed. Inside the house, the midwife and her mother tried to comfort her. Outside, Bill's friend-to-be, Mark Whalon, remembered a crowd of local boys gathered on the porch listening to Emily Wilson's screams as evidence of the strangeness of the adult world. Later, Emily was fond of saying that Bill's birth had almost killed her." (Cheever, p. 18)

The future founder of Alcoholics Anonymous entered the world on November 26th, 1895, "in a little room in back of a bar".

Chapter 2 Young Bill Wilson (Prequel to BILL'S STORY)

The Prequel Begins

It was the night before Thanksgiving when the pains of child labor drove Emily Griffith Wilson from preparations for the next day's meal.

> *Emily's pains drove her from out of the kitchen into the north parlor. She lay on a couch there, trying to breathe, doubling over as the contractions wracked her body… In and out of consciousness, she screamed and cried out as midnight passed. Inside the house, the midwife and her mother tried to comfort her. Outside, Bill's friend-to-be, Mark Whalon, remembered a crowd of local boys gathered on the porch listening to Emily Wilson's screams as evidence of the strangeness of the adult world. Later, Emily was fond of saying that Bill's birth had almost killed her." (My Name Is Bill, Susan Cheever, p. 18)*

The future founder of Alcoholics Anonymous, "William Griffith Wilson was born on November 26, 1895, in a room behind a bar… about 3 am on a wintry morning." (Pass It On, p. 13)

Bill's mother had emotional problems and a low tolerance for stress. Prescribed a "rest cure," Emily went to Florida, where there were family friends, and she stayed for an extended period of time. In this she found salutary benefits, and the process was repeated. She was generally accompanied by her pre-school age daughter, three years Bill's junior, on these sojourns but her young son was left behind.

Rutland

In 1903, when Bill was seven, the family moved to Rutland, a city of about 15,000, twenty-five miles north up the valley. This transition was certainly difficult for a shy lad from a village of perhaps 200. Problems between his parents had been increasing, with Emily spending considerable time away in Florida visiting friends. "The move promised a change in a marriage that had bogged down in the stifling details of domesticity. Emily's life, at this juncture, appears to have been devoted to an effort to analyze and then in some way dominate her circumstances." (Bill W., Robert Thomsen, p. 16)

Fifty years later, in a speech delivered in St. Louis, Bill reflected on the troubled Rutland times. "I was tall and gawky, and I felt pretty bad about it because the smaller kids could push me around in quarrels. I remember being very depressed for a year or more, and then I began to develop a fierce resolve to win. I resolved to be a 'Number One' man." (Licit And Illicit Drugs, E.M. Bruckner) "It was during this period that I can see how my willpower and distinction, later to keynote my whole life, was developed. I had many playmates, but I think I regarded all of them as competitors. At everything I must excel." (My First Forty Years, Bill Wilson, p. 15)

A Series of Unfortunate Events

"But then, in 1905, an incident occurred... There was talk... an affront to dignity... and that was more than the proud Emily could stand. Gilly left town." (Thomsen, p. 17) Biographer, Susan Cheever is more direct: "Gilman apparently got involved with the local minister's daughter. Emily took Dorothy on long visits to Florida that were ostensibly for health. She had a series of what her son heard called nervous breakdowns. For a while, she was sent to a sanitarium. Then she decided her breakdowns were caused by her marriage." (Cheever, p. 20)

Whatever Gilman Wilson's flaws, they did not block the love and admiration of his only son. "When he stood beside his father, Bill Wilson never felt too tall. He never felt skinny then or thought his ears stuck out too far and was never afraid that he was going to do something awkward that would make people call him 'Beanpole.'" (Thomsen, p. 5)

One cool, autumn night a very drunk Gilman Wilson took his son for a late night wagon ride. The quarryman was silent, perhaps in his own thoughts, as they rode out to his little manager's shed. Leaving his son in the cart, the senior Wilson went inside for some time, not forgetting his jug of hard cider. In the carriage, a trepidatious young Bill Wilson, not yet ten years old, waited expectantly, and feared the worst as he remembered his parents' dinnertime argument.

"'You'll take care of her, won't you, Billy?' he said. 'You'll be good to your mother, and to little Dotty too.' And before he could answer, his father reached out a hand and mussed the back of his hair. 'Sure you will,' he said. 'Sure. You're okay, Billy,' then withdrew his hand, and Billy knew this was it." (Thomsen, p. 9) No further explanation was given. "When he awakened in the morning, his sister, Dorothy, was waiting to tell him their father had gone away. This was in the autumn of 1905. Billy didn't see his father again until the summer of 1914, and by then they had discovered they had nothing at all to say to one another." (Thomsen, p. 12)

Easily seen in hindsight, there was a "fundamental and insuperable incompatibility of Bill Wilson's parents, who had little in common... This was a case of opposites attracting, and then colliding." (Bill W and Mr. Wilson, Matthew J. Raphael, pp. 23-24) "Emily had hoped that marriage would turn him (Gilly) into a responsible man." (Cheever, p. 7) It did not. Some people are perhaps not well-suited for parenthood. Young Bill Wilson seems to have had the misfortune of having two parents of such type.

Nonetheless, "Bill suffered loss and abandonment at a tender age, although he never suggested that this had much to do with his alcoholism." (My Search for Bill W., Mel B., p. 9)

Mommie Dearest

In the spring of 1906, Emily Wilson took her children on a picnic to Dorset Pond (aka Emerald Lake), where she made two announcements to her children.

First, their father was never coming back, and secondly, she was moving to Boston to study medicine. The second revelation had a corollary – the children were not going with her, but would be staying with her parents.

"It was an agonizing experience for one who apparently had the emotional sensitivity that I did. I hid the wound, however, and never talked about it with anyone, even my sister." (Pass It On, p. 24) He went into a year-long depression, and Lois later claimed that it had "made him feel set apart and inferior to youngsters who lived with a mother and father." (Pass It On, p. 27)

Number One Man

"Fayette and Ella Griffith proved kindly as surrogate parents. Yet deep within young Bill Wilson ached a feeling of rejection... the more painful because, in his mind, it was deserved... Grandfather Fayette tried hard to be a father to the boy, but he was a taciturn and introverted man, a too quiet person." (Not-God, Ernest Kurtz, p. 10)

"I had to be first in everything because in my perverse heart, I felt I was the least of God's creatures." (Alcoholics Anonymous Comes Of Age, p. 53) It was Fayette who provided the challenge to be the first non-Australian to build a working boomerang, and after six months of frustration and failures, persistence paid off. "I sawed the headboard of my bed to get just the right piece of wood, and... whittled away'... He called his grandfather to watch as he threw the boomerang. It circled the churchyard and almost struck Fayette in the head as it came back. 'I remember how ecstatically happy and stimulated I was by this crowning success,' Bill said. 'I had become a Number One man.'" (Pass It On, p. 30)

"Whenever his proud grandfather reported the tale in Bill's hearing, all the lights in the room seemed to come up brighter. He was filled with a kind of power, and when they went on about his accomplishment, he could feel it growing, spreading through his body, as if some potent drug had been released." (Not-God, p. 11)

An Atheist

The 12 + 12 and Chapter 4 of the Big Book make it quite clear that Bill Wilson was possessed of a somewhat skewed grasp of what lies in the minds of atheists and agnostics. The genesis of these misunderstandings dwells, of course, in his own story.

Until the age of eleven, "Bill Wilson went unquestioningly to the Congregational Sunday School across the green. All the Griffiths went to church." (Cheever, p. 44) One weekend, all the children were asked to sign temperance pledges. "Although Wilson knew a great deal about drinking and what drinking could do to a family, he wasn't about to let some Sunday School temperance preacher tell him what he had to do... He walked away from Sunday School and away from church. He decided he was an atheist. If there was a God, how could he have allowed all this to happen. If he was to have a decent life, he knew he would have to build it for himself, in spite of God, with his own intelligence and determination." (Cheever, p. 45)

Mark Whalon

"Bill's closest friend from about 1908 was Mark Whalon, a university student about ten years his senior. The two... passed much time together when Mark was home on vacation, the boy Bill revelling in his enthusiastic friend's quotations from Shakespeare and Burns, Ingersol and Marx, Charles Darwin and William Graham Sumner." (Not-God, p. 11) "Mark Whalon became Bill's guide through the complications of life, literature and education." (Cheever, p. 37)

One day, they stopped by a tavern, and young Bill Wilson was struck by the atmosphere. "Bill felt nothing but a crazy happy feeling of lightness. He had laughed so hard and so much, the muscles of his stomach ached, but his whole being was relaxed... He wanted it again." (Thomsen, p. 47) For one of the rare times in his life, young Bill experienced the pleasure of fellowship, community with one's fellow men, and he experienced its palpable enervating power. "He knew this was the friendliest gathering he'd ever been in... everybody was talking together." (Thomsen, p. 46) His good friend had introduced him to new 'friends.' "When Mark Whalon died in September of 1956, Bill Wilson collapsed first into hysteria and then into one of the depressions that had become dreadfully familiar to him and to his wife and mother." (Cheever, p. 43)"

It was Lois who opined that in his entire life, Bill Wilson had only had two friends, the second being Dr. Bob.

Burr and Burton

"The teenage Bill Wilson spent most of his high school years at Burr and Burton, a prestigious school in Manchester, Vermont. He had thought of himself as homely, awkward, and vastly inferior to his classmates. In fact, photographs of him at the time show him to be tall, broad shouldered, and handsome, and he became president of the senior class, a star football player, and the star pitcher and captain of the baseball team. Bill also acted in the school's stage productions, and he was first violin in the student orchestra." (Bill W., Francis Hartigan, p. 10) "With each new triumph, a new dimension seemed added to his life... (he) was beginning to develop something of a reputation as a raconteur.... (and) he was proving that if he adhered to his scheme – receiving a challenge, formulating a plan of action and then pursuing the plan – he'd not only be accepted, he would be admired, envied." (Thomsen, p. 51)

And it was while he was at Burr and Burton that Bill met Ebby Thacher, a man he would see, and drink with, occasionally over his adult years, and the man who would re-enter Bill's life in such a dramatic way in November of 1934.

Things were going well for Bill, and they were about to get better.

The Summer of Love

"During the spring of his junior year in 1912, Bill fell 'ecstatically in love,' as he said, with Bertha Bamford, a classmate and the daughter of the local Episcopal minister. (She was) a beautiful, brainy, and popular girl." (Raphael, p. 29) His affection was reciprocated, and her family welcomed him. Bill's autobiography provides a fore-telling of ideas that would years later appear in Chapter 5 of the Big Book:

> I'm going to make quite a point of an easily understood triad of primary drives. The drive for distinction and power; the drive for security – physical, financial and emotional; and the desire to love and to be loved, romantically or otherwise. Well, you see, at this period, now that I am in love, I am fully compensated on all these primary instinctual drives. I have all the prestige there is to have in school. I excel, indeed I'm the number one where I choose to be. Consequently, I am emotionally secure. My grandfather is my protector and is generous with my spending money. And now I love and am loved, fully and completely for the first time in my life. Therefore, I am deliriously happy and am a success according to my specifications. (My First Forty Years, p. 30)

"In November, Bertha went to New York City with her parents, where she underwent surgery (to have a small tumor removed) in Flower Hospital and died from postsurgical hemorrhaging. Bill first learned what had happened when he was summoned to the school chapel along with the other students to hear the tragic news of their classmate... Bill reacted to the loss of Bertha in the same way he had to his parents' divorce and their subsequent departure from his life. This time though his devastation was even more severe. The depression he plunged into... lasted three years." (Hartigan, p. 19-20) "My whole career and my whole life utterly collapsed." (My First Forty Years, p. 30)

"It was simply a cataclysm of such anguish as I've since had but two or three times. It eventuated what was called an old-fashioned nervous breakdown, which meant, I now realize a tremendous depression." (Pass It On, p. 35) The most skeptical among us can be forgiven, perhaps, for wondering if Bertha's tragic demise could have all been the result of a botched abortion.

This tragedy propelled young Bill Wilson to a "crisis of faith," which surely must be doubly troubling for atheists. He "felt all his faith in providence slipping away… all his loving meant nothing to the terrible ongoing forces of creation." (Thomsen, p. 63) "He had discovered his radical powerlessness over his own and other destinies. He had also discovered his proclivity for depression and began to search for an emotional anodyne." (Raphael, p. 31)

Norwich University

At this time of crushing devastation for her only son, Emily interrupted her own busy schedule to tell Bill to "snap out of it."

Bill would move on from Burr and Burton to Norwich University, America's first private military college, in Northfield, Vermont. "In high school Wilson was a star athlete, orchestra leader, and president of his class. But he was also neurasthenic and depressive; after his first year at Norwich University, mysterious heart palpitations, stomach upset, and generalized malaise laid him low for a year." (The Language of the Heart, Trysh Travis, p. 66)

None of the Burr and Burton stardom was relived at Norwich. He was miserable there. This was September, 1914, and in August he had made the continent-wide trek to see his father for the first time in nine years. The reunion was disappointing.

At Norwich, the almost nineteen year old's academic performance had him holding his own, but socially he remained withdrawn. "Early in the second semester, he fell… and injured his elbow. He insisted on going to Boston to be treated by his mother, who was now a practicing osteopath. He had no desire to return to school." (Pass It On, p. 44) Returning to Norwich on the train, Bill had a severe panic attack, and these episodes continued back at school. "No physical cause could be found for his troubles… 'at the end of a couple of weeks, I was sent to my grandfather in East Dorset, which was exactly where I wanted to go.' He was overcome by inertia, unable to do anything… The doctor gave him a bromide and tried to persuade him that there was nothing wrong with his heart." (Pass It On, p. 45)

Lois Burnham

"Eight months after the death of Bertha, Bill had met Lois Burnham while she was vacationing at Emerald Lake near East Dorset. Lois was a receptionist at the YWCA in Brooklyn and four years Bill's senior." (The Roots of Alcoholics Anonymous, Bill Pittman, p. 145) They shared a mutual interest in boating. "They spent sunny summer days racing each other up and down the little lake. There was something about Bill Wilson that intrigued her even though he was a teenager and she was a young lady. Was he letting her win?" (Cheever, p. 61)

The following summer the relationship grew. "Bill confided to Lois his dreams of glory as well as his many doubts and fears. Lois thrilled to and completely believed in the former, sympathized and promised to help with the latter. By the end of the summer they were secretly engaged." (Hartigan, p. 24) "I think Lois came along and picked me up as tenderly as a mother does a child... I began to fall in love with her." (My First Forty Years, p. 32)

He returned to school that fall and once more found himself in trouble. In revealing her secret relationship with Bill to her seventeen year old sister Barb, Lois found out that her beau had been quite flirtatious and had done some kissing with the younger Burnham. Bill sheepishly explained this away as a subterfuge to mask his secret engagement to Lois. She forgave him, and a long pattern of such absolution was begun.

War Fever

Significant events were taking place in Europe and in 1917, all classes at Norwich were cancelled and students automatically became members of the US reserve forces. Young Bill Wilson was saved from poor grades and disciplinary actions by America's looming participation in World War I.

Given options, Bill went with the safest choice, the Coastal Artillery. "In his mind he was a coward for joining the heavy artillery..." (Cheever, p. 73) "I had never had, at least for many years, such a terrible feeling of shame and guilt. How I had let my ancestors down!" (My First Forty Years, p. 41) Following training in Virginia, Bill was sent to Fort Rodman, Mass., where "the first citizens took us to their homes, making us feel heroic." This is where the 'Bronx cocktail' of "Bill's Story" has its origins.

Bill would later described that period in his life, and his compulsion to drink:

> My self-consciousness was such that I simply had to take that drink. So I took it, and another one, and then, lo, the miracle! That strange barrier that had existed between me and all men and women, even the closest, seemed to instantly go down. I felt that I belonged where I was, I belonged to the universe, I

was part of things at last. Oh, the magic of those first three or four drinks! I became the life of the party. I actually could please the guests. I could talk freely, volubly. I could talk well... (T)he next time or two, I passed out completely. (My First Forty Years, p. 43)

It would be another couple of decades before he would climb out of a bed in Towns Hospital, a sober alcoholic, meet Dr. Robert Smith and, just few years after that, write the Big Book.

But let us stop at Bill's Story, the opening to the Big Book. Let us end at the beginning, as it were, having accompanied Bill from his birth in the back of a bar to New England, where "war fever ran high."

Chapter 3 The LSD Experiments

How could Bill W., Grand Poobah of sobriety ever have allowed himself to join the Learyesque acidheads and "turn on, tune in, and drop out?"
(Bill W. and Mr. Wilson, Matthew Raphael, p. 164)

The Juice

Twenty-five years ago, O.J. Simpson was just an ex-football player, a commentator, and a car rental company spokesperson. While some of his movie acting may have bordered on the criminal, he had not yet been the centerpiece in 1995's "trial of the century". Fifty years ago, Simpson had no national notoriety at all. There had been no NFL rushing record (1973), nor even the Heisman Trophy (1968) awarded to the best college football player in America.

Sixty years ago, O.J. Simpson was just another black kid in a poor neighborhood in San Francisco. There had as yet been no "If it does not fit, you must acquit". There had been no "Miami's got the oranges, but Buffalo's got the 'Juice'". In a very real sense, O.J. Simpson was not yet O.J. Simpson.

Of course, it is difficult, if not impossible, to erase from the American consciousness, the various events that brought both fame and infamy to the onetime youngster in "the projects". Perhaps it is even more difficult to imagine a time when LSD was not yet LSD, as we are familiar with it today.

Timothy Leary's admonition to "tune in, turn on, and drop out" has been with us since the mid 1960's.

When Bill Wilson first tried LSD, at the Veterans Administration Hospital in Los Angeles, in 1956, the LSD world of Timothy Leary and hippies was fully ten years away. LSD was a lab experiment. The street drug incarnation of LSD simply hadn't yet happened. In a very real sense, in 1956, LSD was not yet LSD.

Ernie Kurtz

In the 1970s, "Ernest Kurtz was given full and complete access to the archives of the General Service Office of Alcoholics Anonymous in New York. His unhindered research, coupled with extensive interviews of surviving early members and friends of AA, has resulted in an account with documented accuracy". (Not-God, Ernest Kurtz, About the Book, p. vi)

Mr. Kurtz came to the study of history after professional experience in both religion and psychology. His study of the genesis and the workings of AA led to a Ph.D. in the History of American Civilization from Harvard University, in 1978.

In the course of this research, details of Bill Wilson's LSD experimentation were uncovered. "An AA trustee had asked me to consider excluding that part of my dissertation (Not-God) from publication, but after consultation with my mentors, I decided to retain it as an essential part of the story." (The Collected Ernie Kurtz, p. 39)

Dr. Albert Hoffman

The chemical, d-lysergic acid diethylamide, was first produced in 1938 by a Swiss research chemist employed by Sandoz Laboratories, now Novartis, since a 1996 merger. Dr. Albert Hoffman only later, in 1943, discovered LSD's properties. Hoffman's findings "attracted interest, for scientists saw in LSD-25, as it was then called, 'a drug which would make a normal person psychotic.' That implied a chemical basis for insanity". (Collected Kurtz, p. 41)

A chemical cause suggested a possible chemical cure. Sandoz began clinical trials and marketed the substance, from 1947 through the mid-1960s, under the name Delysid as a psychiatric drug, thought useful for treating a wide variety of mental ailments, ranging from alcoholism to sexual deviancy. Sandoz suggested in its marketing literature that psychiatrists take LSD themselves, to gain a better subjective understanding of the schizophrenic experience, and many did exactly that and so did other scientific researchers.

A Time Magazine feature in 1954 had produced a flood of attention to the Sandoz product. "In the 1950s, LSD was widely thought to have psycho-therapeutic potential. Research...was undertaken by some of the most prestigious medical and scientific institutions in the country." (Bill W., Francis Hartigan, p. 177)

Hoffer and Osmond

Doctors Abram Hoffer and Humphrey Osmond worked in a mental hospital in Saskatchewan, Canada, "treating alcoholics as well as schizophrenics, and their interest centered on patients suffering both disorders. These were their toughest cases, for the schizophrenia seemed to impede the kind of insightful experience thought to be required if an alcoholic was to stop drinking". (Collected Kurtz, p. 41)

In 1952, the clinicians began to incorporate the use of LSD in their treatment. The "initial intention was to induce a psychic experience similar to delirium tremens, or DT's, in the hope that it might serve to 'shock' alcoholics out of their dependence on alcohol... LSD was considered as a last resort, to be tried with otherwise unreachable alcoholics... In the aftermath of the DT's, some alcoholics with whom all intervention efforts had failed were capable of understanding the desperation of their condition and responding to treatment". (Hartigan, pp. 177-178)

Bill Wilson was "extremely unthrilled" when he first learned of the Canadians' research through his friend, Gerald Heard. He opposed giving drugs to alcoholics. The psychiatrists had discovered that

> *the main effect of the drug was to bring on an experience of illumination... (which) seemed to allow some of their patients who had previously resisted 'the spiritual' to accept it and thus to 'get' the AA program.*
>
> *The results reported by Hoffer and Osmond fascinated Wilson. When LSD was given to alcoholics in mental hospitals, 'of whom AA could touch and help only about five percent, they had about 15 percent recoveries.' One of the Canadian studies reported a recovery rate of 70 percent. (Collected Kurtz, p. 42)*

Motives

Bill Wilson had replaced his thirst for alcohol with a passionate thirst for helping alcoholics. He "had learned, in those first twenty years, that the main obstacle to drunks 'getting' AA was 'the spiritual'". (Collected Kurtz, p.

42) Here also was an increased hope for helping those previously considered somewhat outside of the prime target market.

> *Those who do not recover are people who cannot or will not completely give themselves to this simple program, usually men and women who are constitutionally incapable of being honest with themselves. There are such unfortunates. They are not at fault; they seem to have been born that way. They are naturally incapable of grasping and developing a manner of living which demands rigorous honesty. Their chances are less than average. (AA Big Book, p. 58)*

The *Common Sense of Drinking* has been acknowledged as having been a powerful influence on Bill Wilson's understanding of alcoholism. The author of the 1931 publication, lay therapist Richard Peabody, had strongly advised against working with "psychotics." Wilson had some experiences which confirmed Peabody's concerns. Dr. Bob and the Good Oldtimers relates the tale of Eddie R., the very first Akron "prospect". Eddie was "a borderline mental case" according to Smitty, Dr. Bob's son.

After a variety of misadventures including wife-beating, escapes and chases, a threatened suicide, and a knife being brandished at Anne Smith, they gave up on Eddie.

The LSD trials were achieving decent success rates with this most unpromising demographic: "Bill became enthusiastic about the potential, saying 'Anything that helps alcoholics is good and shouldn't be dismissed out of hand.' That was typical of his openness to new ideas and therapy." (Grateful to Have Been There, Nell Wing, p. 81)

Bill Wilson

On August 29, 1956, Bill Wilson took LSD in a laboratory setting. "When Bill took LSD, use of the drug was legal. He first took it as a participant in a medically supervised experiment with Gerald Heard and Aldous Huxley in California." (Hartigan, p. 178) To return to the point of the early paragraphs, this was a full ten years before Timothy Leary's "turn on" revolution. There was no incense burning, no Jefferson Airplane on the stereo, and it is highly unlikely that Bill was wearing bell bottoms and a tie-dyed t-shirt.

In a very real sense, LSD wasn't LSD yet.

Its use was limited to hospitals, clinics, labs and universities.

> *"Here, then, is one clear reason why Bill Wilson experimented with LSD: he was seeking still further ways of helping alcoholics, specifically those alcoholics who could not seem to attain sobriety in Alcoholics Anonymous because, apparently, they could not 'get the spiritual'." (Collected Kurtz, p. 42) Support for this research came from a surprising source. When one of his parishioners expressed concern to Sam Shoemaker, the reverend consulted his superior, Bishop Pardue who "declared himself 'in utmost sympathy with what (Bill) is doing.' The bishop, Shoemaker reported to Wilson, 'is convinced that the biochemical factor is of the greatest importance...half our problems are bio-chemical and do not go back to sin and cannot be wholly governed by prayer'." (Collected Kurtz, p. 43)*

Wilson was insightful in noting, "the probability that prayer, fasting, meditation, despair and other conditions that predispose one to classical mystical experiences do have their chemical components". (Wilson letter to Shoemaker, 1958) "Bill W. was himself drawn to seek ways of making more available the 'sudden and spectacular upheavals' that although not necessary seemed very, very useful." (Collected Kurtz, p. 45)

"Wilson faced the classic problem of religious mystics: how to speak of that which cannot be captured by words? AA spirituality is founded in an experience of release, a free-ing – the sense that one has been saved... The co-founder felt a responsibility to make that deeper less glib experience available to a wider population of alcoholics... Bill realized... his own background in matters of 'the spiritual' was hardly typical." (Collected Kurtz, p. 46)

There was an additional benefit ensuing from the LSD trials. "I am certain that the LSD experiment has helped me very much... I find myself with a heightened color perception and an appreciation of beauty almost destroyed by my years of depression." (Letter to Gerald Heard, 1957)

Transparency

Once more, we return to our attempt to capture the perspective of the time. "The 1950s were not the 1990s... Far from keeping secret his experience with LSD, AA's co-founder judiciously but eagerly spread the word, inviting not only his wife and his secretary but also trusted friends to join his experiments... Clearly, Bill experienced no sense of shame or guilt over his activities... Bill was still seeking a cure for alcoholism... a way of helping more alcoholics get sober in Alcoholics Anonymous... one more facet in his persistent pursuit of 'the spiritual.'" (Collected Kurtz, pp. 40-41)

Bill had "a major enthusiasm for LSD, and, later, for niacin, a B-complex vitamin". (Hartigan, p. 9) There were of course, objections from a variety of sources and pressure to "cease and desist", which ultimately, but grudgingly, he did. A clear consensus of when the experimentation was halted is not available. Matthew Raphael and Nell Wing have the end in late 1959, Kurtz the early 1960s, and Francis Hartigan has the activity continuing well into the 1960s.

Cool Wind A'blowin'

"Perhaps the best understanding of addiction presents it as an attempt to fill a spiritual void with a material reality." (Collected Kurtz, p. 48) Twenty years of working with alcoholics had convinced Bill Wilson that his Towns Hospital "hot flash," whatever the exact cause, had given him an advantage over those not sharing such experiences themselves. If LSD could produce some sort of transformative event, then the AA founder was interested in looking into it. Hoffer and Osmond's early results were encouraging.

> *A friend of mine, saved from alcoholism, during the last fatal phases of the disease, by a spontaneous theophany which changed his life as completely as St. Paul's was changed on the road to Damascus, has taken lysergic acid two or three times and affirms that his experience under the drug is identical with the spontaneous experience which changed his life - the only difference being that the spontaneous experience did not last as long as the chemically induced one. There is, obviously, a field here for serious and reverent experimentation.(Aldous Huxley to Father Thomas Merton, 10 January 1959)*

Lessons

Although prompted by motives that were pure, the LSD experimentation may indicate a lack of good judgment, or the alcoholic's common propensity for flying headlong into projects with an enthusiastic intensity, perhaps indicative of the "malady".

Damn the torpedoes, full speed ahead!!

"The 'lesson' of Bill Wilson's experimentation with LSD? If perfection is your goal, don't go looking for models among the members - or even the founders - of Alcoholics Anonymous." (Collected Kurtz, p. 49)

Ours is truly, a spirituality of imperfection.

Chapter 4 Bill and Rumors of Other Women

> *History cannot proceed by silences. The chronicler of ill-recorded times has none the less to tell the tale. If facts are lacking, rumors must serve. Failing affidavits, he must build with gossip.*
>
> Winston Churchill

In "Bill's Story," the protagonist lets us know that among his problems as a drinker, there were assignations with "other women," leading to remonstrations from his aggrieved wife.

> *"There were many unhappy scenes in our sumptuous apartment. There had been no real infidelity, for loyalty to my wife, helped at times by extreme drunkenness, kept me out of those scrapes."* (Big Book, p. 3)

"Despite his technical innocence, something at least imaginably adulterous did occur, and more than once." (Bill W. and Mr. Wilson, Matthew Raphael, p. 53)

Decades later, a non-inhaling U.S. President would sound much the same – "I did NOT have sex with that woman!" And, of course, "It depends on what the meaning of the word 'is' is."

Innocence, by way of technicality. Or, in the case of the AA founder, possibly a white lie for the protection of Lois Wilson.

It is worth remembering that this was a different era, an age in which many wives of the men of power or prestige, wealth or genius, turned a blind eye to a certain amount of sexual philandering, if they were able to "keep up appearances."

In one of the many films about JFK, Jacqueline becomes enraged, not by her husband's infidelity, but by his lack of discretion.

Pass It On

"Pass It On," first published in 1984, documents some bizarre, and possibly embarrassing scenarios involving clinical depression, Ouija boards, séances, vitamin therapy, and LSD experimentation, but there are no accounts of marital infidelity. That there is not the barest mention of Bill's most serious lover, Helen Wynn, belies any attempts to present "Pass It On" as less than sanitized.

Helen Wynn was bequeathed ten percent of Wilson's book royalties. This was both in his will, and in an agreement with GSO.

It is likely that AA's "official" account, "Pass It On" would have been further redacted if not for an injudicious granting of full archives access to Ernest Kurtz in the late 70s, when he was researching the incomparable chronicle of AA history, "Not-God." The "cat was out of the bag" on LSD, etc. in 1979.

Robert Thomsen

Of all the Wilson biographers, no one had greater direct access to the founder than Robert Thomsen. He worked directly alongside Bill for twelve years, from 1959 to 1971. Published in 1975, the Thomsen biography, "Bill W." as would be the case with the Conference-approved "Pass It On", was "authorized". "Lois read and approved (it)." (Bill W., Susan Cheever, p. 224)

Under such scrutiny, Thomsen was a co-conspirator in the "code of silence" and was able only to hint at matters sexual. "...Fitz, Hank and Bill were three extraordinarily healthy males... men who had meant to live life passionately..." (Bill W., Robert Thomsen, p. 226)

In spite of being undeniably "sanitized," the Thomsen effort is worth reading, although not above legitimate criticism. "That the book contains neither documentation nor index reinforces the notion that Bill W. is more of a biographical novel than a biography." (Raphael, p. 19)

His description of a Clinton St. meeting of the 1930s is particularly heartening for non-believing AA members who would arrive in the decades to come.

> "There were agnostics in the Tuesday night group, and several hardcore atheists who objected to any mention of God. On many evenings Bill had to remember his first meeting with Ebby. He'd been told to ask for help from anything he believed in. These men, he could see, believed in each other and in the strength of the group. At some time each of them had been totally unable to stop drinking on his own, yet when two of them had worked at it together, somehow they had become more powerful and they had finally been able to stop. This, then – whatever it was that occurred between them – was what they could accept as a power greater than themselves." (Thomsen, p. 230)

Francis Hartigan

Pulitzer Prize winner, "Nan Robertson in her 1988 book, 'Getting Better,'… briefly discusses Bill's sex life." (Cheever, p. 227)

> "She (Lois) believed in him fiercely and tended his flame. Yet, particularly during his sober decades in AA in the forties, fifties and sixties, Bill Wilson was a compulsive womanizer. His flirtations and his adulterous behavior filled him with guilt, according to old-timers close to him, but he continued to stray off the reservation." (Getting Better, Nan Robertson, p. 36)

These peccadilloes received an even greater airing in the 2000 Francis Hartigan bio, once again titled "Bill W." Hartigan was Lois' secretary in the 1980s, and was given access to her voluminous supply of records and letters relating to her husband, and to AA itself.

> "Bill Wilson's personal popularity in AA circles was enormous. People would wait in line at large AA gatherings just to touch his sleeve. Many treated him like the Messiah or, in today's world, a rock star… Wilson also had his enemies, many of them people who were previously among his staunchest allies. They accused him of betrayal, of power mongering, of lacking principle… of personal immorality, and even of insanity… With the exception of the womanizing, none of those charges were true." (Hartigan, p. 1)

Clearly, Hartigan was not out to do a hatchet job, but to present a picture of Bill Wilson without the customary air-brushing.

James Houck, an old Oxford Grouper who has been brought to some notoriety by "Back To Basics" founder, Wally P., "recalls that he (Bill) often regaled its (Oxford Group's) male members with tales of his exploits... Bill was frequently 'checked' for his smoking and womanizing, but he simply ignored these admonitions." (Hartigan, pp. 68-69)

Hartigan also interviewed Tom Powers Sr., Bill's writing partner on the "Twelve & Twelve," who stated that "Bill was frequently overwhelmed by the guilt and remorse he felt as a consequence of his infidelities and the turmoil his affairs were causing within the Fellowship." (Hartigan, p. 170) Powers insisted that Wilson's guilt over his infidelities was responsible for his depression. No argument was returned. "You're right... But I can't give it up." (Hartigan, p. 171)

> *"While other people I spoke with insisted that Lois never knew about Bill's affairs, Tom insisted that 'Lois knew everything and she didn't have to guess about it, either. A lot of people tried to protect her, but there were others who would run to Stepping Stones to tell Lois all about it when they saw Bill with another woman." (Hartigan, p. 171)*

Sexual fidelity does not seem to be something of which Bill Wilson was capable.

> *"His father was not faithful, and it was not something he had been brought up to consider a value... Barry Leach, a longtime AA member who was a close friend of Bill's for more than twenty-five years, Jack Norris, and Nell Wing all said that Bill had let them know how badly he felt about his unfaithfulness to Lois." (Hartigan, p. 172-173)*

Two Wynns, No Losses

Bill met Helen Wynn at an AA meeting, when he was about sixty. Eighteen years his junior, the former actress was by all accounts a very attractive woman with tremendous charisma. "Of all the women Bill was close to outside his marriage, none had as much impact as Helen Wynn." (Cheever, p. 229) This one was different, and the liaison was to continue for fifteen years.

> *"Soon after the affair began (in the mid 1950s), Bill got Helen, who had been sober only a short time, a job at AA Grapevine... (where) she worked her way up over a period of years to become the managing editor. After Helen left the Grapevine in*

> *1962, Bill contributed to her support, though when he wanted to direct a portion of his royalty income to her, the AA trustees refused to do it. Bill was furious."* (Hartigan, p. 192)

In the end, she inherited a royalty share but lived on only a few years beyond Bill's death. This relationship went way beyond any previous involvements. This was a "soul-mate" situation, and it seems that Bill had to be talked out of "divorcing Lois so that he could marry Helen. A number of people thought that, given the strength of his feelings for Wynn, only his sense of obligation toward Lois kept him from going through with it." (Hartigan, p. 195)

Some years earlier, there had been another Wynn.

> *"Another alleged mistress has been outed by novelist Carolyn See in a memoir of her familial drinking life. It seems that Wynn C., See's father's second wife, had once 'come within a hair's breadth of becoming the First Lady of AA.' For a while during the late 1940's or early 1950's, 'she and Bill had been a mighty item.' A tall and buxom beauty...Wynn 'was a knockout, and she knew it, and dressed like a chorus girl.'"* (Raphael, p. 130)

Bill wouldn't, and couldn't, marry her, but he put her story in the book, the second edition of Alcoholics Anonymous. In her tale, "Freedom From Bondage," she takes a self-deprecatory jab at her succession of relationships. "I had always been a cinch for the program, for I had always been interested in mankind – I was just taking them one man at a time." (BB, p. 548)

Founder's Watch

Bill sometimes went to AA events alone.

> *"When Bill wasn't accompanied by Lois (or later, Helen) he could often be observed engaged in animated conversation with an attractive young newcomer. His interest in younger women seemed to grow more intense with age. Barry Leach... told me that in the 1960s he and other friends of Bill's formed what they came to refer to as the 'Founder's Watch' committee."* (Hartigan, p. 192)

This group had the specific mission of short-circuiting these flirtations before they could become potentially inappropriate involvements.

Susan Cheever

Of the Bill W. biographers, Susan Cheever is the most controversial, while at the same time, perhaps the finest writer. Her descriptions of the Vermont mining town of Wilson's youth are outstanding, and we are treated to a sense of history in tales of Ethan Allen and the Green Mountain Boys.

Cheever, herself an "un-anonymous" AA member, also delves into Bill's sexuality, and the code of silence surrounding it. "Bill's sex life is still a secret, something AA members buzz about over coffee after meetings, but something which has been excised from the official literature and – for the most part from the official AA archives." (Cheever, p. 224)

According to Cheever, there are letters from Bill to Lois, in which he tries desperately to explain away a flirtation and kissing incident with Lois' younger sister, Barb. To prove his straightforwardness Bill offers full disclosure of his sexual history, which began when he was young. "His first sexual experience occurred when he was thirteen, and it was with an older girl who worked at the hotel." (Cheever, p. 68)

And, there were more.

In getting past the incident with Barb, "...they set the pattern for their long marriage. Bill was passionate, and abashed by his behavior; Lois was forgiving and comforting." (Cheever, p. 68)

Bill's writing reflects an inner acquaintance with immoderation. "In Step Six (of the Twelve and Twelve), he notes that 'since most of us are born an abundance of natural desires, it isn't strange that we often let those far exceed their intended purpose.'" (Cheever, p. 233)

"I can resist anything but temptation."- Oscar Wilde

The Big Book

> "We all have sex problems. We'd hardly be human if we didn't." (BB, p. 69) Ideally, in AA, sex can be treated like any other problem, but it's clear that "sex is not just 'any other problem' for Wilson". (Raphael, pp. 127-128)

> "We want to stay out of this controversy. We do not want to be the arbiter of anyone's sex conduct... God alone can judge our sex situation... We earnestly pray for the right ideal... If sex is

very troublesome, we throw ourselves the harder into helping others... It quiets the imperious urge..." (BB, p. 69-70)

AA's fifth step is a confession, but Wilson warns that "we cannot disclose anything to our wives...which will hurt them and make them unhappy." (BB, p. 74) And what if, (in sobriety): "Perhaps we are mixed up with women in a fashion we wouldn't care to have advertised... If we are sure our wife does not know, should we tell her? Not always, we think... If we can forget, so can she. It is better, however, that one does not needlessly name a person upon whom she can vent jealousy." (BB, p. 81-82)

Biographer, Matthew Raphael (a pseudonym), himself an AA member, finds this whole approach astonishingly convenient. "In its scrupulous desire to protect the 'innocent' third party, such a passage seems remarkably self-serving, exculpatory of the husband's 'wild' behavior, but admonishing the wife's 'natural' (but potentially hysterical) 'jealousy.' If we choose to forget the offense, then why shouldn't she?"

Indeed!

To Wives

"What's truly incredible in Wilson's handling of adultery is his impersonation of a woman's point of view in the chapter he would not permit Lois to write." (Raphael, p. 129)

"He will tell you he is misunderstood. This may lead to lonely evenings for you. He may even seek someone else to console him – not always another man." (BB, p. 111) "The menacing coyness of this threat is calculated to put any uppity wife in her place, which is to be seen, perhaps, but definitely not to be heard." (Raphael, p. 129)

"His preoccupation with infidelity, however likely sprang from his own history of philandering, no trace of which, unsurprisingly, is to be found in official AA publications." (Raphael, p. 130)

Perspective

There are many men of achievement who have exhibited a preoccupation with sex. Are their accomplishments diminished by this? For some, a great deal. For others, not at all. Some undoubtedly see a level of hypocrisy separating AA's spiritual "code of conduct," and the actions and attitudes of its founder.

"It is worth remembering that Bill was raised almost a century ago (written in 2000), and while he could justifiably be accused of possessing sexist attitudes, he was also capable of treating the women who worked with him with dignity and respect. When Bill wrote the literature now being objected to as sexist, he was reflecting the prevailing attitude of his time." (Hartigan, p. 197)

In 1964, shortly after the JFK assassination, Arthur Crock, the grand old conservative columnist of "The New York Times" wrote of President John F. Kennedy, "The truth explains what the gathering myth obscures – that he was endearingly and admirably human."

The same could be as easily be said of William Griffith Wilson.

Chapter 5 Doctor Bob - Part One (1879-1935)

St. Johnsbury, Vermont

Dr. Bob Smith remembers his childhood hometown of St. Johnsbury, some 100 miles northeast of the East Dorset birthplace of Bill Wilson, as having a general moral standard "far above the average". The consumption of alcohol was considered a question of morality. "No beer or liquor was sold in the neighborhood, except at the State liquor agency where perhaps one might procure a pint if he could convince the agent that he really needed it... Men who had liquor shipped in from Boston or New York by express were looked upon with great distrust and disfavor." (Doctor Bob's Nightmare, p. 171)

Judge and Mrs. Walter Perrin Smith were prominent citizens in the archetypical New England village of about 7,000. "Judge Smith sat on the Caledonia County Probate Court. He was also, at various times, state's attorney, member of the state legislature, superintendent of St. Johnsbury schools, director of the Merchants National Bank, and president of the Passumpsic Savings Bank. In addition, he taught Sunday school for 40 years. Dr. Bob, who rarely discussed family background, described his father as being a typical Vermont Yankee - reserved and taciturn." (Dr. Bob and The Good Oldtimers, p. 9) Beneath the granite surface, the Judge had warmth and passion, and considerable indulgence toward his only son.

That son was Robert Holbrook Smith, who was born in their large home on August 8th, of 1879. He had a much older foster sister, Amanda Northrup, but he essentially grew up as an only child. "Mrs. Smith… was… a stern, tight-lipped, churchgoing lady who busied herself with the countless social and religious activities of St. Johnsbury's towering, gray stone North Congregational Church. 'Grandma Smith was a cold woman,' said Sue Windows, Dr. Bob's adopted daughter." (Good Oldtimers, p. 10) Mrs. Smith did live to see her sybaritic son become sober. The Judge died in 1918.

A "Churchy" Childhood and a Taste of Hard Cider

Young Bob was forced to go to church, Sunday school and other prayer meetings, as many as four or five times per week. "This had the effect of making me resolve that when I was free from parental domination, I would never again darken the doors of a church." (Good Oldtimers, p. 12) A second rebellion was more immediate. Sent to bed at five o'clock every evening, he went without argument, but stealthily slipped out to join his friends, once he thought the coast was clear.

Bob was a boy who liked the outdoors - hunting, fishing, hiking and swimming. One day, while at a neighbor's farm helping the men bale hay, he discovered the "secret stash" of one of the workmen, a jug of "hard cider", and the irresistible lure prompted a large swallow. He liked the taste. He was barely nine. Although he was not to drink again for ten more years, this single event was memorable.

At school he managed creditable grades in spite of an effort level that was less than diligent. He was popular, having plenty of friends. At a high school dance at the St. Johnsbury Academy, he met Anne Robinson Ripley who would, many years later, become Mrs. Robert Smith.

The "Drinkingest of Ivy League Schools"

Dr. Bob attended Dartmouth which "had a name then for being a rugged backwoods school where the 800 or so students spent the long winters ignoring their books and drinking as much beer and hard cider as they could hold". (Good Oldtimers, p. 18) Bob Smith could hold a lot - he was a prodigious drinker. At university, sixty miles from parental supervision, he was unrestrained.

Regarding his college drinking, Smith writes, "I did it more and more, and had lots of fun without much grief, either physical or financial. I seemed to be able to snap back the next morning better than most of my fellow drinkers… Never once in my life have I had a headache, which fact lends me to believe that I was an alcoholic almost from the start. My whole life seemed to be centered around doing what I wanted to do, without regard for the rights, wishes, or privileges of anyone else; a state of mind which became more and more predominant as the years passed. I was graduated 'summa cum laude' in the eyes of the drinking fraternity, but not in the eyes of the Dean." (Nightmare, p. 172) At college, he developed a fondness for billiards, horseshoe pitching, and several forms of cards, including the beginnings of a lifelong passion for bridge. Highly competitive, he played to win. He was also a very skilled chugalugger.

"My Son the Doctor? No, I Don't Think So!"

"When it came to things he really wanted, Bob was hardworking. He was also ambitious, and he wanted to become a medical doctor like his maternal grandfather. For some reason we have never learned, his mother opposed this quite strongly. He had no choice but to get a job." (Good Oldtimers, p. 24) He became a salesman for Fairbanks Morse, a St. Johnsbury manufacturer of platform scales. The future doctor was uninspired by "heavy hardware", and was not particularly successful. Weekends were spent bingeing. After two years, a change of companies took him to Montreal, and then to Boston.

With pledges and sweet promises, he finally persuaded his parents to send him to medical school, but his reckless drinking caused him to get expelled from the University of Michigan after his second year. The assistance of his father enabled a transfer to Rush University, where his jitters caused him to miss several classes, and "his life in school became one long binge after another, and he was no longer drinking for the sheer fun of it". (Good Oldtimers, p. 25) His worsened imbibing prompted his fraternity brothers to send for his father, whose quiet attempts at understanding only heightened Bob's feelings of remorse. Hard liquor replaced beer, binges lengthened, and shakes intensified. At one final exam, he could not hold a pencil, and turned in three absolutely blank booklets.

Two Dry Quarters, Eight Dry Months

On the carpet once more, Bob was given a final chance. The dean of the medical school decided that if Bob wished to graduate, he needed to come back for two quarters, remaining completely dry. This he was able to accomplish, and in 1910, at age 31, he was finally Dr. Bob Smith.

City Hospital, Akron, Ohio

"I conducted myself so creditably that I was able to secure a much coveted internship in a western city, where I spent two years. During these two years I was kept so busy that I hardly left the hospital at all. Consequently, I could not get into any trouble." (Nightmare, p. 174) The new doctor opened an office downtown, in the Second National Bank Building, where he was to remain until he retired in 1948.

"Perhaps as a result of the irregular hours and tense work of a new GP, Dr. Bob developed considerable stomach trouble. "I soon discovered that a couple of drinks would alleviate my gastric distress, at least for a few hours at a time", he said. It didn't take him long to return to the old drinking habits. Almost immediately, he began to 'pay very dearly physically,' to know the real horror and suffering of alcoholism." (Good Oldtimers, p. 28)

Drying-Out Spots

When so bad that he could not function, the new medical practitioner put himself into one of the local "drying-out" spots. This happened at least a dozen times. In one small hospital for patients with socially unacceptable ailments, he sabotaged the sincere efforts of the staff by getting friends to smuggle in whiskey by the quart. If unavailable, he then stole medicinal alcohol.

Sobriety And Tranquil Domesticity

In 1914, Judge Smith dispatched a doctor to bring Bob home where he remained in bed for two full months before daring to venture out. He was utterly demoralized. "Scared straight" Smith stayed sober, and believed he was that way to stay. He went to Chicago to finally marry Anne, which he did on January 25, 1915. It was about a full year since his last drink.

"The first three years of the Smiths' married life were ideal, free from the unhappiness that was to come later. Dr. Bob continued to stay sober, and any lingering doubts Anne may have had were stilled. They were then, as always, an extremely devoted couple... Dr. Bob's professional life was going smoothly, too; he was developing a reputation as a physician, work he loved... A bit authoritative and difficult to approach, he was sympathetic and understanding once you started talking." (Good Oldtimers, p. 30) In 1918, the Smiths became the parents of Robert Jr., later known as "Smitty".

The Volstead Act

Activism by the very vocal forces of Temperance, the Anti-Saloon League, and other anti-alcohol groups had successfully pushed for a dramatic end to the explosively expanding problems with drunkenness in America. By late 1917, the Eighteenth Amendment, prohibiting the manufacture, sale, and transportation of intoxication liquors, had been passed by Congress, and was awaiting ratification by the states. The drunkenness problem would be ended (in theory) by a complete shutdown of supply. America would become "dry".

"With the passing of the Eighteenth Amendment I felt quite safe. I knew everyone would buy a few bottles, or cases, of liquor as their exchequers permitted, and that it would soon be gone. Therefore it would make no great difference, even if I should do some drinking. At that time I was not aware of the almost unlimited supply the government made it possible for us doctors to obtain, neither had I any knowledge of the bootlegger who soon appeared on the horizon... During the next few years I developed two distinct phobias. One was the fear of not sleeping, and the other was the fear of running out of liquor." (Nightmare, p. 175)

Of course, it was not only physicians who were able to get liquor during Prohibition. The Ebby Thachers, Rowland Hazards, and Bill Wilsons of the world did the worst of their drinking during America's grand failed experiment. The thirty-sixth state (of forty-eight) provided ratification on January 16th, 1919, and the legislation would be in force one year later. The Amendment was repealed in 1933, ironically, not long after the time a rapidly deteriorating Bill Wilson entered the Towns Hospital for the first time.

855 Ahdmaw Avunuh

The Smith family home at 855 Ardmore (Ahdmaw, with Bob's heavy New England drawl) Avenue, purchased new in 1915 for $4,000. is quite ordinary by the standards of physicians' homes in the current era. "This house, neither modest nor opulent, speaks of unadorned respectability. It recalls that Dr. Bob shared the stolidly simple ways of his Vermont ancestors, including their moral and verbal austerity." (Bill W. and Mr. Wilson, Matthew J. Raphael)

Visited annually by many thousand alcoholics and addicts in recovery, anxious to be near "where it all began", the now famous residence has been designated a "National Historical Landmark" and a museum. Founders Day, held each June, is a weekend of the celebration of sobriety, with a very large component of bikers. Gigantic men, muscled and leather clad, tattooed and pierced, some former gang members, are seen bawling like babies, overwhelmed by the enormity of being at the site of the birth of a life-altering process.

For Mrs. Smith, it must have been more of a hysterical landmark as her husband once more fell into the pit of destructive drinking. The good doctor, of course, needing to earn an income, had various ways of "managing" his drinking, such as no morning drinking (usually), taking sedatives instead, to quiet the "jitters". Today, he would recognize a "dual addiction". "I had sense enough never to go to the hospital if I had been drinking, and very seldom did I receive patients." (Good Oldtimers, p. 33) On a good day, he would stay "dry" but well-sedated until four o'clock, then go home, acquiring a good supply along the way. Thus, he preserved his great "secret", discovering later that he had fooled himself far more than anyone else.

Amazingly, this life went on and on and on.

The Oxford Group

Five years after the birth of Robert Jr., a daughter Sue was adopted. As the children aged, they grew more and more aware of their father's alcoholism. They retained fond childhood memories, nonetheless. Possibly to counterbalance his own strict upbringing, Dr. Bob was the most liberal of parents. The long-suffering and frustrated Mrs. Smith, however, took up cigarettes in her fifties, and became a chain smoker. "She was broiling inside. She had to be." (Good Oldtimers, p. 37) Bob's promises to his wife and children, though sincerely made, barely got him through a day.

By 1933, the country's full-blown Depression, combined with a bread winner who only rarely made it to work, left the Smiths in economic desperation. Only the national mortgage moratorium kept the family from losing their house. Dr. Bob was often irritable, and this tetchiness was without doubt magnified when Anne dragged him to the Oxford Group. In spite of bitter remembrances of the "force-fed" religion of his childhood, the guilt-ridden inebriate could hardly refuse the pleadings of his more devout spouse who surely clung to the faint hope of a religious cure.

The Oxford Group had burst dramatically onto the Akron scene in January of 1933, when "a rubber company president [Harvey Firestone], grateful because the Oxford Group had sobered up his son (Russell, 'Bud'), brought some sixty OG leaders and team members to Akron for a ten day 'house party,' as their gatherings were called. They held meetings throughout the day, and it all culminated in a dinner for 400 prominent citizens of the community". (Good Oldtimers, p. 55) This group profoundly attracted Anne Smith, who dragged her recalcitrant husband to this altar of potential redemption.

Despite his original antipathy, Smith was somewhat drawn to the Oxford folks, "... because of their seeming poise, health, and happiness. They spoke with great freedom from embarrassment, which I could never do, and they seemed more at ease on all occasions.. I was self-conscious and ill at ease most of the time, my health was at the breaking point, and I was thoroughly miserable... I gave the matter much time and study for the next two and one half years, but I still got tight every night nevertheless". (Nightmare, p. 178)

"My wife became deeply interested and it was her interest that had sustained mine, though I at no time thought it might be the answer to my liquor problem." (Nightmare, p. 178)

By the Spring of 1935, even the dedicated and ever hopeful Anne Smith must have realized, in her heart of hearts, that the desperately desired spiritual cure was not to be forthcoming.

The Mayflower Hotel and The Seiberling Gatehouse

By the Spring of 1935, there were things that Bill Wilson, now five months sober, knew as well. His Towns Hospital "spiritual experience" along with the religious practices of the Oxford Group, were insufficient, in and of themselves, to sustain his sobriety. A few years later, he would write, "... I soon found that when all other measures failed, work with another alcoholic would save the day". (Bill's Story, p. 15) And, "Practical experience shows that nothing will so much insure immunity from drinking as intensive work with other alcoholics. It works, when other activities fail". (Alcoholics Anonymous, p. 89) Lest the key point be missed: "... it is well to let him (alcoholic dad) go as far as he likes in helping other alcoholics. During those first few days of convalescence, this will do more to ensure his sobriety than anything else". (Alcoholics Anonymous, p. 129)

Bill Wilson's "clean wind of a mountaintop" spiritual experience was a mere five months removed, but possibly already past its "best before" date, when at the Mayflower Hotel, on May 11th of 1935, "his self-pity and resentment began to rise. He was lonely... Now began the personal crisis that was to set in motion a series of life-changing events for Bill. There was a bar at one end of the lobby, and Bill felt himself drawn to it... the idea was loaded with danger... For the first time in months, Bill had the panicky feeling of being in trouble... I thought, 'You need another alcoholic to talk to. You need another alcoholic just as much as he needs you!'" (Pass It On, p. 135-136)

And thus the phone calls were made that led Bill Wilson to Dr. Bob, through Reverend Tunks, Norman Sheppard, and Henrietta Seiberling. Beyond this point the events are well known, recorded in some detail in the "Foreword To The Second Edition". It is worth revisiting Bob Smith's own words regarding what was magical about this first meeting, and more impactful than thirty months of Oxford Group religiosity: "He gave me information about the subject of alcoholism which was undoubtedly helpful. Of far more importance was the fact that he was the first living human with whom I had ever talked, who knew what he was talking about in regard to alcoholism from actual experience. In other words, he talked my language." (Nightmare, p. 180)

Dr. Bob stopped drinking and Bill Wilson moved into the Smith home. There was to be one more relapse at the AMA Convention about a month later, but the physician then sobered permanently in June of 1935, the date memorialized as the start of AA. Perhaps fittingly in an organization priding itself on a lack of organization, the famous date was incorrectly remembered as June 10th, but is now thought to have been June 17th.

Chapter 6 Doctor Bob - Part Two (1935-1950)

From his last drink in June, 1935, AA became the centerpiece of Dr. Bob's life... (He) worked with Sister Ignatia... to treat thousands of alcoholics, who were then channeled into AA. He provided all of these services without charge.(Slaying The Dragon, William L. White, p. 186)

Before getting sober, Bob had been active with the Oxford Group. "They told me that I should go to meetings and I did, every week. They said I should affiliate myself with some church, and we did that. And they also said that I should cultivate the habit of prayer, and I did that - at least to quite a considerable extent for me. But I got tight every night. And I mean that. It wasn't every once in a while." (Detroit Talk, 1948)

Bill Wilson's instruction to attempt to be helpful to others is what turned the trick.

Two Women Smackers

"During the summer of 1935, both co-founders worked tirelessly to maintain their own sobriety while trying to help others." (Dr. Bob and Bill W. Speak, Michael Fitzpatrick, pp. 62-63) Even before the trip to the AMA convention "...they found a young guy by the name of Eddie R. He had just been thrown out in the street... with his cute little blond wife and two kids. So they decided to move the whole shebang into our home. They locked Eddie upstairs in the bedroom". (Bob Smith Jr. Talk, Kerrville, Texas, 1986)

Eddie got out a few times, by sliding down the downspouts, once making it all the way to Cleveland, where he was going to commit suicide. "When he sobered up he had a few things that hadn't shown up immediately. And he began beating up on his little blonde wife; and he began chasing my mother around the house with a butcher knife." (Bob Jr., Texas) Eventually, Eddie was recommitted to a mental Institution.

The first success was with Bill Dotson. "He was a lawyer, who had been in the hospital six times in the preceding four months. He went completely out of his mind when drinking, and he had just roughed up a couple of nurses... 'He's a grand chap when he's sober.'" (Dr. Bob and the Good Oldtimers, p. 82) Bill D.'s sobriety date was June 26, 1935.

By the time Bill returned to New York, they also had added Ernie G. (The Seven Month Slip), and had some other strong prospects.

The Prince of Twelfth-Steppers

"Lois described Dr. Bob as being full of humanity. 'He definitely wanted to help people in trouble. And he was so excited and enthusiastic about this new thing he and Bill had... Bill realized, too, that he got things from Bob that he needed to complement his work. He always consulted with Bob... (who) usually went along with Bill.'" (Oldtimers, p. 91)

"Beginning in 1935, Dr. Bob quickly became an extraordinarily effective worker with active alcoholics. He was tough. He was inflexible. He told his prospects: 'Do you want to surrender to God? Take it or leave it.'...The doctor was authoritative, and he was impressive." (Getting Better, Nan Robertson, p. 61) There had been a lesson learned from the failure with Eddie R. "The men he sobered up... asked themselves about any new alcoholic prospect: 'Does he want to stop badly enough? Is he mentally sound apart from his alcoholism?'" (Robertson, p. 62)

Women were not welcome. The young were not welcome.

What existed at the time was very much a "Christian fellowship". Quiet time, prayer and bible reading were integral parts of the healing process. "Dr. Bob continued his efforts with alcoholics in Akron in close connection with the Oxford Group." (Not-God, Ernest Kurtz, p. 53) Jim Burwell would not have survived the Akron vetting.

AA Number 12

Interviews with Bob E., who got sober in February 1937, provide much of the information about what was happening in Akron during the early years. He was hospitalized, but "clear-headed enough to begin to wonder about this 'new therapy,' for over the next five days it seemed to consist simply of being visited by groups of two or three men. 'None of them said anything about what I had to do - they just introduced themselves and started to tell me their experiences'". (Not-God, p. 54)

On the fifth day, his friend Paul returned to indoctrinate him in the "spiritual side". "'The surrender was more than important; it was a must...' they told you to get down on your knees and say a prayer to God... They demanded it. You couldn't go to a meeting until you did it.'" (Oldtimers, p. 101) It is downplayed in the literature, but it's quite clear that in the circumstances of the time, these were "surrenders to Christ".

"'I often wonder how many people that come in now would survive an experience like that - a regular old-fashioned prayer meeting,' said Dorothy, who was then married to an AA member, Clarence S.." (Oldtimers, p. 101) Hospitalization was another "must" in the early days, to the point that when Warren C. came to AA in Cleveland, in July 1939, there was much debate about admitting him to the Fellowship, as he had not been hospitalized.

Change of Venue

"In the spring of 1939, administrators at the Akron City and Green Cross Hospitals, noting that Dr. Smith's mysterious patients owed over five thousand dollars, began scrutinizing his admissions more carefully." (Not-God, Ernest Kurtz, p. 79) He asked Sister Ignatia, the admissions officer of St. Thomas if he could smuggle in some alcoholic patients. Dr. Bob knew that the good sister was sympathetic to the cause. "'We often discussed the problem of alcoholism and the tragedies caused by excessive drinking,' according to Sister Ignatia." (Oldtimers, p. 185)

There is absolutely no denying the convincing evidence that throughout his fifteen years of sobriety, Dr. Bob labored in the service of his fellow alcoholic at a level that, to this day, remains virtually unparalleled.

Throughout the larger AA world, the more flamboyant Bill Wilson was the public face of the society, but in Ohio, the iconic figure was the curt, but devoted, medical man. The tarnishing of Bill W.'s star in the past few decades has led to an elevation of his co-founder's legacy. As happens with other mythic figures, elements of the saga have been aggrandized, and even altered.

Free Medical Care

A total of "4,800 alcoholics were admitted into St. Thomas under his care." (Oldtimers, p. 188) Before the first of the St. Thomas admissions, starting in August 1939, there had been many others treated in the previous four years at the two hospitals where Dr. Bob had his principal affiliations. What an enormous humanity this reflects! One would think that no aggrandizement is required.

But!!

One often hears that Dr. Bob "sponsored" 5,000 people. That's a lot of sponsoring!! Better than one a day, granting Sundays off. Free medical care to 5,000 is admirable and astonishing. Enough in itself, one would think.

The Myth of Unification

Every political party's leadership convention ends the same way. There is a final vote in which 100% of the delegates vote for the candidate who hours earlier was one of seven contenders, and perhaps the first choice of a mere 25%. The last vote, of course, is ceremonial, an act of "manufactured" unity. The disappointed 75%, supporters of the losing candidates, participate in the unanimous ratification, but do they adopt every policy of the winner, policies against which they were struggling an hour earlier?

The great AA myth is that ALL of the original folks were delighted with the book, and that the book then ascended to a position of "authority," for one and all. The truth is that compromises like "God, as we understood Him", were disappointing to both the "radicals" and the "conservatives." For those whose lives were so positively transformed with a decision for Christ, it's hard to picture them telling prospects to "pick a God, any God".

There is nothing in the history of Dr. Bob Smith, until possibly late in life, that indicates he had much regard for "as we understood Him". For Bob, God was God. His side, those lobbying for a fully Christian book featuring a fully Christian God, had lost in the voting. But, did they change immediately the way they operated by adopting all of the book's "middle ground" path? No, they did not. Not even close.

Akron-Style AA

There is a lot of whining today about the watering down of AA, and the past is glorified. Akron-style AA of the 1940s is the Holy Grail. (Cue Bruce Springsteen - "Glory Days".) Many of those idealizing the AA of that era and locale, would be surprised at the pervasive Christianity. Although they had lost the battle for a fully and openly Christian book, it is clear that the Akronites changed very little about their procedures, even after the split from the Oxford Group in the autumn of 1939.

Group autonomy existed even the early days when AA was present in only three cities. In the summer of 1939, Clarence S. reported on Cleveland AA, in a letter to Bill W. "Not too much emphasis on spiritual business at meetings. Have discussions after meetings of any business or questions arising. Plenty of fellowship all the time." (Oldtimers, p. 167) Of the three locations, Cleveland seems to have made the most use of the Big Book.

Akron meetings were more solemn, with quiet time, prayer, and bible readings. The Oxforders' 4 Absolutes and 5 "C's" remained in high regard. Drunkalogs were discouraged. "Spirituality" lacked today's diversity. Prospects absorbed, or adapted to what was offered or they moved on.

The Akron Manual

There were other problems with AA's new book for the folks in Akron. In the 1930s the American economy was still not strong, and with many members and new prospects struggling, the Big Book was very expensive, about equivalent to a current price of sixty dollars. There was no lack of cynicism in Ohio about this "New York project", and its commercial aspects.

Under the guidance of Dr. Bob, some Akron members, in 1940, assembled "A Manual for Alcoholics Anonymous". Its Foreword explains, "This booklet is intended to be a practical guide for new members and sponsors... The booklet should be used in conjunction with the larger book, Alcoholics Anonymous, the Bible, the daily lesson... and other constructive literature". This pamphlet became known as the Akron Manual, and very quickly went into wide usage in Ohio. It contained specific Dr. Bob prescriptions, and it had the enormous advantage of being obtainable for ten or fifteen cents.

Sponsor responsibilities are delineated. "You have in your hands the most valuable property in the world... the future of a fellow man. Treat his life as carefully as you would your own. You are literally responsible for his life." (Manual, p. 5)

Helpful reading material is recommended. "You should make it a point to supply your patient with the proper literature... the big AA book, this pamphlet, a Bible...." (Manual, p. 6)

The sponsor essentially co-signed on the hospital fees, and set up a schedule of visits from other members. "It is desirable that the patient's visitors be confined to members of Alcoholics Anonymous." (Manual, p. 7) A quiet talk with the wife was suggested, explaining that family and friends were asked to stay away.

The prospect is also guided. "The Bible tells us to put first things first. Alcohol is obviously the first thing in your life. So concentrate on conquering that...There is the Bible you haven't opened for years. Get acquainted with it. Read it with an open mind. You will find things that will amaze you." (Manual, p. 11) Specific passages were recommended. Recruits were told that the AA book could become their "second bible."

Newly sober members fresh from the hospital themselves were encouraged to visit those in the position they had themselves occupied only days before. "You feel that you have nothing to say to a new patient. Nonsense. You have been sober for a day, or a week. Obviously you must have done something to stay sober, even for that short length of time. That is your story... Definitely you have something to say." (Manual, p. 12)

This directly contradicts all of the talk exhorting newer folks to "Sit down and shut up", like it was done "in the old days". The Akron Manual expresses the direct opposite of "Take the cotton from your ears and put it in your mouth" tough-talking approach.

A Salute to Human Power

"The harder you work at sobriety, the easier it is to remain sober." (p. 12) This runs somewhat counter to the Big Book notion of turning it ALL over to God, as human power is of no avail whatever. Slogans such as One Day at a Time are often mocked by modern AA fundamentalists who sometimes refer to the absolute futility of going to "the human power gym".

And yet, the Akron Manual conveys a contradictory philosophy. "One of the easiest, most practical ways of keeping sober ever devised is the day by day plan - the 24-hour plan." (p. 18) The fired-up modernists also will find more to displease them in an advocacy for prudent deliberation. "WHAT'S YOUR HURRY?... There is an old saying 'Easy Does It.' It is a motto any alcoholic could well ponder... Sobriety is a thing that you must do step by step. If anything puzzles you... forget about it the time being... Meanwhile, EASY DOES IT." (p. 20)

There is even some outright "treatment center-style" advice. "Diet and rest play an important part in the rehabilitation of an alcoholic... We find it wise to eat balanced meals at regular hours, and get the proper amount of sleep." (p. 21) Vitamins, fresh vegetables and fruits are recommended, as is getting a physical. Extra carbohydrates are advised to supply sugar. "When we deprive ourselves of alcohol our bodies cry for sugar. This often manifests itself in a form of nervousness." (p. 22) Candy and sweets calm the nerves.

The Manual is very pro-meetings which "provide a means for an exchange of ideas, the renewing of fellowships... a sense of security, and an additional reminder that we are alcoholics and must be continually on the alert against temptation to slip backwards into the old drunken way of living. In large communities where there are several groups it is recommended that newer members attend as many meetings as possible... Remember that attendance at meetings is one of the most important requisites of remaining sober." (p. 22)

The Akron Manual was "written and distributed by Dr. Bob's Home Group, Akron AA group #1." (barefootsworld.net) After listing the 12 Steps, the Manual continues with - "The Twelve Steps are more fully explained in another pamphlet... called 'A Guide to the Twelve Steps of Alcoholics Anonymous,' available at 12 cents a single copy."

Tenth Step Promises

The Big Book of Alcoholics Anonymous promises an entirely new state of being for the recovered alcoholic. "We will see that our new attitude towards liquor has been given us without any thought or effort on our part. It just comes. That is the miracle of it. We are not fighting it, neither are we avoiding temptation. We feel as though we had been placed in a position of neutrality - safe and protected. We have not even sworn off. Instead, the problem has been removed. It does not exist." (BB, p. 85)

POOF!!!! Cue Cecil B. DeMille! The implication is quite obvious.

For the fundamentalist, this result is inevitable, for those diligently following the process. Here lies the "cake recipe" metaphor. Notwithstanding the normal irregularities found in all human endeavor, this "miracle" is viewed as absolute and unvarying.

Thus the problem that arises in attempting to explain why Bob Smith, one of the most godly and selfless of AA practitioners, did not get the promised results. Many will say that the good doctor did not get these tenth step promises until he was two and a half years sober. Doctor Bob's Nightmare is the source of this "cited" information, but the text, in reality, says something different. "Unlike most of our crowd, I did not get over my craving for liquor MUCH during the first two and a half years of abstinence." (BB, p. 181)

From what has been written elsewhere, it is clear that he continued to struggle, albeit in a battle that was less intense and less constant. Speaking to Dan K. well into the 1940s, "'Dr. Bob said that even then, it wasn't Easy Does It for him. "In the morning, when I get up and put my feet on the floor... I have to battle all day to stay away from that drink.'" (Oldtimers, p. 282)

Mirroring his own experience, "Dr. Bob advocated that members stay in dry places whenever possible. 'You don't ask the Lord not to lead you into temptation, then turn around and walk right into it,' he said." (Oldtimers, p. 281)

Biographer Robert Thomsen had the best direct access to Bill Wilson, of all who have told AA's story. "He (Bob) had had to struggle... with his obsession always, and far more than Bill. There was never a two-day period, he told Bill once, when at some point he did not have a physical craving for booze. Still he'd gone on. He'd won... In his unpretentious way he'd fought his obsession." (Bill W., Robert Thompsen, p. 310)

Life

AA's Big Book states that "when all other measures failed, work with another alcoholic would save the day." (BB, p. 15) Bob Smith worked tirelessly with other alcoholics. Such work was likely critical in his struggle to stay sober. He clearly also enjoyed it, and delighted in the reclaimed lives of a great number of followers. The diligent efforts on behalf of alcoholics left him with an income far below that of the average medical professional.

Although gruff and reserved, he loved people. He was a giver of nicknames and a lover of slang. Dr. Bob very much enjoyed cards, especially bridge, and he was extremely competitive. He played to win.

In sobriety, he made efforts to be a better father, and a better husband to Anne. One wonders if the family members were ever resentful that even in their new life, Dr. Bob was less than an outstanding provider. Nonetheless, there was a warmth. Smitty in particular, spoke well of his father. Anne was deeply involved in the AA work herself.

Death

Dr. Bob was a tremendous supporter of Bill Wilson, and frequently sacrificed his own instincts in order to side with Bill. Bob remained opposed to Bill's push for AA's self-governance. When his spouse passed on June 1, 1949, Bob may have been confronted with his own mortality. In July of 1950, at the First International Convention, then in failing health, he made a brief speech.

Herein is a good portion:

> *It would be fitting to lay a little emphasis (on a few things); one is the simplicity of our Program. Let's not louse it all up with Freudian complexes and things that are interesting to the scientific mind, but have very little to do with our actual AA work. Our 12 Steps, when simmered down to the last, resolve themselves into the words love and service. We understand what love is and we understand what service is. So let's bear those two things in mind.*
>
> *Let us also remember to guard that erring member - the tongue, and if we must use it, let's use it with kindness and consideration and tolerance.*
>
> *And one more thing; none of us would be here today if somebody hadn't taken time to explain things to us, to give us a little pat on the back, to take us to a meeting or two, to have done numerous little kind and thoughtful acts in our behalf. So let us never get the degree of smug complacency so that we're not willing to extend or attempt to, that help which has been so beneficial to us, to our less fortunate brothers. Thank you very much. (barefootsworld.net)*

He survived only until November 16 of that year. Dr. Bob was 71 years of age and 15 1/2 years sober.

SECTION II PRE-HISTORY

Chapter 7 Dr. Benjamin Rush

"Dr. Benjamin Rush, one of the signers of the Declaration of Independence, was the first member of the (American) medical community to write about alcoholism and suggest it might be an illness... a 'disease process'". (The Roundtable of AA History, Silkworth.net) This was fully one hundred years before the disease concept of alcoholism was fully developed and articulated in the 1870s.

Rush was born on January 4, 1746, on a plantation, a dozen miles outside of Philidelphia. "His interest in alcohol and alcohol-related problems sprang from personal as well was professional experience. Rush's father was an alcoholic whose drinking led to his parents' divorce, and his mother's second husband was a distiller who abused her." (Silkworth.net) His biological father died when the future founding father was five or six.

At the age of eight, Rush was put under the tutelage of his uncle, the Reverend Samuel Finley, who would later become president of the College of New Jersey, which became Princeton in 1896. There was some thought of his becoming a lawyer, but after graduating with a B.A. from the College of New Jersey, Rush began an apprenticeship as a physician's assistant to Dr. John Redman.

In 1766, he went to study at the University of Edinburgh, where he completed an MD degree in 1769. While in Europe studying and touring, the young Pennsylvanian became fluent in French, Italian and Spanish. Returning to America, Rush set up a medical practice and became North America's first ever chemistry professor, when he began teaching the subject at the College of Philadelphia's medical department. He taught more physicians than any other educator of his era.

Social Activism

Upon his return to America, Rush also became active as a publisher of tracts lobbying for the elimination of slavery. His social activism eventually branched into other areas. He opposed slavery, advocated for free public schools, sought improved education for women and a more enlightened penal system.

"Rush was a prolific writer and social activist. If a health or social issue arose during this period, Benjamin Rush was likely to be in the middle of the debate. He was often called the 'father of American Psychiatry' and was unquestionably the first American authority on alcohol and alcoholism." (Slaying The Dragon - The History of Addiction Treatment and Recovery in America, William L. White, Second Edition, p. 2)

During the Revolutionary War, Rush was in the field with the colonial military. In this capacity, the physician's

> *first professional recognition of the problem of alcohol involved the level of drunkenness among soldiers of the Continental Army - an issue of concern to George Washington as well. In 1777, Rush issued a strong condemnation of the use of distilled spirits that was published and distributed to all soldiers.*
>
> *This was followed in 1782 with a newspaper article entitled 'Against Spirituous Liquors,' in which Rush recommended that farmers cease the practice of providing daily rations of liquor to their laborers... Two years later, in 1784, Rush published a pamphlet entitled "An Enquiry into the Effects of Spirituous Liquors Upon the Human Body, and Their Influence Upon the Happiness of Society". This 36-page tract was reprinted by the thousands and stands as the most influential piece of early American writing on alcohol and alcoholism." (Dragon, p. 2)*

Some Injudicious Criticisms

Dr. Rush seems to have been an outspoken man, possibly lacking in political savvy. While representing Philadelphia at Pennsylvania's own Constitutional

Convention, he aroused controversy and some antipathy when he criticized the new Pennsylvania Constitution.

During the early stages of the Revolutionary War, the Army Medical Service was in disarray as the result of the high level of military casualties and deaths due to typhoid, yellow fever and other camp illnesses. There were also political conflicts, and inadequate supplies.

Then surgeon-general of the middle department of the Continental Army, Rush sided with John Morgan in criticizing a one-time mentor William Shippen Jr., for misappropriating supplies. When their complaint to George Washington was referred to Congress, and they then sided with Shippen, Rush resigned in disgust.

The early prosecution of the war did not go well for the colonials, and many were critical of the generalship of George Washington. Some sought to have him replaced. Rush penned two letters of criticism that he wanted communicated orally to Washington, leaving Rush's reproaches conveyed, but anonymous. Washington saw the letters, recognized the doctor's handwriting, and Rush was compelled to sever himself completely from the war effort.

In later years, Rush deeply regretted his criticisms of the national hero, and issued statements of great praise of the military leader.

Abolition, Indiscretion and Inconsistency

Dr. Benjamin Rush vociferously opposed slavery, and argued scientifically that Negroes were not, by nature, intellectually or morally inferior. Unfortunately, he went into greater detail. "In 1792, Rush read a paper before the American Philosophical Society which argued that the 'color' and 'figure' of blacks were derived from a form of leprosy. He argued that with proper treatment, blacks could be cured and become white." (Racial Formation in the United States, M. Omi and H. Winant, 1986)

Say whaaaaaat?????

The physician's conclusions were based, at least in part, by his review of the case of Henry Moss, a slave who had lost his dark skin color, probably due to vitiligo.

"Despite his public condemnation of slavery, Dr. Rush purchased a slave named William Grubber in 1776. To the consternation of many, he still owned Grubber when he joined the Pennsylvania Abolition Society in 1784." (African American Lives, Clayborne Carson, p. 119)

SAY WHAAAAAAAAT?????!!!!!!!

Rush the Physician

Rush thought that illness was the result of imbalances in the body's physical system and was caused by malfunctions in the brain. He stressed diligence in personal hygiene, and a clean environment. The colonial doctor was overly enamored of bleeding and purges using calomel and other toxic substances. The forced blood loss was thought to relieve pressure to the brain.

The Yellow Fever epidemic of 1793 brought great acclaim to the physician. He was seen as courageous for remaining in town, and treating up to 100 patients per day. Unfortunately, a great number of these patients died. In fairness to Benjamin Rush, this was an era in which the healer was often more dangerous than the affliction.

Not all were enthralled by his efforts. Journalist and pamphleteer, William Cobbett attacked Rush's extreme use of bloodletting, a practice increasingly being abandoned by many of his fellow physicians on the scientific grounds of its danger and ineffectiveness.

Cobbett accused Rush of killing more patients than he saved. Rush sued and won a judgment of $8,000, his victory in part possibly being due to his critic being a controversial figure, and an openly British sympathizer. Cobbett soon fled to New York, then Halifax, and back to England, still owing the lion's share of the penalty.

Notwithstanding this "moral victory", Rush's practice waned as he continued to advocate for leeches and purges, much to the chagrin of his friend Thomas Jefferson.

Conception of Drunkenness

> Rush first suggested that chronic drunkenness was a progressive medical condition... He called the process through which the drunkard became progressively addicted to and finally destroyed by alcohol a 'disease of the will.' Rush further recognized that the tendency toward drunkenness was transmitted intergenerationally within families.

> Rush's belief that distilled spirits were the cause of most drunkenness was so strong that he miscalculated the potential for similar effects from wine and beer.... (His) essay, which suggested that alcoholism should be viewed as a self-contained

disease, broke from the traditional view that excessive drinking was either a reflection of moral depravity or a cause or symptom of mental illness.

Disease references helped buttress the move toward total abstinence from alcohol...

Rush referred to the disease of drunkenness as "suicide perpetrated gradually" - an idea that Dr. Karl Menninger would revive and elaborate on 152 years later... some people's drunkenness sprang from a hidden desire for self-injury..." (Dragon, pp. 3-4)

Cotton in Their Ears

Cautions regarding the dangers of distilled spirits seems to have found an audience with cotton in their ears, and corn liquor jugs at their mouths. Considerable segments of the population were drinking, the pace being both startling and escalating.

At a time when the newly born nation "was reveling in its newfound freedom, Rush challenged in his tract that 'a nation corrupted by alcohol can never be free'". (Dragon, p. 3) The citizens of the new republic continued to run up this "corruption" to unprecedented levels. By 1810, the per capita consumption of pure alcohol per person was almost double the 1792 figure, and by 1830, it was triple.

This 40 year period of the highest alcohol consumption in America's history brought with it a variety of social problems, and prompted a strengthening of the countering forces of temperance. The temperance advocates reacted surprisingly well to the "disease concept". Without surrendering their basic "Satan and sin" message, the disease idea buttressed the move toward total abstinence from alcohol.

Treatment of Drunkards

As did other physicians of the day, Dr. Rush "believed that health and disease were determined by the relative balance or imbalance of the body's four humors (fluids): blood, phlegm, black bile and yellow bile... re-establishing the balance... by sweating, bleeding (via lancing or leeches), purging... blistering the skin, or ingesting various drugs... Many of his 'heroic' methods were clearly harmful". (Dragon, p. 4)

The refusal to alter his aggressive treatments led to a collapse of his practice, and financial disaster was averted by his appointment as Treasurer of the US Mint in 1797, a position he held until 1813, the year of his passing.

On the plus side, he "was the first American physician to posit that continued abstinence from alcohol was the only hope for the confirmed drunkard". (Dragon, p. 4) This idea did not gain a broad acceptance until the "AA era" was firmly established.

In one case, Rush produced a "cure" by inducing vomiting through an emetic mixed with alcohol, essentially inventing "aversion therapy" 156 years before Dr. Walter Voegtlin. He also had some success with what would much later be called "occupational therapy". Those assigned menial daily tasks did better in their recuperation than those left idle.

At a time when drunks, unwed mothers, and STD sufferers were seen as agents of their own misfortune, unworthy of community hospital care, Rush pushed for the creation of a "Sober House" where inebriates could be medically treated and rehabilitated. It was a visionary proposal.

The Weird and the Wonderful

Perhaps the majority of human beings are a mix of the weird and the wonderful, the stories of those in "high profile" remaining in the public consciousness. "A wildly popular and much beloved man, he was nonetheless a fallible character." (ushistory.org) That he practiced extensively among the poor, and lobbied for the general betterment of the working class, he was, to some extent, a champion of the masses. This was the man risking his own life to help others, in the 1793 Yellow Fever epidemic.

He made clear political errors. Both Benjamin Franklin and John Adams had some harsh observations to make about Rush. He had a reputation for gossip, and he was quick to pronounce judgments on others. While he considered himself scientific, he clung tenaciously to the old ideas of medical practice that others saw as obsolete.

"He was supremely confident of his own opinion and decisions, yet shallow and unscientific in practice." (ushistory.org)

His resolute abhorrence of distilled spirits, possibly rooted in unpleasant experiences with a liquor-producing step-father, tempered his call for drunkards' "total abstinence", sometimes prescribing wine, beer, cider and opium as replacements.

He lobbied for blacks to not be seen as inferior, but theorized that their "negroidism" was a curable disease.

He was an abolitionist who owned a slave.

America's most famous physician's practice was so diminished that his acceptance of a political appointment was, at least in part, motivated by economic considerations. Nonetheless, in some circles he remained much admired. Several of his students established Rush Medical College in Chicago, naming it in his honor.

Two notable graduates of Rush Medical were the very entrepreneurial Leslie Keeley, and a lanky Vermonter, Robert Holbrook Smith.

The Disease Concept

Rush's advocacy for viewing inebriety as an illness was a brave one. A religious man himself, he understood the dangers of lobbying for the medical treatment of "sin".

"I am aware that the efforts of science and humanity, in applying their resources to the cure of a disease induced by a vice, will meet with a cold reception from many people." (An inquiry Into the Effects of Ardent Spirits Upon the Human Body & Mind, Benjamin Rush, p. 29)

The modern disease/not disease debate is a complex one based largely on technicalities and terms of definition. The debate of Rush's time was disease vs. "moral depravity." The AA era moves forward in a now much easier battle.

The wisdom gleaned from William White's four decades of experience emerges in these words: "We have both an individual and collective need for this concept to be 'true,' regardless of its scientific status… Science is unlikely to destroy the popularity of the disease metaphor, but a better metaphor could." (Dragon, p. 512)

As the first American physician to challenge the old, intractable metaphor of dysfunctional drinking as "moral degeneracy", Dr. Benjamin Rush merits a nod from AA.

Chapter 8 The Washingtonian Society

"Jack Alexander, Saturday Evening Post, was also one of the friends to whom Bill sent material. Of the Twelve Tradition essays, Alexander has this to say: 'The only serious (in my view) defect is that you have treated the old Washingtonian Society too briefly; most people never heard of it.'" (Pass It On, p. 354)

In the twenty-first century, AA members generally have heard of the movement, but often in snippets that have been distorted in the various re-transmissions. With thanks mainly to William L. White, here is an account of the principal details of the early mutual-aid group.

The Drunkard's Mind and Heart

> *How much more influence then has the man who stands before an audience to persuade them to abandon the use of strong drink, when he can himself tell them of its ruinous and blasting effects on his own life and character - trace the program of his own habits of intemperance - and warn others to avoid the rock on which he spit. A reformed man has the best access to a drunkard's mind and heart, because he best knows, and can enter into a drunkard's feelings. And such appeals from such sources, properly directed, can rarely fail of entire success. John Zug (The Foundation, Progress and Principles of the*

Washington Temperance Society of Baltimore, John D Troy, 1842)

The arrival of 1840 in America saw a temperance movement that was fragmented and in decline. The shift from moderation to total abstinence, emerging advocacy for the legal prohibition of alcohol, and conflict regarding its stand on the abolition of slavery, had hurt the organization's membership.

It was also recognized that what was needed was some means of reforming the drunkard.

The Chase Tavern

"On April 2, 1840, six members of a drinking club at the Chase Tavern in Baltimore, Maryland were prompted, by an argument with the proprietor, to send a delegation to investigate a temperance lecture being given that very night by the Reverend Matthew Hale Smith." (Slaying The Dragon, The History of Addiction and Recovery in America, Second Edition, p. 13)

Further discussion led, the following day, to the formation of the Washingtonian Total Abstinence Society. William Mitchell, John Hoss, David Anderson, George Steers, James McCurley, and Archibald Campbell all signed the pledge drafted by Mitchell:

> *We, whose names are annexed, desirous of forming a society for mutual benefit, and to guard against a pernicious practice which is injurious to our health, standing and families, do pledge ourselves as gentlemen, that we will not drink any spirituous or malt liquor, wine or cider.*

Unlike other temperance groups which tended to be led by, and composed of, the social elite, the Washingtonians were from the artisan and working classes.

Experiencing Sharing

"The main bill of fare at a Washingtonian meeting was experience sharing - confessions of alcoholic debauchery followed by glorious accounts of personal reformation... As each newcomer came forward, he was asked to tell a little of his own story, then sign the abstinence pledge amid the cheers of onlookers. This ritual of public confession and public signing of the pledge carried great emotional power for those participating. It evoked, at least temporarily, what would be described one hundred years later as ego deflation and surrender." (Dragon, p. 14)

The converts immediately sought others.

"Let every man be present, and every man bring a man."

The proselytizing effort was highly organized, with "ward committees" taking charge of given areas. The sequence of drinker recruiting drinker led to rapid growth.

"From the beginnings as a working class movement, the Washingtonians recruited a growing number of the affluent and famous... (including) two men who became mayors, one who became governor of his state, and several members of Congress." (Dragon, p. 14)

Closed Meetings

Until November of 1840, Washingtonian meetings were not open to outsiders, and as such, constituted "the first widespread 'closed meetings' of alcoholics banded together for mutual support and recovery". (Dragon, p. 15) All of this took place a full century before Alcoholics Anonymous.

Public meetings led to a change in primary purpose. Initially a society for reformed drunks, "the only requirement for membership became the pledge of personal abstinence... The speed with which the membership changed was quite remarkable... by June of 1841, the Washingtonian Society in Worcester had 500 members, only 50 of which had been hard cases." (Dragon, p. 15)

Abe Lincoln and Good Press

One sympathetic guest speaker was Abraham Lincoln, who on February 22, 1842, addressed the Springfield, Illinois branch with these words: "In my judgment such of us who have never fallen victims have been spared more by the absence of appetite than from any mental or moral superiority over those who have".

The group's results were so remarkable, and often with those considered beyond redemption, that they were sometimes referred to as the "Resurrection Society". "The Press of the day gave the society uncounted columns of publicity." (AA Grapevine, July 1945, History Offers Good Lesson For AA) "The drunkard has taken the cause in his own hands - analyzed his disease and wrought his own cure." (Baltimore Sun)

"Never in history had an alcohol abstinence movement taken off so explosively... At the height of the movement, more than 600,000 pledges were signed, thousands marched in Washingtonian temperance parades, and a weekly newspaper was launched." (Dragon, p. 15)

Martha Anon and Marthateen

Special meetings were organized for women and children. The first Martha Washington Society was... May 12, 1844, in New York. The goals... were to provide moral and material support to reforming inebriates, and to provide special support to female inebriates and to the wives and children of inebriates... Although other temperance societies were quite conscious of the social class and reputation of those they recruited, the Martha Washington Societies extended support to some of 'the most disreputable members of their communities.'

One of their parade banners, "Total abstinence or no husband" indicates that they may have scored a "first" in the use of "detachment", loving, or otherwise. Other temperance movement "firsts" were in helping inebriate women, and in having females in leadership roles.

John Hawkins

As these successes were reported, requests for speakers flooded in from all over the country. Various pairs went on extended tours propelled by a single purpose: to spread the Washingtonian message of hope to the alcoholic.

John Henry Hawkins, having lost two wives and a career as a hatter, was approached by his daughter who begged him to not send her for more whiskey again. He joined the original Baltimore group two months after its founding. "His organizational skills and charismatic speeches contributed to the spread of the movement... Hawkins made a profession of lecturing on the temperance circuit and held a paid position with the Massachusetts Temperance Society." (Dragon, p. 17)

Hawkins was convinced of the role of religion in long term recovery, and became a Methodist minister. He is said to have travelled in excess of 200,000 miles, and delivered more than 5,000 speeches in the eighteen years between his reformation and death.

John Gough

"John Gough was popular during his drinking years. His imitations, stories, and songs brightened many a tavern and street corner. Through the years of his drinking, he descended from a light-hearted man of the town to a drunken buffoon." (Dragon, p. 17)

Touched by what he heard at a temperance meeting in October, 1842, he signed a pledge and almost immediately began a career as a speech maker. The former bookbinder had a flair for it.

"His emotional and highly dramatic presentations were in high demand. He was paid $2 for his first lecture, $10 per lecture in a 1844 tour of New York, and as much as $170 per lecture in the years following the Civil War ($2,800 in 2014 money). Thirty years after signing the pledge, John Gough has amassed a small fortune from his skills on the lecture stage." (Dragon, p. 17)

Gough was not without relapses, the first possibly triggered by tincture of opium prescribed by his physician. He confessed to that particular fall, and gained a new understanding of the insidious nature of addiction. However, after being found in a "house of ill-repute" following a later relapse, his claim of being drugged and abducted by the enemies of temperance was less credible.

Other Washingtonians disagreed with his advocacy of the legal prohibition of alcohol, and some colleagues accused him of exploiting temperance for his own financial gain. Some of this sprung from obvious jealousies over his legendary oratorical skills.

"On February 15, 1886, John Gough collapsed and died while giving a speech. He was 69 years old. In his lifetime, he had travelled more than 450,000 miles and delivered more than 8,600 temperance addresses." (Dragon, p. 18)

Carrying the Message

Hawkins and Gough, and others like them, carried the Washingtonian message across the nation. They shared openly and intensely the stories of their lives, before and after they quit drinking. In doing so, they inspired many to reach for a pledge card and to tell their own tales. Rehabilitated inebriates sought out others of their ilk who might be open to being inspired to a new way of living.

Gough also pushed religion, and was especially high on the importance of a posture of humility.

"Key leaders of the Washingtonian Movement such as John Hawkins and John Gough continued their travels long after the movement's demise…

Hawkins and Gough were among the first recovered alcoholics working in paid roles to carry a message of hope to other alcoholics." (Dragon, p. 19)

Demise and Lessons for AA

As quickly as it had come about, so did it dematerialize. "By 1845, the Washingtonian movement's energy was spent. Almost none of the Washingtonian Societies were active beyond 1847, with the exception of those in Boston." (Dragon, p. 19)

Even to this day, some mystery surrounds the downfall. The multiplicity of possible contributory causes are excellently reviewed in Mr. White's "Slaying the Dragon - The History of Addiction Treatment in America."

Although they lacked an unambiguously articulated ideology,

> *their core activities are clearly identifiable. The Washingtonian program of recovery consisted of:*
>
> - *public confession;*
> - *public commitment;*
> - *visits from older members;*
> - *economic assistance;*
> - *continued participation in experience sharing;*
> - *acts of service toward other alcoholics;*
> - *sober entertainment. (Dragon, p. 16)*

The criticisms are varied, and in some instances, reflect the prejudices or agendas of the detractors. Those favoring legal prohibition of alcohol saw "moral suasion" as inherently inadequate as a strategy. Religious leaders attacked the lack of religion and the reliance on social camaraderie. Some even went so far as leveling charges of "humanism".

Land O Goshen!!

In a Grapevine article published in July, 1945, a Michigan writer brought the Washingtonians story to the attention of Bill Wilson and other AA members... at that time, merely an arcane bit of recovery history. Regarding the ruination of the group, he wrote, "politicians looked hungrily at its swelling membership. Some of them climbed aboard the wagon and they helped to wreck local groups through their efforts to line up votes". (Lesson For AA)

The essayist's personal agenda was reflected in his own summary of the Washingtonians "real" problem - that "its organizers thought they could get along without a 'Higher Power'". (Lesson For AA)

As speakers attempted to "outdo" each other, there were charges of sensationalism, even fabrication. Meetings were criticized for vulgarity, and instances of relapse were particularly damaging.

As Bill Sees It

The article above prompted Bill W. to explore, then weigh in on, the Washingtonians, and the "Lessons" article, in the very next issue. "Those who read the July Grapevine were startled, then sobered, by the account which it carried of the Washingtonian movement." (AA Grapevine, August, 1945, Modesty One Good Plank For Public Relations)

He found the reports of "triumphal parades in Boston" to be "overdone self-advertising". The stories of members who were hungry politicians reflected dangerous "personal ambition", and also injudicious was the "unnecessary group participation in controversial issues... (such as) the abolition of slavery". (Modesty)

The Washingtonians were "too cocksure, maybe. Couldn't learn from others and became competitive instead of cooperative". (Modesty)

A crucial error was made in the society's deviation from its initial prime directive. "The original strong and simple group purpose was thus dissipated in fruitless controversy and divergent aims." On the issue of the general proscription of alcohol, members and spokespersons debated each other, the prohibitionists alienating manufacturers and distributors in the process.

Ultimately, it was a death blow that there was "no national public relations policy which all members were willing to follow".

Summary

> *The Washingtonian Society contributed many firsts. It was the first widely available mass mutual-aid society organized by and for alcoholics in American history... Washingtonian legacies included:*
>
> - *the importance of maintaining a focus on the welfare and reformation of the individual alcoholic;*

- *the potential power of a personal and public commitment to total abstinence from alcohol;*
- *the benefit of regular sober fellowship...*
- *the power of experience sharing...*
- *the use of recovered alcoholics as charismatic speakers and in service work to other alcoholics, and;*
- *the use of a spiritual religious foundation for sustained recovery (not part of the official program but incorporated by key Washingtonian leaders. (Dragon, p. 21)*

The lessons to AA came in the greater part from an examination of the Washingtonians errors. AA's Traditions were formed, in the main, from mistakes made, and lessons learned.

"Those who cannot remember the past are condemned to repeat it." - George Santayana

History has value.

Chapter 9 What is "New Thought"?

> *The most obvious connecting link between Alcoholics Anonymous and the New Thought movement comes through William James who "had found answers to his own depression and doubts about his self-worth from... New Thought teachings, which he termed 'mind-cure'... While New Thought organizations never became very large, their ideas have wide acceptance in general society and also influenced early AA.... The principal benefit... was much like the program of the Oxford Group and the claims of William James in his seminal book. It transformed religious beliefs into a plan of action that individuals could follow for their own benefit in solving problems here and now."*
>
> *(New Wine - The Spiritual Roots of the Twelve Step Miracle, Mel B., p. 105)*

The powers of the universe will directly respond to your individual appeals and needs.

Nice!!!

"Mind-cure" is discussed at length in the Varieties lectures. James sees roots of New Thought ideas in the four Gospels, Emersonian transcendentalism,

Berkeleyian idealism, spiritism, evolutionism, and Hinduism. Others see an origin that dates back to Plato's cave, where "ideas" had greater reality than matter. The New Thought philosophy also appears to have been influenced by the works of Emmanuel Swedenborg who held the view that the material realm is one of the effects whose causes are spiritual, and whose purpose is divine.

Lois Wilson's family, the Burnhams, were staunchly ensconced in this faction - her grandfather was a Swedenborgian minister.

What Is "New Thought"?

"New Thought is a spiritual movement, sometimes classed as a Christian denomination, which developed in the United States in the 19th Century, following the teachings of Phineas Quimby. It is a mind healing movement... based on religious and metaphysical presuppositions." (Encyclopaedia Britannica) New Thought is "an umbrella term for diverse beliefs that emphasize experiencing God's presence for practical purposes, such as healing or success." (beliefnet.com)

Or getting sober, perhaps.

> *(a) We were alcoholic and could not manage our own lives.*
> *(b) That probably no human power could have relieved our alcoholism.*
> *(c) That God could and would if He were sought. (BB, p. 60)*

"The New Thought person was to be free from the principles of a declared belief, instead being in touch with the omnipresent Indwelling Presence of God." (The Road To Fellowship, Richard Dubiel, p. 3) Unlike most religious societies, there is no sacred text, or immutable canon. "Truth is viewed as a matter of continuing revelation, and no one leader or institution can declare with finality what is the nature of truth." (newthoughtalliance.org)

This is not so unlike "Our book is meant to be suggestive only. We realize we know only a little. God will constantly disclose more to you and to us." (BB, p. 164) AA is not frozen in 1939.

In theory, at least.

For a relatively small organization, New Thought has experienced much fragmentation. Beliefs are varied, and thus, difficult to summarize. The three major factions today are: 1. Religious Science; 2. Unity Church; 3. Church of Divine Science. Bill Wilson's close friend, Marty Mann, was a longtime member of the Church of Religious Science.

The bulk of the remaining sects have unified under the banner of the International New Thought Alliance (INTA).

INTA

In 1914, various New Thought splinter groups formed an association, and in 1916, put out a "mission statement".

"To teach the Infinitude of the Supreme One, the Divinity of Man and his Infinite Possibilities through the creative power of constructive thinking and obedience to the voice of the indwelling Presence which is our source of Inspiration, Power, Health and Prosperity." (newthoughtalliance.org)

The 1917 "Declaration of Principles", modified in 1919, "emphasized the immanence of God, the divine nature of man, the immediate availability of God's power to man, the spiritual character of the universe, and the fact that sin, and human disorders are basically matters of incorrect thinking". (Britannica)

The modern INTA website lists New Thought's "affirmations" which include:

> *We affirm the power of prayer and the capacity of each person to have mystical experience with God, and to enjoy the grace of God.*
>
> *We affirm the manifestation of the kingdom of heaven here and now.*
>
> *We affirm...loving one another unconditionally... (and) ministering to one another.*

(newthoughtalliance.org)

Phineas Quimby

Phineas Quimby (1806-1866) "a self-educated clockmaker from Portland, Maine, is generally acknowledged as the founder of New Thought". (New Wine, p. 104) Quimby "practiced mesmerism and developed his concepts of mental and spiritual healing, and health based on the view that illness is a matter of the mind". (Britannica)

Anton Mesmer (1734-1815), a physician who practiced hypnotism, and other forms of psychic healing, attributed his successes to a natural energetic transference that he called "animal magnetism". A Royal Commission investigating the "cures" wrought by one of Mesmer's disciples concluded the cause to be "imagination".

Quimby, the former clockmaker, thought that his healings were not from animal magnetism. He thought he was duplicating the works of Christ, and other prophets. The Skeptic's Dictionary agrees, seeing a sameness in the biblical and Quimby phenomena. "The power of suggestion, the optimism of the healer, the strong motivation of the sick to be rid of their various ailments (many of them psychological), the faith of the patient in the cure of the healer, the rituals and theater of the healing all combine to produce what we now loosely call the placebo effect." (Skeptic's Dictionary)

Many years earlier, the comments of Mark Twain were more succinct. He proclaimed that "all the various forms of New Thought, as well as Christian Science, were cut from the same cloth... they all do their miracles with the same old powerful instrument – the patient's imagination". (Dubiel, p. 3)

Although she denied it, Quimby can be seen to have influenced Mary Baker Eddy, the founder of Christian Science, a movement which was explosively popular at the turn of the 20th century. Eddy had been a "patient" of Quimby's.

"Did Christian Science teachings have anything to do with the forming of AA and the evolution of the Twelve Steps? Bill Wilson, months before he met up with the Oxford Group, had read and reread Mary Baker Eddy's Science and Health with Key to the Scriptures in the hope of overcoming his drinking by strengthening his willpower." (New Wine, p. 104)

Fire and Brimstone

New Thought was, in many ways, a reaction to the existing intellectual and religious climates of the era. It can be "traced to the dissatisfaction on the part of many persons with scientific empiricism and their reaction to religious skepticism in the 17th and 18th centuries". (Britannica) As well, the "fire and brimstone" that constituted the Christian reign of terror being foisted on the majority of Americans, left an opening for something more positive.

"Man... is reared in fear; all his life is passed in bondage to fear of death and disease; and thus his whole mentality becomes cramped, limited, and depressed, and his body follows its shrunken pattern and specification... a perpetual nightmare... an ocean of morbidity." (Ideal Suggestion through Mental Photography, p. 54)

And then, Hell awaits.

"New Thought counters with an unflinchingly positive and optimistic view of life and its outcome. By... resigning the care of your destiny to higher powers... the believer gives the little private convulsive self a rest." (Language of the Heart, Trysh Travis, p. 77)

William James and Eldwood Worcester

"James disaggregated spirituality from specific theologies... and thus made it available for use by anti-authoritarian alcoholics." (Travis, p. 78) Further, "James characterized New Thought's highest aim as an undoing of the modern norms of vigilance and aggression, the cultivation of 'passivity, not activity; relaxation, not intentness'". These ideas invite comparison to the relaxation techniques employed by lay therapists Courtenay Baylor and Richard Peabody of the Emmanuel Movement, which was influenced by Christian Science and New Thought concepts.

Elwood Worcester was an Episcopal minister with a PhD in psychology. His Emmanuel Movement was, at least in part, a response to Christian Science and New Thought, both claiming to heal various diseases by Christian methods. These are "'harmonial religions' ...in which spiritual composure, physical health, and even economic well-being are understood to flow from a personal rapport with the cosmos". (Dubiel, p. 2) The Emmanuels attempted to reconcile psychotherapy and Christianity. Their efforts in bringing "free religious psychotherapy" led to conflicts with the medical authorities, but not before they were brought into contact with many alcoholics among the populations of tuberculosis, and neurasthenia sufferers they targeted to help.

> *And we have ceased fighting anything or anyone - even alcohol. For by this time sanity will have returned. We will seldom be interested in liquor. If tempted, we recoil from it as from a hot flame. We react sanely and normally, and we will find that this has happened automatically. We will see that our new attitude toward liquor has been given us without any thought or effort on our part. It just comes! That is the miracle of it. We are not fighting it, neither are we avoiding temptation. We feel as though we had been placed in a position of neutrality - safe and protected. We have not even sworn off. Instead, the problem has been removed. It does not exist for us. We are neither cocky nor are we afraid. (BB, pp. 84-85)*

The famous 10th step promises are dripping with passivity!

Early AA

Early AA members were encouraged to read New Thought literature such as Emmet Fox's The Sermon on the Mount and Thomas Troward's Edinburgh Lectures on Mental Science. Some went to the Ministry of High Watch retreat, based on the teaching of Eddy disciple, Emma Hopkins. High Watch was "one of the first treatment communities to address alcoholism solely through spiritual means". (Travis, p. 79)

Richmond Walker, an AA member who got sober in Boston in 1942, penned a daily meditation book, Twenty-Four Hours A Day, in 1948, after moving to spend winters in Daytona Beach. This book was instantly popular, and it has been conjectured that there may have been a time when more AA members owned Walker's volume that owned the rather expensive Big Book. According to historian Glenn Chesnut, "there are flashes of the Emmanuel Movement's New Thought mysticism scattered throughout the text". (hindsfoot.org)

As we have learned from Mel B., Bill Wilson was familiar with the writings and philosophy of Mary Baker Eddy. Various aspects of Alcoholics Anonymous reflect the influences of both Christian Science and the overall "New Thought" movement.

Letting Go

A fundamental and critical AA method involves "letting go". "Some of us have tried to hold onto our old ideas and the result was nil until we let go absolutely." (BB, p. 58) Change through religion sprouts from similar seeds. "The individual becomes willing to give up the old self or the old ways… and the answers come. James called this 'surrender' the 'way of success.'" (New Wine, p. 104)

"It's not hard to see that this same idea was transferred to AA." (New Wine, p. 104) A Second Edition story, The Professor and the Paradox, lists four paradoxes of how AA works. Number One is "We Surrender to Win". Although Bill Wilson judiciously avoided using the specific term "surrender" in writing the Big Book, the concept is easily discernible.

AA, in its book, expresses disdain for the "self-propulsion" and "self-will run riot" of alcoholics in their former lives, these ambitions going hand in hand with compulsive drinking. "Influenced by both the evangelical Oxford Group… and New Thought religions, AA's created a sense of self and of community loosely premised on what (sociologist) Max Weber has called a 'religious rejection of the world.'" (Travis, p. 62)

"Alcoholics Anonymous... is premised on a 'rejection of the world' ...AA's versions of asceticism and mysticism derive from... the active and evangelical Protestantism of Frank Buchman's Oxford Group and the passive, idealist, harmonial optimism of New Thought religions... By vigorously embracing the ascetic 'surrendered life', AA's became able to pursue a deliberately diffuse, non-creedal, and sometimes mystical spirituality." (Travis, p. 70)

"To the New Thought idealist, it is the world's false definitions of health, wealth, and happiness that weigh down and sicken the soul. Devotional practice - affirmations, prayers, meditations - works to loosen the hold of those false definitions on the spirit and thus restore its 'natural' health and prosperity." (Travis, p. 77)

New Thought in the Modern World

The 21st Century incarnations of the New Thought Movement are largely commercial. The positive thinking that was believed capable of spiritual regeneration, or even of physical healing by those in the Eddy camp, now appears in the self-help world as the "golden ticket" to all that the avaricious heart may desire.

Phineas Quimby might flinch at The Secret, or possibly bemoan his lack of foresight in not himself venturing down the yellow brick road of gold ingots. The notion that positive thoughts have an all-encompassing power over future results, supplies more than ample fodder for critics. Even more so, perhaps, does the corollary that negative thinking is at the root of every tribulation.

The number of healed amputees, of course, remains at zero.

Can anyone believe that if you happen to have the misfortune of being born, say, in a squalid Indian village governed by a caste system, that all you have to do is believe your way out?

In a harshly critical 2010 review, The New York Times states: "'The Power' and 'The Secret' are larded with references to magnets, energy and quantum mechanics. This last is a dead giveaway: whenever you hear someone appeal to impenetrable physics to explain the workings of the mind, run away - we already have disciplines called "psychology" and "neuroscience" to deal with those questions. Byrne's onslaught of pseudoscientific jargon serves mostly to establish an "illusion of knowledge", as social scientists call our tendency to believe we understand something much better than we really do".

The "Law of Attraction" is about as much a law as AA "statistics" are statistics.

Rhonda's Byrne's enormously successful book has spawned many imitators, while itself being an imitation of the "positive thinking" efforts of generations ago. Napoleon Hill and Norman Vincent Peale grew out of the basic New

Thought mentality. The torch bearer of the movement's "spiritually-focused" aspect is Oprah Winfrey, who is also no opponent of financial windfall, but don't go dissing Oprah! Like AA, Oprah is a national institution.

Alcoholics Anonymous

AA's ideas of taking the drink problem in its entirety and turning it over to God is fully compatible with core "New Thought" strategy. When one reads the Big Book looking for positive affirmations, there are many to be found. Journeying through the philosophy and writings of William James, and also the Emmanuel Movement, New Thought's principles have arrived in AA.

Phineas Quimby probably did not foresee that.

Chapter 10 Jerry McAuley and The Water Street Mission

Salvation from alcoholic dissipation through religious conversion is not unprecedented. The tale of Jerry McAuley is a classic one, as he was able to achieve sobriety via a spiritual experience, and then to maintain this new lifestyle by means of service to his fellow man. His story is in William James *Varieties of Religious Experience*, a book given to Bill Wilson in Towns Hospital by his new evangelistic friends. Bill Wilson went on to found AA.

Sixty years earlier, McAuley had gone on to establish "the world's first rescue mission - where the drunkard was more welcome than the sober man, the thief preferred to the honest man, the harlot favored over the beautiful woman". (The Roots of Alcoholics Anonymous, Bill Pittman, p. 80) This took place in New York City on October 8th, 1872.

A Misspent Youth

The future founder of the McAuley Water Street Mission was born in Ireland, circa 1839. He had no recollection of a father who had fled from the law which sought to arrest him for counterfeiting. His mother either could not, or would not raise him, so he was deposited with a grandmother while he was still a very young child. The grandmother, "a devout Romanist", could not instill those values into a rebellious young Jerry who threw clumps of dirt at the old woman when she was prostrate in rosary-reciting devotions.

As a youth, he never went to school. Instead, he would "roam about in idleness, doing mischief continually, and suffering from the cruel and harsh treatment of those who had the care of me". (Jerry McAuley: His life and Work, Robert M. Offord, 1885, p. 10) At the age of thirteen, the youthful miscreant was sent to live with relatives in New York City.

A "River Thief" Gets Framed

In America, teen-aged Jerry McAuley continued his apprenticeship as a minor criminal and a "street tough". He became a "river thief", pillaging whatever he could from boats and waterfront warehouses. "In the daytime we went up into the city and sold our ill-gotten goods, and with the proceeds dressed up, then spent our time, as long as the money lasted, in the vice dens of Water Street practising all sorts of wickedness."(JM, p. 11)

The young thug became highly skilled as a fighter and became hated not only by the "straight" citizens but by his confrères in the underworld. At the age of nineteen, he was accused of highway robbery, convicted, and sentenced to fifteen years of hard labor. Thus he was off to Sing Sing, for a crime he forever claimed he had not committed.

"Awful" Gardner

Orville Gardner who had converted to Christianity, leaving behind a life of crime, was allowed to come to Sing Sing to preach. Jerry McAuley was about five years into his sentence when one Sunday he listened to "Awful" Gardner's tearful tale of reformation. Convinced of the sincerity of the former criminal, McAuley began to read the Bible. No immediate transformation was wrought, and for several weeks he was conflicted.

Then one day in his tiny cell, an inner voice directed him, "Pray". A spiritual experience ensued leaving him with a conviction that his sins were forgiven and that life had become "new". "I was happy, for Jesus was my friend; my sins were washed away and my heart was full of love." (JM, p. 20) Feeling the call to evangelize, he had some success in converting others. When mocked by the other inmates, he prayed to forgive them. This reformation impressed the Governor, and a pardon was issued. On March 8th, 1864, the twenty-six year old convict was set free, the latter half of his sentence commuted.

A Funny Thing Happened on the Way to Salvation

Released from prison, McAuley set out to associate with Christians. Unfortunately, he had a chance encounter with an old friend who persuaded him to try the new and "harmless" lager beer. "I drank it, and thus began my downfall... The old appetite was awakened. From that time, I drank every day... Satan got completely the upper hand of me." (JM, p. 23) In a short time, lager beer was replaced with stronger liquors.

For a time, McAuley worked as a bounty hunter, getting young men very drunk and enlisted into the Union army. Smuggling and counterfeiting were added to his resume. A boat was acquired and, with a partner, the old river thievery was resumed. One night, a fire aboard the "Idaho", a ferry, provided a great opportunity for looting, but McAuley instead was inspired to rescue passengers from the river after they had abandoned the flaming craft.

Possibly already reconsidering his life of crime, one night he was very nearly shot by a ship's captain while trying to steal from his vessel a part that would fetch less than two dollars. However, the "devil-may-care" criminals had no rainy day reserve of funds, and were propelled by need to a continuation of the pilfering. One night while too drunk to assist his cohort, McAuley fell into the water and knowing he was about to drown, a voice told him to call out to God, which he did. "I seemed to be lifted right up to the surface of the water and the boat... was brought right to me, so that I could get a hold of it... It always seemed to me a miracle." (p. 26)

A sobering experience! Or possibly not.

A Pledge and a Coat

"I drank, and drank, and drank. But no amount of liquor could drown that inward voice." (JM, p. 27) At the Howard Mission, he signed a temperance pledge. Recounting this to his partner only an hour later, the man laughed at him and proffered a glass of gin. Perhaps conflicted once again, McAuley downed the spirits but declared that it was his last drink. Nonetheless, financial destitution was compelling him back to his familiar means of "earning" a dishonest living, when a missionary offered to sell his coat, so that Jerry would not go out on the river to steal.

He was moved.

The good man went away and returned with fifty cents, which he turned over with the words, "Pray for yourself, and God will save you". This elicited a second spiritual experience, this one "more calm and peaceful". (JM, p. 31)

McAuley stayed sober under the close ministrations of his new friend. After a few months, the mentor went away and "the devil made me drink again". (JM, p. 32)

There's a Train A'comin'

Plagued with guilt, the fallen sinner found a church where he was unrelieved by his prayers and came up with a plan to kill himself. Saved by the conductor from a very slow-moving train, McAuley found a meeting and confessed his sins, seeking God's forgiveness. "I fell once after that, but God lifted me up again". (JM, p. 33)

Alfrederick Hatch

Jerry McAuley had gone straight, and a fellow Christian from the opposite end of the social spectrum was impressed, and became his "confidant". Businessman, Alfrederick Hatch was a Wall Street banker who had been president of the New York Stock Exchange. In October of 1872, Hatch donated a house at 316 Water St., and funds were raised to repair the property. The McAuley Water Street Mission was founded, America's first ever "Rescue Mission". (There are over 300 today in North America.)

A very shaky post Civil War economy, as well as a giant wave of European immigration to New York, made this a time of exceptional hardship and poverty. The Water Street Mission provided food and shelter for the body and an offer of Christ for the soul. "They were the first to open the doors of a religious institution every night of the year to the outcasts of society." (NYC Rescue Mission Website)

Recovery

Among those assisted by the operation were a number of drunkards, some of which were led to sobriety through the channel of Christian surrender, but also under the very practical mentoring of Jerry McAuley. Some sixty-five years later, Dr. Bob Smith would write of Bill Wilson and the impact of their first meeting, "... he was the first human being with whom I had ever talked, who knew what he was talking about in regard to alcoholism from actual experience. In other words, he talked my language". (Big Book, p. 180) Jerry McAuley also spoke that language.

The Mission motto was "Helping Hand For Men". The sobered drunks were encouraged to "pass it on" to others. The "helped" became helpers.

Times Square and Time's Up

In 1882, McAuley left Water St. in the care of others and moved on to start the Cremorne Mission near Times Square. Similar works were done there. In 1884, tuberculosis ended the life of a still young Jerry McAuley, but had he continued drinking he very likely would have gone far sooner.

Hadleys

> One Wednesday evening in 1882, Jerry McAuley helped convert a drunkard by the name of Samuel Hopkins Hadley. After Hadley's conversion, he became an active and successful member of McAuley's Water St. Mission. He even lured his drunkard brother, Colonel Henry Harrison Hadley, down to Water Street one night in July, 1886 and helped to convert him... From the 1890s until his death in 1906, Samuel Hadley traveled to Winona to participate in the annual Great Bible Conference, as did representatives from missions across the nation... Whenever it was known that S.H. Hadley was to speak the people with one accord rushed to hear him...

> Hadley's son was converted three days after his father's death. Henry Harrison Hadley II became a missionary like his father and traveled throughout the United States doing Christian work. In 1926 he helped open Calvary Mission in New York City with Rev. Sam Shoemaker. Over the years, many drunkards were converted at this mission... On December 7, 1934, Calvary Mission had a first-time visitor, William Griffith Wilson. This visit helped precipitate Wilson's last debauche and four days later on December 11, 1934, he entered Towns Hospital which was to become his final detoxification. (Pittman, pp. 80-81)

Conclusions

It remains, and will continue to be, a matter of debate as to what were the exact causative factors, in these "religious" redemptions. For some, these transformations lie beyond the scope of human manipulation, and are wrought only through unmerited grace bestowed by some Ultimate Power. Perhaps this is so.

Perhaps not.

Others lacking belief in the Power, readily acknowledge the power of belief.

It is fascinating that surrender to the divine produced in Jerry McAuley spiritual experiences that had no lasting effect until he had, what AA would call, a "practical program of action". For the secularist, helping others may have been the definitive factor in his long term success. As McAuley shared with others, the role of identification is difficult to deny. Within the Mission, and its broader purposes, a small aggregation of alcoholics was able to gather and develop a community of like-minded fellows, a formula previously proven highly effective with the Washingtonians. Early in the twentieth century, the Jacoby Club in Boston followed their slogan of "Men Helping Themselves By Helping Others" to a significant number of reclamations.

Other groups in other locales did likewise, and forged a path for the most efficacious and enduring of them all, Alcoholics Anonymous. How does it all work?

Who's to say?

Chapter 11 20th Century Influences on AA

It is fairly common knowledge that there are religious roots to AA. Much has been written about our earliest existence as part of the Christian revivalist Oxford Group. From Carl Jung comes the need in the chronic alcoholic for some form of "spiritual awakening". These awakenings are also described as "huge emotional displacements and rearrangements", "personality changes", "a profound alteration in his reaction to life", and the like. One man's miracle is another's psychology.

Our great medical benefactor, Dr. William Silkworth also was more convinced of the power of belief, than belief in the Power. "We doctors have known for a long time that some form of 'moral psychology' was of urgent importance to alcoholics". Silkworth's first letter to the fledgling Alcoholics Anonymous refers to Bill Wilson's new plan of treatment for alcoholics, the core being presenting "his conceptions to other alcoholics, impressing upon them that they must do likewise with still others".

Helping others in order to stay sober oneself was not unprecedented. The Baltimore Washingtonian Society, in the previous century, had had tremendous short term success, as had Richard R. Peabody in the 1920s and 1930s. Peabody used his firsthand experience as an alcoholic to create a program for sobriety that was deliciously secular, kept himself sober for years, helped many others, and produced a book, "The Common Sense of Drinking". (1930)

"Alcoholism is a disease of immaturity", "The conviction that abstinence from alcohol is of SUPREME IMPORTANCE is an absolute necessity", "The alcoholic has already found out that he cannot learn to drink normally, and he is convinced that his habit is progressive", "A man who is on the wagon may be sober physically, but mentally he may be almost as alcohol-minded as if he were drunk". These quotations could have easily come from an early draft of the Big Book, but in fact, they are from Peabody's book.

Any doubt regarding Bill Wilson's familiarity with "The Common Sense of Drinking" is removed by the following, "A man must do everything in his power to cooperate in such work as there is to be done. Halfway measures are of no avail". Sound familiar?

Richard Rogers Peabody

Richard R. Peabody was born in January, 1892, and grew up as a member of the upper class in Boston. Great-great-grandfather Joseph, a Salem shipowner and privateer, had amassed a mammoth fortune by importing pepper from Sumatra and opium from Eastern Asia. At the time of his death in 1844, he was one of America's wealthiest men. Succeeding generations of Peabodys ranked with the Cabots and the Lodges among the region's most prominent families.

A young Dick Peabody attended Groton School, a small and elite prep school (2011 tuition: $40K to $50K) founded, in 1884, by his uncle, the Reverend Endicott Peabody. Moving on to Harvard, he failed to graduate, at least in part owing to a burgeoning fondness for liquor. After courting and then marrying, in 1915, fellow "blue-blood" Polly Jacobs, Peabody started a shipping business. The onset of World War I brought prosperity to many American entrepreneurs, but Peabody lost money.

In April of 1916, the young husband's excessive drinking was being scrutinized by his in-laws. This precipitated a rather hasty flight from Massachusetts to Mexico, where Peabody enlisted in Battery "A", Boston's crack militia, a unit engaged in defending against border raids by Pancho Villa. By 1917, American troops were readying to join the European conflict, and summer found the young officer in the very same town of Plattsburgh, where "war fever ran high" for a young lieutenant, William Griffith Wilson. In the homes of New England's "first citizens", the future founder of Alcoholics Anonymous made the life-changing discovery that his shyness and social awkwardness vanished amidst the clinking of cocktail glasses. Dick Peabody, some four years older, and among his peers, would have been much more at ease at these soirées. He was, after all, a Peabody. It is not overly far-fetched to speculate that the two men may have raised glasses, and wished each other well.

Armistice did not immediately return Captain Peabody to America. Instead he basked in revelry and French gratitude in post-war Paris. When he did get back home, the young man, still in his twenties, brought with him a full-blown and debilitating alcohol problem. His wife Polly, who in his absence had become involved in a long-term, and not-so-secret affair, made efforts to rebuild her marriage. Unfortunately, she found her husband to be "a well-educated but undirected man, and a reluctant father". Large promise and poor performance, perhaps. For his own part, Peabody found domestic tranquility to be stultifyingly dull in comparison to his recent grand adventures.

Peabody's alcoholism, which had earlier led to disinheritance, now brought divorce, depression, and institutionalization. The summer of 1922 found him committed to a sanitarium, and subsequently he sought sobriety with some desperation at the Emmanuel Church, where some enlightened clerics were achieving some substantial victories against the age-old opponent.

The Emmanuel Movement

In 1906, Elwood Worcester, pastor of Boston's Emmanuel Church began a free clinic providing medical, and mental health care for the disadvantaged. Both Worcester and his younger associate, Samuel McComb were clergymen, but with doctorates in psychology and a belief that methods beyond mere religion could be brought to bear in solving some very human problems. Influenced by the rise of psychiatry in Europe, the principles of Christian Science, Darwin's anthropological work, and the American psychologist William James, these men tested their theory that psychological principles could be usefully applied in the fields of religion and health. At their clinic, physical medicine, psychological suggestion, and the resources of religion were integrated and the efficacy of a therapeutic approach merging body, mind, and spirit was tested.

"Religion and Medicine" (1908), written in conjunction with Isodor Coriat, the clinic's physician, documents their work "on behalf of nervous sufferers". Of course, these patients included a significant sub-set of alcoholics. Enough of these drunkards were getting sober through this new methodology, that the day soon came for them to have their own group and their own gatherings.

The Jacoby Club

In 1908, or 1909, rubber merchant and Emmanuel Episcopal Church member, Ernest Jacoby began sponsoring a Saturday night get-together, "a meeting place for Boston citizens recovering from alcoholism". His "men meeting men" idea was not a new one, and had been effective elsewhere. Newcomers were welcome, of course, and were given very "sponsor-like" assistance from those further along on the recovery path.

Several Jacoby features were later replicated in Alcoholics Anonymous, including an emphasis on sober leisure and "fellowship", an aversion to dogma, and special support for the new members. Their formula was successful and the club grew, eventually separating from the Emmanuels in 1913. The group's motto, "A Club for Men to Help Themselves by Helping Others", is evocative of AA's twelfth step and core principle - "Practical experience shows that nothing will so much insure immunity from drinking as intensive work with other alcoholics".

The rapid expansion of the Jacoby Club faltered at about five hundred plus, with some disagreements over "primary purpose", some for concentrating on the alcohol issue, and others in favor of expanding the mission to include bringing succour to ALL indigent old men. Nonetheless, the organization continued, and Boston AA founder, Paddy K. got sober in the club around 1940. The Jacoby Club and early Boston AA were closely affiliated until AA's rapid growth in the city took it to a position of dominance.

Courtenay Baylor

In 1912, possibly 1913, reformed drunkard Courtenay Baylor began working under the Emmanuel Movement umbrella as a "lay therapist", a specialist in the treatment of alcoholism. In so doing, he earned a place in addiction treatment history as, likely, the first paid alcoholism therapist. At the time, psychiatry had yet to come to view alcoholism as something which fell within its province, and thus a door was open for the notion of lay therapy.

Although neither clergyman nor medically trained professional, Baylor did bring the unique perspective of an intimate, "insider's knowledge" of the malady. Additionally, clients could readily acknowledge his unique credibility as a living example - "proof positive" of his own solution. This was not a mere theory. Real results were being attained, and Baylor's therapeutic ideas and practices were given a broader audience with the publication, in 1919, of "Remaking a Man". Both physicians, and some of those who had been "cured", picked up on his techniques, and increased numbers were reached.

Baylor's claimed "cure rate" of 65 per cent is given much credibility by the fact that his critics assailed not his numbers, but the possibility that his remarkable degree of success was due in large part to his tremendous personal charisma, more so than his methodology. However, similar numbers were achieved by his followers. One reason for the strength of the percentages came as a result of the procedure of strictly "pre-qualifying" potential clients for motivation, wasting little time with the "wishy-washy". Earliest AA's did much the same.

Two of Baylor's clients are of a particular historical interest. The story of "a certain American businessman" appears in Chapter 2 of AA's Big Book. This man of "ability, good sense, and high character" travels to Switzerland on a "money is no object" quest for treatment for his alcoholism at the hands of pre-eminent psychiatrist, Carl Jung. Extensive therapy is followed by almost immediate relapse. Memorialized in the Big Book, this story is iconic in AA lore as the great allegory demonstrating the inefficacy of "human power". Jung, the embodiment of psychiatry and medicine, even science as a whole, fails and thus "proves" the need for "something more". Human foibles are sometimes revealed when, in the retelling of the parable, Dr. Jung is described as "the world's foremost expert in alcoholism", a claim with no basis in reality.

Rowland Hazard, although unnamed in the Big Book, is well-known to most AA's as "the American businessman" who later got sober in the Oxford Group, and assisted Ebby Thacher in doing the same. The untold portion of the story is that Hazard was being treated by lay therapist, Courtenay Baylor in late 1933 and well into 1934. It seems that sobriety was achieved at a time when both resources were being applied!

Baylor's other very notable client was Richard Peabody, successfully treated in 1922.

Emmanuel Movement Methodology

Worcester and McComb are particularly interesting in that they ventured away from conventional 'ministering' by merging scientific, psychological methods to the more traditional approaches of their clerical colleagues. Along with their medical associate, Isador H. Coriat M.D., they authored, in 1908, "Religion and Medicine", in which they describe their work with "nervous sufferers". Their original goal of a clinic serving tuberculosis victims rapidly altered to a primary focus on mental health issues, including many alcoholics.

In their clinic, "physical medicine, psychological suggestion, and the resources of religion were integrated, stressing the interrelatedness of body, mind and spirit". Physical checkups were followed by a course in relaxation and suggestion with hypnosis sometimes employed. The Emmanuels stressed the power of the mind, medicine, nutrition, good physical health, and a wholesome, well-regulated life. In their own words, "most religious workers in this field have made the mistake of supposing that God can cure in only one way, and that the employment of physical means indicates a lack of faith". Over a hundred years later, it is apparent that many AA fundamentalists have reverted to a 'God-Only' policy, denigrating any sobering techniques evincing the faintest tinge of "human power".

Of course, the Emmanuel Movement was hardly secular, and encouraged "the return to the Gospels of Christ and the acceptance of His words in a more literal sense". Their ideas that revisiting first century Christianity would be more helpful than "ritual and dogmatic ceremonies" clearly influenced the subsequent formulae of the Oxford Group. The movement away from dogma doubtlessly was critical in their more far-reaching accomplishments with alcoholics. Fully believing in both the therapeutic benefit of prayer, and value "in man's dependence on a Higher Power", they nonetheless opted for a "soft-sell" approach.

Robert MacDonald, a New York minister and admirer of the movement contributed "Mind, Religion and Health", in 1909, in which he reviews the phases of the "cure". Confession, wherein the patient unburdened himself of his worries, and opened up about his follies and indulgences, has been viewed as beneficial in many philosophies. Freeing one's mind to a "sympathetic listener" is an age-old practice. Next, the imparting of religious faith was hoped to bring both allies, and optimism, and to serve the very practical purpose of "quieting the mind". Remoralising one's life was to bring a new "positivity". Finally, hypnosis and auto-suggestion have modern equivalents in meditation and positive affirmations.

"Remaking A Man"

Courtenay Baylor may have been the first recovering alcoholic to present a workable, concise treatment program for alcoholics. Wasting no efforts with those who were too far gone, he also saw no great hope for the psychotic, and did not work with them. AA later on followed a similar tack - "There are those who do not recover... usually men and women who are constitutionally incapable of being honest with themselves. They are not at fault. They seem to have been born that way". Dr. Silkworth's frustration in trying to help alcoholic "psychopaths" was evident: "They are always 'going on the wagon for keeps.' They are over-remorseful and make many resolutions, but never a decision". Baylor viewed the bulk of alcoholics as suffering from an "alcoholic neurosis", and that the craving for a drink was the result of a state of "mental tension that was akin to physical tension".

Patients were taught techniques of relaxation, in the short-term, with the goal of making permanent the state of relaxation, in the long term. The alcoholic, for his part, was to re-outfit his life and acquire an entirely new set of values. Jung's talk of "huge emotional displacements and rearrangements", comes to mind. "Ideas, emotions, and attitudes which were once the guiding forces of the lives of these men are suddenly cast aside, and a completely new set of conceptions and motives begin to dominate them." In a similar vein, Dr. Silkworth recognized the transformative power of "moral psychology".

An underlying brain condition of "tenseness" is postulated which produces "new and imaginary values". Baylor writes, "I have found that with a release of this 'tenseness,' a normal coordination does come about, bringing impulses and rational thinking". (Restoration to sanity?) The mental state preceding drinking - "fear, depression, and irritability", is much like the unbearable state of the sober alcoholic, as later described by Silkworth. "They are restless, irritable and discontented unless they can again experience the sense of ease and comfort which comes at once by taking a few drinks... drinks which they see others take with impunity." The alcoholic transitions back and forth between "normal" and "tense" states. Illogical and irrational thinking, easily scorned or unnoticed at normal times, become "insistent and controlling" under tenseness.

As Silkworth would later write, "... they cannot after a time differentiate the true from the false". Monday's sincere and firm resolve to never again take another drop, vanishes completely under Thursday's emotional tenseness. Mental confusion and distorted values then succumb to some unlikely proposition of "having one drink". As AAs are sometimes heard to say, "Willpower works until it doesn't".

Although he did not use the specific term "denial", Baylor understood, and gave credence to, the concept. In his words, "The patient wishes to have the acute symptoms allayed, but there is an unconscious tendency to secretly hold on to his difficulties while making believe that he is trying to surmount them".

Baylor's core solution of relaxation, he sees as "a combination of suppleness, vitality, strength and force - a certain intentional elasticity". The therapist attempted to inspire his client to develop "an entirely new outlook on life - a new scale of values". These ideas are entirely compatible with AA's conceptions of "spiritual awakening" or, more broadly "psychic change".

The therapist or "instructor" is cautioned that he must first gain the patient's confidence and cooperation and, at all costs, "to avoid any air of superiority or dogmatic statements". AA's Big Book promises the reader that there should be "no Holier Than Thou attitude... no lectures to be endured". "Sponsors" are advised to "never talk down from any moral or spiritual hilltop". A marvelous theory, but in many AA quarters, the spiritual hilltops are sadly overflowing with the "enlightened".

By the time patients came for treatment, they were in such a state of mind that they were aware of their inability to make "a consistent and persistent effort in any one direction". Guilt and anxiety over these failings contributed to the alcoholic's general nervousness, and needed to be eliminated. Thus, for the first week Baylor insisted that clients attempt to DO NOTHING, a sort of precursor of AA's "letting go". "There is a great mental and moral relief to the patient in the fact that he is told definitely that he must not even try to do anything about his drinking. Now for the first time since his illness, he is making his mind and body do what he tells them to do." Meditation techniques were then taught "to slow the patient's racing thoughts".

To "incorporate new thoughts", readings were assigned and patients were given daily writing tasks, urged to record innermost notions and reflections. These the therapist used to familiarize himself with the patient's "mental process". In the long-term, Baylor hoped that the physical and mental relaxation processes would become an involuntary action. The patient also came "to distinguish almost unconsciously between true and false thinking. The patient's new 'self-confidence'... the glorious certainty that he need never fail again brings perfect freedom and happiness".

Baylor's methods were used extensively by others during the 1920s. Several alcoholics sobered and became lay therapists themselves. Treated and then trained by Baylor, Richard R. Peabody became the best known of these, and with Baylor's encouragement, produced his own volume, "The Common Sense of Drinking" in 1931 (possibly 1930). AA members will instantly recognize that the work of these men had an ancillary, but vital side effect - it helped to keep themselves sober!

Peabodyism

Following his own recovery, Peabody studied abnormal psychology, and thus augmented what he had learned from Courtenay Baylor. Peabody developed a system of re-education incorporating modern psychological principles into the treatment of alcoholism. He professionalized the lay therapist position to the point of not telling clients of his own alcoholic history, and totally secularized the therapeutic process. His nine step treatment process sought three reactions from his patients – surrender, relaxation, and catharsis.

From the outset, the patient was shown that his problem was thoroughly understood, and that he would not be scolded or preached at. It was made very clear that the process would require "a sustained effort". Surrender (though not in any religious sense), must be made to the idea of "total abstinence", and to the difficulty of the alcoholic's situation. The "misplaced pride" that insisted on trying to use alcohol ran far into the unconscious. "Halfway measures are of no avail." As willpower was seen as relatively impotent against misdirected thinking, changes were to be effected in the "thought process itself". A believer in the merits of discipline and order, Peabody imposed rigid daily schedules preventing idleness. Adherence to these schedules gave clients a sense that they were taking concrete action affecting their conditions.

Self-esteem and self-confidence grew with each new day, week, and month of sobriety. The enforced schedule served the purpose of reintegrating a demoralized person, and "absolute honesty" was insisted upon regarding the rationalizations for any changes in to the schedule. This honesty with self became habitual and became automatic in other decision making as well, including temptations to drink.

More interesting than the specifics of Peabody's treatment modalities, were his insights into the nature of the illness itself, the peculiarities of an alcoholic's mental twists, and the quite obvious but unacknowledged (in any major way), influence on the ideas which took form in the book, Alcoholics Anonymous. Apart from the manifest similarity of AA's iconic "Half measures availed us nothing" to a line from Peabody's book, other subtler likenesses permeate AA's basic text. Bill Wilson and other AA's WERE familiar with Peabodyism.

"Once a drunkard, always a drunkard." Peabody was possibly the first to express the idea that there was no "cure". (Notwithstanding CNN infomercials to the contrary.) As much as anyone, he was responsible for introducing into the popular vocabulary the terms "alcoholism" and substituting "alcoholic" for the more emotionally charged "inebriate". He also introduced the idea of a "dry drunk:" "A man who is on the wagon may be sober physically, but mentally he may be almost as alcohol-minded as if he were drunk". Modern AA much ballyhoos the need to "do it for yourself". Peabody: "The minute a man seeks to reform for somebody else, no matter how deeply he may care for the other person, he is headed for failure in the long run".

Here are a few more of many possible other quotations from "The Common Sense of Drinking:" "Alcohol for inebriates acts as a mental nerve poison in a manner that it does not for the normal drinker". "Alcoholism is a disease of immaturity... " "The conviction that abstinence for the alcoholic is of supreme importance (First Things First?) is an absolute necessity". "The alcoholic has already found out that he cannot learn to drink normally, and he is convinced that his habit is progressive". "The patient cannot afford to become 'cocky' about his temperance". "Warnings as to future disasters seldom do any good".

Some words about Peabody appear in the exceptional AA history, "Not-God" by Ernest Kurtz. "Alcoholics Anonymous was not the only therapy for alcoholism that flourished in its time. Other approaches to treating alcoholism, although they derived from sources very different from the influences that impinged upon AA, used similar methods and even incorporated some of the same ideas that a forgetfulness of history leads later thinkers to associate exclusively with Alcoholics Anonymous. In particular, the approach of Richard R. Peabody... not only preceded in time Wilson's own sobriety but was well into the fifties accepted and endorsed by many doctors and clergy much more enthusiastically than was Alcoholics Anonymous." (p. 158)

Conclusions

AA did not in fact originate in the absence of other effective treatments for alcoholism. "The Varieties of Religious Experience" by William James, the failure of Carl Jung to rehabilitate "a certain American businessman", and Rowland Hazard's regeneration through a "spiritual experience" as a result of his involvement with the Oxford Group - all of these are used to sell a story of the complete uselessness of "human power" in the battle against alcoholism. In order to promote the absolute need of a supernatural answer, science, reason, psychiatry, psychology, medicine, fellowship, and all other "human" solutions are denigrated as totally ineffectual in relieving the "real" alcoholic.

A review of history reveals something quite different. Churches have always had some successes in redeeming "ones and twos" of alcoholics through conversion. Worcester and McComb went well beyond the norm of occasional church driven "redemptions" by moving away from the typical religious approach, even "augmenting" the power of "god" with science, psychology, psychiatry, reason and medicine. One can speculate on the sharp criticisms from the majority of their fellow clergymen. The Jacoby Club's impressive growth within a small geographical area can well be attributed to the wonderful effects which often result through fellowship, and the "collective human power" arising when one alcoholic helps another. Almost hidden among the extolling of the "One who has all power" is Bill Wilson's view of what is THE most important ingredient in maintaining sobriety - "... when all other measures fail, work with another alcoholic would save the day".

Courtenay Baylor moved further from the religious solution, and surpassed the successes of the Emmanuel Movement. Richard Peabody and his followers reached even more significant numbers of recoveries with an entirely secular approach. The lay therapists inevitably limited the spread of their recoveries for a variety of reasons. That they were not free, and that they were delivered one-on-one, seriously limited the reach of these services. Peabody's $20. per hour fee in the midst of the Great Depression restricted access to his services to the very "well-heeled". Peabody also moved entirely away from the multiple benefits of fellowship. AA had fellowship, and it was and is free - the perfect price for most alcoholics. It appears that Richard Peabody's personal story did not end well. His death in 1936 is rumored to have followed a return to drinking. Nonetheless, the success of these predecessors shows not that their systems were superior to AA, but that there exists a history of human solutions and that these human solutions profoundly influenced Bill Wilson and his authorship of the Big Book. Some of us, of course, think that all solutions including AA are understandable at a human level.

Vive la différence!

Chapter 12 Charles Towns

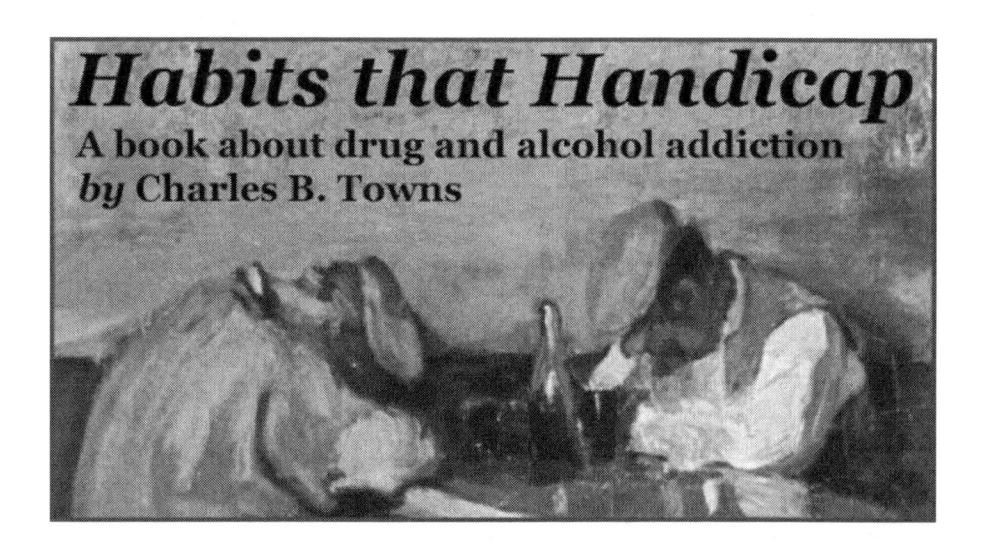

Habits that Handicap
A book about drug and alcohol addiction
by Charles B. Towns

December 11, 1934

Bill Wilson should have been desperate, depressed, and beyond all optimism, when he arrived at Towns Hospital to undergo a fourth and final detox. Following his Armistice Day relapse, "Bill settled hopelessly and without heart into a sort of bottomless bingeing. He no longer made any pretense of going out, save to replenish his supply. He could barely eat; he was forty pounds underweight". (Pass It On, p. 111) Some months earlier, he had left the same hospital terror-stricken, having heard the kind and gentle Dr. Silkworth tell Lois, "I'm fearful for his sanity if he goes on drinking... He can't go on this way another year possibly". (Pass It On, p. 108)

Yet, Bill arrived in high spirits. Buoyed by the tenacity of the human spirit, the newfound sobriety of his old friend, and the three beers consumed along the way, he waved around the fourth bottle and boldly announced that he had "found something". "Silkworth remembered that Bill was carrying two books on philosophy, from which he hoped to get a new inspiration". (Pass It On, p. 120) Following the then-current treatment of sedatives and belladonna, the effects of the alcohol wore away and "he fell into deep depression and rebellion. He wanted the sobriety Ebby had found, but he couldn't believe in the God Ebby had talked about". (Pass It On, p. 120)

Nonetheless, Bill Wilson never had another drink. Over the years, much credit has been graciously offered to "the little doctor who loved drunks", viewed as a medical saint by the AA community. But it is unlikely that Wilson and Silkworth would have ever met, had it not been for the hospital's founder, Charles Towns.

The Movement Toward Prohibition

As the twentieth Century dawned on the United States of America, there was much to celebrate, but in the eyes of a significant portion of the population, the most egregious of enemies needed to be met, battled, and vanquished lest the very fabric of God-loving American families be destroyed.

That adversary was alcohol.

"The Anti-Saloon League emerged toward the end of the nineteenth century: it was to be the last and most effective of the prohibition-temperance movements. Their strategy was to make saloons the target of their efforts." (The Roots Of Alcoholics Anonymous, Bill Pittman, p. 82) Carrie Nation and others led hatchet-wielding hordes, convinced of the righteousness of their cause.

The view of these reformers was typically expressed:

> *The saloon is the storm center; the devil's headquarters on earth; the school-master of a broken decalogue; the defiler of youth; the enemy of the home; the foe of peace; the deceiver of nations; the beast of sensuality; the past master of intrigue; the vagabond of poverty; the social vulture; the rendezvous of demagogues; the enlisting officer of sin; the serpent of Eden; a ponderous second edition of hell, revised, enlarged, and illuminated. (Pressure Politics, P.H. Odegard, 1928, p. 150)*

All of these "anti-alcohol" forces were coming together in moving toward an ultimate solution of the total prohibition, that was to come in only a few short years. Individually, problem drinkers were seeking remedies of their own. Violent or impoverished intemperate drinkers had no options, and were incarcerated. In the higher classes, consultations with physicians rarely produced lasting change. Religion had some very occasional successes with rich and poor, while the pleadings and remonstrances of wives, parents, and children garnered pledges and promises quickly broken. Magazine ads offering remedies for alcoholic dissipation were as commonplace as those offering cures for baldness , and about equally effective. Some provided invigorating "tonics," as strong as Jamaican rum!

Such were the conditions in the turbulent times at which the Towns Hospital was founded, variously reported to be either 1909 or 1901.

Entrepreneur, Salesman Extraordinaire

Charles B. Towns was born in Georgia, during the early part of the American Civil War, a conflict that was to shatter the fortune of Colonel Oliver Towns, his father. Limited means prevented the Colonel from providing his elder children the benefits of an education, other than what was to be obtained from the common country schools, which were at that time, very inadequate. Forced to leave school in order to assist his father, Young Charlie embraced the challenge. His extraordinary competitiveness and ambition were in evidence early on as he won several ranching and farming contests in his county.

Whatever the challenge, the teenager embraced it, striving to be the best. His ambition is evocative of young Bill Wilson's quest to be a "Number One man". "During his youth he (Towns) broke horses and mules and steers that no other person could conquer." (Roots Of AA, p. 84) At twenty, he moved to Florida where he worked in the railroad industry. Starting as a clerk, he advanced rapidly to management, and his company flourished. During this "railwayman" phase, "he used his spare time to study arithmetic and grammar". (Roots Of AA, p. 84) His bosses were sorry to see him go.

At twenty-seven, he found far greater success as a pioneer in the sale of insurance, and "in 1892 he wrote more insurance than was ever written before by any other company in the history of the state, second in the nation only to the general agent in Boston whose territory was all of New England." (Duval County Gen Web) "Towns, with his threatening index finger, with his hypnotic eye and prehensile jaw, could convince a granite gatepost that it stood in immediate need of life insurance!" (Roots of AA, p. 84)

New York and a Rare Failure

"He had set a record for selling more life insurance than any other man had ever written south of the Mason-Dixon Line up to that time (1901). Soon after, he went to New York to seek a larger arena for his talents. There he found something that excited him even more - the stock market. From 1901 to 1904 he was a partner in a brokerage firm that eventually failed." (Roots Of AA, p. 4)

A Whispered "Cure"

Around this time Towns was approached by a mysterious man who whispered to him, "I have got a cure for drug habits, morphine, opium, heroin, codeine, alcohol - any of 'em. We can make a lot of money out of it". (Collier's Magazine, The "White Hope" for Drug Victims, P.C. MacFarlane, Nov. 29, 1913, p. 17) Although his own physician viewed the idea as ridiculous, Towns was intrigued and placed ads seeking "drug fiends" who wanted to be cured. Finding a "patient", he took the "Whisperer", the "fiend", and himself to the Abingdon Square Hotel, along with a few vials of medicine.

The "fiend" seems to have experienced a change of heart and "wanted to leave, but Towns restrained him and gave him a strong sedative. A doctor and a stomach pump were sent for, as the patient became violently ill. After forty-eight hours, the patient was able to leave. Towns and his accomplice decided the 'cure' needed additional refinement, so Towns began reading all the known literature on drug addiction and alcoholism. Unable to find any more willing patients, he kidnapped a racetrack agent and forced him through the treatment, which was successful. His reputation soon spread through New York's criminal underworld and he treated many addicted gangsters. During this time, he eliminated the distressing features of the original formula." (Roots Of AA, p. 85)

Belladonna

We have no way of knowing precisely what constituted the earliest formula. We do know that in later years the Towns-Lambert "cure" involved two full days of hourly doses of a combination of the deliriant *Atropa Belladonna* (aka Deadly Nightshade), henbane (also a deliriant), and prickly ash, which helped with intestinal cramps. The belladonna produced delirium and hallucinations. Delirium tremens also produces hallucinations that "tend to be transmogrifications of things the alcoholic is actually seeing or experiencing". (An Alcoholic's Savior, New York Times Health, April 20, 2010)

Presumably, an open window could produce "the great clean wind of a mountain top", and a "blinding light" could be the result of staring at an overhead bulb. Patients also received cathartics and mercury pills, an all-purpose purgative with a variety of other claimed benefits. Castor oil was also administered. Patients routinely did a lot of vomiting while undergoing the therapy, which was idiomatically referred to as "puke and purge". A number of the listed ingredients prompted purging.

Theoretically, at least, the treatment "successfully and completely removes the poison from the system and obliterates the craving for drugs and alcohol". (Alcoholic's Savior)

It was a very expensive detox. At Bill Wilson's fourth visit to Towns, "Silkworth sedated him with chloral hydrate and paraldehyde, two agents guaranteed to help an agitated drunk to sleep". (Alcoholic's Savior) In later years, Towns alleged that he had obtained the original formula from a "country doctor."

The "Towns Cure" Goes To China

Believing the formula to be now ready for more widespread use, he had interested Dr. Alexander Lambert, professor of clinical medicine at Cornell University Medical College, in his therapy. Lambert, one of then-President Theodore Roosevelt's physicians, began telling government officials about the "Towns Cure". Towns had been sent to China where the drug addiction problem was enormous, and in 1908, claimed to have cured 4,000 opium addicts by his method. Association with the distinguished physician gave Towns credibility among the many naysayers, who viewed him as a complete fraud.

Towns was heralded as "an everyday American fighter. Between 1910 and 1920, he helped to frame the Boylan Bill and testified before Congress in favor of the Harrison Narcotics Tax Act (to regulate the distribution of opiates and cocaine). At the same time he operated a very lucrative hospital, located on fashionable Central Park West, which catered to New York's social elite. It was no more than a fancy, very expensive detoxification facility; Towns would not admit anyone unless the fee was paid upon admission or a 'backer' guaranteed to pay the fee, which was $200. to $350. for a five-day stay". (Roots of AA, p. 86)

(Bill Wilson's four trips to Towns Hospital were of course, not financed by his own, or Lois' meager resources, but were paid for by Dr. Leonard Strong, husband of Bill's younger sister, Dorothy. Setting out on December 11, 1934, for a fourth trip to the "high-end" detox, "he had only six cents, and that left a penny after the subway fare. Along the way, he managed to obtain four bottles of beer from a grocery store where he had a little credit". (Pass It On, p. 120))

Stats? We Got Stats!

No doubt playing on the association with the esteemed one-time physician to a President of the United States, the treatment had become known as the

"Towns-Lambert Cure". Towns claimed a cure rate at 75-90% "based on the (rather clever) reasoning that if you never heard from a patient again, HE NO LONGER NEEDED YOUR SERVICES". (Roots of AA, p. 86)

In his own words, "We have never had a negative result in any case, free from disability, or from an incurable painful condition which enforced the continued use of an addictive drug - such as gall stones, cancer, etc. A little less than ten percent returned to us for a second treatment, a reasonable presumption being that ninety percent from whom we have never heard further after they left our care had no need to consult with us a second time". (Drug And Alcohol Sickness, C.B. Towns, 1932)

In Decline

"After 1920, Towns standing in the medical community fell while his claims became more and more extravagant. The substances he claimed he could help people with included tobacco, coffee, tea, bromides, marijuana, cocaine, and paraldehyde in addition to opiates and alcohol. The Towns Cure appears to border on quackery..." (Roots Of AA, p. 87) His lasting contribution may be that in encouraging directors of large corporations to help save alcoholics, while still on the job, he was one of the precursors of Employee Assistance Programs (EAP), which have found ubiquity in the modern workplace.

From the perspective of Alcoholics Anonymous, Towns' more significant contribution was in providing William D. Silkworth M.D. an almost endless parade of the helpless and hopeless alcoholics he was so desperate to help, and a venue in which to do his research. The serendipitous meeting of the absolutely right patient with the absolutely right physician, led to the passing on of the absolutely vital information about the inevitable consequences, fatality or insanity, of the malady.

Charles Towns was enthusiastic about AA, and loaned a considerable sum of money to the fledgling group so that they get their book published. In 1937, he offered Bill Wilson "an office, a decent drawing account , and a very healthy slice of the profits... Some day this bunch of ex-drunks of yours will fill Madison Square Gardens, and I don't see why you should starve meanwhile... You can become a lay therapist, and more successful than anybody in the business". (12 + 12, p. 136) Various Traditions reflect the lessons learned in this. Bill's "the laborer is worthy of his hire" thought was overridden by the greater wisdom of the collective whole. "Don't you realize... that you can never become a professional?... we can't tie this thing up with his hospital or any other." (12 + 12, p. 137)

Recruiting Ground

Even prior to Charles Towns offer to employ Bill Wilson, which would have made him the "de facto" proprietor of what would become AA, Towns allowed Bill to speak to alcoholic patients at his hospital. Two of the more noteworthy recruits were Hank Parkhurst and Fitz Mayo, his earliest "successes," following abundant failures during which "the work" kept Wilson himself sober.

Legacy

Towns wrote three books on alcoholism, and possibly influenced by Richard Peabody, he felt strongly that idleness was a great producer of relapse in alcoholics, thus rendering the rich and the poor more vulnerable than the middle class. He urged employers to NOT dismiss their wayward workers. Years later, the physician, Alexander Lambert, who had brought credibility to Towns' outrageous claims, distanced himself from Towns and his treatment. The toxic ingredients of the "cure" may have posed a greater risk to the patient than the original malady. There were fatalities.

Charles B. Towns certainly had far more than his fifteen minutes of fame. Somewhere along the way he had acquired a fictitious PhD. He was a daunting presence, both in personality and physicality. Well into his seventies, the one-time bronco buster worked out daily at the gymnasium. He was a "super salesman," but ultimately his wares were "snake oil."

In 1965, the Towns Hospital, a five story yellow brick building with 50 beds, where alcoholics and addicts had been treated for more than fifty years, closed its doors.

Charles B. Towns, history would suggest, was far more L. Ron Hubbard and P.T. Barnum, than Walter Reed or William Worrell Mayo.

Chapter 13 Frank Buchman and The Oxford Group

The founder of the Oxford Group – a Christian evangelical movement and the birthplace of AA – Frank Nathaniel Daniel Buchman was born in the small town (pop. 1,200) of Pennsburg, Pennsylvania, on June 4th, 1878, fourteen months earlier than AA's future co-founder, Bob Smith. Pennsburg's population was almost exclusively German, morally conservative, "where the only permissible vice was overeating". (Frank Buchman – A Life, Garth Lean, p. 3)

Buchman's mother was a devout Lutheran, with grand ambitions for her son. His father was entrepreneurial, operating first a General Store, and later a railroad inn with a restaurant and bar. Pennsburg had no high school which prompted the family to move to nearby Allentown, which was larger (pop. 18,000) and rapidly growing.

In Allentown, Frank attended high school and his father became a wholesale liquor distributor. The teenager was no more than an average student. Nonetheless, he moved on to Muhlenberg College and Mount Airy Seminary, and was ordained a Lutheran minister in 1902. Accurately seen as ambitious by his fellow students, Buchman had aspirations of being called to an important city church. When instead he was offered an unprestigious posting in the Pennsylvania suburb of Overbrook, a new parish lacking even a building, he accepted, possibly to evidence his humility. With diligent effort, he arranged rental of an old storefront with living quarters for himself above.

"Within three years he had built up the vigor and life of the church, and had established a hospice for young men. Differences (over finances) arose between him and the official board of the hospice, however, and he resigned his position." (*Roots Of Alcoholics Anonymous*, Bill Pittman, p. 114)

Exhausted and depressed, Buchman embarked on an extensive holiday abroad. Seething with resentment over his unjust treatment at the hands of bureaucrats, Buchman flitted about Europe for several month's at his parents' expense. The elder Buchmans were frustrated by their son's seeming contentment with this leisurely lifestyle, but nonetheless were persuaded to furnish him with additional funds to go to the 1908 Keswick Convention.

The Birth of AA's Steps 4 to 9

The Keswick Convention was an annual gathering of evangelical Christians in Cumbria, England. In a small, half-empty chapel, he was deeply moved by the preaching of Jessie Penn-Lewis.

> *I thought of those six men back in Philadelphia who I felt had wronged me. They probably had, but I got so mixed in the wrong that I was the seventh wrong man... I can only tell you I sat there and realized how my sin, my pride, my selfishness and my ill-will had eclipsed me from God in Christ. I was the center of my own life. That big "I" had to be crossed out. I saw my resentments against those men standing out like tombstones in my heart. I asked God to change me, and He told me to put things right with them. It produced in me a vibrant feeling, as though a strong current of life had suddenly been poured into me, and afterwards a dazed sense of a great spiritual shaking up. (Lean, p. 30-31)*

In letters of apology to these former "bosses", he took ownership of his own prideful behavior in holding resentments. This action brought much relief. Bill Wilson expanded on the self-analysis, confession, and amends process and incorporated them in Steps 4 through 9.

Religiosity aside, the wisdom of letting go of resentment and moving away from concentration on "self" are age-old, widespread, almost universal, philosophical ideas. Although far from being the exclusive purview of alcoholics, these ideas are prominent in AA. Thus, the Step 3 problem is presented as: "Selfishness-self-centeredness! That, we think, is the root of our troubles. Driven by a hundred forms of fear, self-delusion, self-seeking, and self-pity, we step on the toes of our fellows and they retaliate. Sometimes they hurt us, seemingly without provocation, but we invariably find that at some time in the past we have made decisions based on self which later placed us in a position to be hurt". (Alcoholics Anonymous, 4th Edition, p. 62) Also aligning with Mr. Buchman's experience: "Resentment is the 'number one' offender. It destroys more alcoholics than anything else". (AA Big Book, p. 64)

Down at the YMCA

Young man, there's no need to feel down.
I said, young man, pick yourself off the ground.
I said, young man, 'cause you're in a new town
There's no need to be unhappy.
Young man, there's a place you can go.
I said, young man, when you're short on your dough.
You can stay there, and I'm sure you will find
Many ways to have a good time.
It's fun to stay at the YMCA.
It's fun to stay at the YMCA.
They have everything for you men to enjoy,
You can hang out with all the boys ... (Village People, 1978)

It was a calmer and happier Frank Buchman who returned to the United States, and was hired as Secretary of the Penn State College YMCA. He had grave reservations about the scraps, hazing, and drunkenness at "the most godless university in the country". (Lean, p. 33) Initially he worked hard and was ridiculed by the students, but eventually he doubled membership and got various groups studying the Bible. However he feared that decisions for Christ were shallow, as "the alcohol consumption had hardly decreased and the general tone of the college had not greatly altered". (Lean, p. 35)

It was at Penn State that the minister discovered the enormous power in working one-on-one, as he was able to bring "change" to some unlikely candidates. Football coach, 'Pop' Golden gave up a life of dissipation under Buchman's ministration. The conversion of other notables had a great impact on the regular folks. As a young man, much as was the case with Bill Wilson, Buchman "was dazzled by the elegance and wealth" of the social elite. (Lean, P.11) His recruitment system became very organized, and other religious leaders came to study his methods and the conversion movement spread to other colleges. "It really began at Penn State College last year under Frank N.D. Buchman. 'This new evangelism of the second decade of the twentieth century is transforming our colleges.'" (Yale Paper, Mar. 3, 1915)

Samuel Shoemaker

In April, 1915, Buchman left Penn State College for India, and then China. His hope to convert a few key players, which in turn would bring huge nations to Christianity, was seen as naïve by his critics. A second China mission had an early setback as his colleagues "became critical of each other, and Buchman in particular". (Lean, p. 52) During this 1917 tour to China, Buchman met recent Princeton grad, Sam Shoemaker, who found the Pennsylvanian to be abrupt, but insightful. The two men would later share common bonds of their work with the Oxford Group, and their influence on the formation and practices of Alcoholics Anonymous.

The Asian trips were ultimately failed efforts, but "he remarked one day that it had only been in China that (he had learned) the confession of one's own shortcomings, privately or publicly, was an important way to help others". (Lean, P.63) It was time to go back to the States, where he continued with the "Hartford Theological Seminary" which had supported his forays into the Orient.

Sam Shoemaker, meanwhile, would work with Buchman for twenty years, as the American head of the Oxford Group movement. He was the Episcopalian minister at the Calvary Mission in New York. Encouraged by Ebby Thacher and other Oxford Group members, when Bill Wilson got out of the Towns Hospital after his last drink, "still shaky, he visited Dr. Shoemaker at Calvary Mission and made a decision to become very active in the Missions work and to try and bring other alcoholics from Towns to the (Oxford) Group". (*The Evolution of Alcoholics Anonymous*, Jim Burwell)

Bill would later acknowledge that, "The early AA got its ideas of self-examination, acknowledgment of character defects, restitution for harm done, and working with others straight from the Oxford Group and directly from Sam Shoemaker, their former leader in America, and from nowhere else". (AA Comes of Age, p. 39)

A "Spiritual Adjunct" to the Christian Church

Throughout Buchman's career, "in each instance, conflicts with institutional authorities prompted his departure. In 1921, this history of friction culminated in his decision to quit the church proper and create his own organization, which he vowed would be a 'voice of protest against the organised, committeeised, and lifeless Christian work' of doctrinal and institution-based religion". (*The Language of the Heart: A Cultural History of the Recovery Movement from Alcoholics Anonymous to Oprah Winfrey*, Trysh Travis, 2009, p. 71) These efforts were financed by wealthy "sponsors".

"His primary focus was on 'soul sickness'… He saw the contemporary glorification of the physical and the material as a kind of debased Mammonism; what he called 'materialism' encompassed sexual acting out, profligacy, vanity, envy, gluttony, and of course excessive drinking." (Travis, p. 71) The theme of anti-materialism comports well with Bill Wilson's later ideas regarding the futility of "self-propulsion" in the quest to become a self-made "Number One man".

Buchman traveled a great deal. His right hand man, Sam Shoemaker, held the fort in United States.

A regular meeting held a Corpus Christi College grew so popular that, by 1928, the group moved to the ballroom of the Randolph Hotel, and then to the library of the Oxford University Church, St. Mary's. The movement got its name when, in the same year, six Oxford students on a mission to South Africa, were branded the "Oxford Group" by the press.

Russel "Bud" Firestone and Dr. Bob

A few years later, Oxford Groupers assisted Russell "Bud" Firestone in conquering a severe drinking problem by turning to God. Bud's father, Harvey, had four things the Oxford Group liked, wealth, fame, generosity, and gratitude. The rubber magnate in his appreciation hosted a ten day gala, in January, 1933, that brought the religious group to the forefront of Akron society. This set the table for Oxford Group members to arrange the famous Mother's Day meeting, two and one half years later, of Bill Wilson and Dr. Bob Smith.

It is worth noting that at about this time, Buchman had an even more notable candidate in mind for religious conversion, Adolph Hitler. At least two approaches were made, in 1932 and 1933, to get a Buchman audience with the German leader. The extraordinarily optimistic thinking was that the Fuhrer could be led to a "decision for Christ", millions would follow, and the world would be changed. Some Buchman critics, former colleagues among them have levelled the charge of megalomania. Not without grounds.

Reinhold Niebuhr – author of the Serenity Prayer – was a prominent, contemporary critic of Buchman and the Oxford Group. "We can see how unbelievably naïve this movement is in its efforts to save the world. If it would content itself with preaching repentance to drunkards and adulterers one might be willing to respect it as a religious revival method which knows how to confront the sinner with God," Niebuhr wrote. "But when it runs to... Hitler, or to any seat of power, always with the idea that it is on the verge of saving the world by bringing the people who control the world under God-control, it is difficult to restrain the contempt which one feels for this dangerous childishness." (The Christian Century magazine, Oct. 7, 1936, pp. 1315-1316)

Nevertheless, the Russell Firestone conversion brought about a rapid ascension in Akron, Ohio, and the group came to the attention of Anne Smith, desperate wife of the drunken and deteriorating physician, Dr. Bob.

Initially, merely as an attempt to appease his spouse, Dr. Bob began to attend the Christian gatherings, no doubt remembering the mandatory, unpleasant forced Church attendance of his childhood. Despite his original antipathy, Smith was somewhat drawn to the Oxford folks, "...because of their seeming poise, health, and happiness. They spoke with great freedom from embarrassment, which I could never do, and they seemed more at ease on all occasions... I was self-conscious and ill at ease most of the time, my health was at the breaking point, and I was thoroughly miserable... I gave the matter much time and study for the next two and one half years, but I still got tight every night nevertheless". (Nightmare, p. 178)

"My wife became deeply interested and it was her interest that had sustained mine, though I at no time thought it might be the answer to my liquor problem." (Nightmare, p. 178)

Oxford Group Practices

The Oxford Group was "a non-denominational Christian fellowship... devoted to 'world-changing through life-changing'". (Travis, P.30) It profoundly influenced AA and our 12 Steps, but the statement that the Oxford Group had a six Step program is incorrect. They had no Steps. They were guided by "The Four Absolutes" (or Standards) – Honesty, Unselfishness, Purity and Love. Any behavior could be judged by how well it adhered to these principles.

Action was also directed by the 5 C's – Conviction, Confession, Contrition, Conversion, and Continuance. Much of this continued for years as AA practices, in some areas, most especially in Ohio.

"The 5 Procedures" represented another formalized Oxford "plan of action".

1. Give in to God;

2. Listen to God's direction;
3. Check guidance;
4. Restitution;
5. Sharing – for witness and for confession.

It is quite obvious that the bulk of what is in our Steps, is present here.

The 5 Procedures are clearly seen in AA's process of transformation. "The two other AA practices present in the Oxford Group were the insistence that its workers–and especially its founder–never be paid for the 'soul surgery' of aiding others to attain the 'changed life'; and an emphasis on the obligation to engage in personal work with others in order to change the *helpers'* lives." (Not-God, P.49)

The Oxford Group "operated under "six basic assumptions":

1. Men are sinners;
2. men can be changed;
3. confession is prerequisite to change;
4. the changed soul has direct access to God;
5. the 'Age of Miracles' has returned;
6. those who have been "changed" must "change others." (Not-God, p. 49)

Positives and negatives

The alcoholics used the Oxford Group methods as a way to solve their own specific issues (see Pass It On, p. 197), including the vital, "We admitted we were licked, that we were powerless over alcohol". And yet AA broke away, New York in 1937, Cleveland next in May of 1939, and Akron last, and most reluctantly, in the autumn of 1939.

The best analysis of the positives and negatives of the Oxford/AA relationship can be found in Ernie Kurtz' masterful AA history, *Not-God: A History of Alcoholics Anonymous* (Hazelden, 1979). Some of the most pressing reasons for the separation were that AA steadfastly and consistently:

1. avoided absolutes;
2. avoided aggressive evangelism;
3. embraced anonymity;
4. strove to avoid offending anyone who might need the program.

Of these and others, the most cogent reason for the split was likely Bill Wilson's vision of the future. In the history of mankind, it may be that there was no one who understood alcoholics better than AA's founder. The earliest years convinced him that for AA to have a religious attachment would be a mistake. Bill's unexpected ally in separating AA from the Christian Protestant Oxfords was Clarence Snyder of Cleveland, who was concerned that Cleveland's many Catholics would be prevented from seeking sobriety through a group with a Protestant affiliation. In 2013, it is hard to imagine the power held over citizens by organized religion in the 1930s, nor will younger people easily grasp the one-time impassable chasm dividing these two Christian groups.

It is abundantly clear that a great debt is owed to these Oxford folks. Self-examination, acknowledgment of character defects, restitution for harms done, working with others, quiet time (meditation), and the quest for change are all practices alive and well in AA. The use of slogans was an Oxford custom; "Study men, not books", "Give news, not views". At its peak just prior to World War II, the group had a membership of 50,000, but Mr. Buchman made a major misstep in endorsing Hitler's anti-Communism, making some statements in a press interview that were seen as pro-Nazi. That AA distanced itself from its Oxford roots may have had much to do with the negative publicity that attached itself to the group. Alcoholics had their own significant PR issues with which to be concerned.

AA World Services

In 1938, the Oxford Group was renamed "Moral Rearmament" and continues today as "Initiatives of Change," but its heyday is long past. In 1978, a 100th birthday memorial was organized for founder Frank Buchman, who had died on August 7, 1961.

According to Mel B. (*New Wine: The Spriritual Roots of the Twelve Step Miracle*, p. 27), this "drew cooperation from a number of prominent individuals who had benefitted from Buchman's work. But an invitation to Alcoholics Anonymous – perhaps the greatest beneficiary of all – was politely declined... there were two problems: (1) the anonymity principle ruled out anyone speaking for AA; and (2) as Bob P. put it (then GM of AA World Services) 'I think some of our members would say that we got out of bed with those people – why should we now get back in?'"

A good question.

Perhaps a better (if more complicated) question today is: Having decided to climb out of bed with those fellows, had our pioneers already borrowed too much from Frank Buchman and the Oxford Group as part the program of Alcoholics Anonymous?

Chapter 14 Sam Shoemaker

> *The basic principles which the Oxford Groupers had taught were ancient and universal ones, the common property of mankind... The early AA got its ideas of self-examination, acknowledgement of character defects, restitution for harm done, and working with others straight from the Oxford Groups and directly from Sam Shoemaker.*
> (Alcoholics Anonymous Comes Of Age, p. 39)

Burnside

Samuel Moor Shoemaker Jr. was born in Baltimore, Maryland, on December 27, 1893, making him about 2 years older than Bill Wilson. His ancestors had been Schumachers of Germany, Holland, and Switzerland who had converted to Quakerism under William Penn.

Sam's father "was intelligent... but was terribly handicapped by a shyness that would see him cut off from many persons including his young son". (The Virginian, bbsgsonj. com) Nonetheless, he would one day be the chairman of the board of regents at the University of Maryland. His mother Nellie "was a dedicated church woman and president of the Woman's Auxiliary of the Diocese of Maryland". (The Virginian, bbsgwsonj.com)

"A central figure in young Sam's life at Burnside was his grandmother. 'Nana' was an avid story teller, reader of the Bible, and an accomplished musician... more Victorian than Victoria herself." (The Virginian, bbsgsonj.com)

When Sam was two, his parents joined his paternal grandmother on the 467 acres estate, 10 miles north of Baltimore, that had been acquired by his grandfather during the Civil War. The patriarch, also a Sam, had made his fortune organizing the Great Western Express transportation line between Philadelphia and Baltimore, then operated his cattle ranch, Burnside, before passing on in 1884.

Located at the edge of the Green Spring Valley, this was fox-hunting territory, a verdant land of rolling hills and marvelous panoramas. In 1898, Sam's father converted Burnside to a dairy farm. The Shoemakers enjoyed the privileged existence of the American aristocracy, complete with Negro servants.

St George's and Princeton

At 14, Sam was sent to an Episcopal boarding school in Newport, Rhode Island. He was initially homesick, and not fully comfortable among the "Yankee" student body at St. George's. Nonetheless, he held several positions, including president of the mission society. After graduation in 1912, he went on to Princeton, the alma mater of his father.

After his sophomore year, he traveled to Europe. Upon his return, he expressed a newfound political interest by joining protests against war propaganda and military drills at the university. It was at Princeton that Sam discovered his interest in personal evangelism and missionary work as well as the relatively new, at that time, ecumenical movement.

China and Buchman

In 1917, with the blessing of Rt. Rev. John Gardner Murray, bishop of Maryland, Sam Shoemaker went to China to start a branch of the YMCA and teach business courses at the Princeton-in-China Program. Shoemaker was frustratingly unsuccessful in converting the Chinese to Christianity, a failing he confessed on meeting Frank Buchman, perhaps seeking a sympathetic ear. The somewhat brash Buchman suggested that Shoemaker look at his own shortcomings.

Although he was at first offended, Shoemaker reflected upon what the older cleric had told him. Contemplation of the 4 absolutes of honesty, purity, love and unselfishness brought Shoemaker into an intense awareness of his own inadequacies, and he made the humbling decision to let God guide his life.

Buchman had also stressed to the young missionary the value of sharing personal experience, a practice that would later form a key component in Alcoholics Anonymous. The very next day, he shared this personal experience with a young Chinese businessman who, as a result, "wanted what he had", and made a decision for Christ. These experiences left Shoemaker with an enormously high regard for Frank Buchman, a man he viewed as "a born mystic".

In 1919, Shoemaker returned to Princeton to head the Philadelphia Society, a campus Christian organization.

The Calvary Church

In 1920, Shoemaker was ordained a deacon in the Episcopal Church. He returned to missionary work at Princeton, an institution frequently visited by Buchman. In the early twenties, he attended the General Theological Seminary in New York, and after graduation and ordination, got his bishop's permission to travel with Buchman through Europe and the Middle East.

These journeys were cut short when Sam received a cable and letter from Manhattan. The Calvary Church in the Gramercy Park neighborhood, a once more vibrant ministry, wanted the energetic young man to be their rector. Shoemaker accepted, and returned to New York. This was 1925, also the year in which he married Helen Smith, whom he had met at Princeton. Helen was an author, a sculptor, and a church leader.

After a two year trial, Sam was confirmed in the new position. He was able to almost immediately boost the church's flagging attendance. In the summer of 1927, he began outdoor services in nearby Madison Square.

His mission was not without controversy. Shoemaker was now fully immersed in Buchman's approach, and the "hot gospelling" of the Oxford Group was not universally appreciated. Also contentious was the decision to sell some vacant property, and use the funds to construct the 7-story Calvary House, adjacent to the church. This building became the American headquarters of the Oxford Group.

At a different location, the church also owned and operated the Calvary Mission, an outreach project to serve the disadvantaged. The facility could house up to 57 homeless men, and served over 200,000 meals in its 10 years of operation. Ebby Thacher was living at Calvary Mission at the time of his famous "twelfth step" call on Bill Wilson.

On another front, Shoemaker initiated a Faith At Work program in which dedicated Christians were trained to witness in the workplace. In 1932, he requested, and was granted, an extended leave so that he might pursue his ambition to bring his ideas to a wider audience. This continued as a problem, the division of his energies between his local responsibilities, and the worldwide evangelical effort.

Moral Dis-armament

From 1926 to 1936, the Faith At Work (later called LUMUNOS) group held Thursday night meetings. Around 1938, it transformed into Moral Re-Armament. These discretionary activities were taking increasing amounts of the rector's time, and this now unpopular group occupied a significant share of the Calvary House's facilities.

Rev. Shoemaker spent 1940 and 1941 assessing priorities, and the conflicting demands on his time, and near the end of 1941, separated himself entirely from the Oxforders, now known as Moral Re-Armament. It is unlikely that mere scheduling issues led to the split. In 1936, Frank Buchman had made some extremely injudicious remarks in an interview. The remarks were somewhat laudatory of Adolf Hitler, and affected the public's perception of the group.

Throughout 1941, the involvement of the United States in the European conflict was increasingly seen as inevitable. As the nation was about to declare war on Hitler's Germany, it was not a time to be seen to be affiliated with individuals or organizations which had demonstrated ANY friendliness toward Hitler.

Another probable consideration was Buchman himself, a man with a reputation for not getting along with colleagues. Through the 1930's, he was viewed by many as having crossed the line into megalomania.

Reverend Sam detached.

On the Radio and Off to Pittsburgh

In the forties, Shoemaker became involved in "radio preaching", and a 5-minute daily show on one station led to a half hour Sunday broadcast, and then another half hour program called Faith in Our Time. His growing fame led, in 1950, to an offer to become Dean of the San Francisco Cathedral. He declined.

Following the split from Buchman, Rev. Sam reactivated the Faith At Work program.

The following year he yielded to personal urgings from the Bishop of Pittsburgh to accept the position of "rector" at the Calvary Church of Pittsburgh. From his Pittsburgh base, he was encouraged to evangelize the entire area, including nearby Akron, Ohio.

Reverend Sam and AA

Samuel Shoemaker grew up in a privileged environment, but "his own conversion experience gave him an interest in helping people life had dealt with much more severely than most". (Hartigan, p. 70) Calvary House was sheltering Ebby in December, 1934; it was also where Bill Wilson "came to know Sam Shoemaker who would become a lifelong friend". (Hartigan, p. 64) It was not a friendship without problems.

Calvary House, along with Towns Hospital, was where an enthusiastic Bill Wilson found drunks to tell of his dramatic spiritual experience. Although Bill and Lois, and later, other of their recruits like Hank P., attended Oxford Group meetings, "it was clear almost from the beginning that Bill Wilson was not well-suited to be an Oxford Group member… He never shared in, or had much sympathy for, the Oxford Group's goals". (Hartigan, p. 65)

Whether the Wilsons quit, or were thrown out, remains uncertain, but Shoemaker was upset and did not speak to Bill again until after he detached from Buchman's group. "He later wrote a letter of apology to Bill stating that he and other OG members were wrong to oppose Bill's desire to work solely with alcoholics and to focus only on helping these individuals to stop drinking." (Hartigan, pp. 97-98)

Wilson then took the opportunity to extend gratitude and credit to Shoemaker and the Oxforders, a debt that had been minimized or ignored throughout the estrangement, and in the book Alcoholics Anonymous. Rev. Sam was a prolific author, and half of his 30+ books were in circulation before the publication of the Big Book, likely reading material for the pre-book AA'ers.

Thus, Bill Wilson credited Sam Shoemaker as a key source of the ideas underpinning Alcoholics Anonymous:

> *It was from Sam Shoemaker that we absorbed most of the Twelve Steps of Alcoholics Anonymous, steps that express the heart of AA's way of life. Dr. Silkworth gave us the needed*

> *knowledge of our illness, but Sam Shoemaker had given us the concrete knowledge of what we could do about it, he passed on the spiritual keys by which we were liberated. The early AA got its ideas of self-examination, acknowledgment of character defects, restitution for harm done, and working with others straight from the Oxford Group and directly from Sam Shoemaker, their former leader in America, and from nowhere else. (AACOA, pp. 38-39)*

And Bill Wilson later said the following in an address about Rev. Shoemaker at the St Louis AA convention in 1955:

> *It is through Sam, that most of our principles have come, that is he has been the connecting link for them, it is what Ebby learned from Sam and what Ebby told me that makes up the linkage between Sam the man of religion, and ourselves. How well I remember that first day I caught sight of Sam, it was a Sunday service in his church. I was still rather gun-shy and diffident about churches. I can still see him standing there before the lectern, and Sam's utter honesty, his tremendous forthrightness, his almost terrible sincerity struck me deep. I shall never forget it. (AACOA, p. 261)*

Reverend Shoemaker continued in the service of his church until his retirement in 1961, and he remained throughout his life a friend and supporter of Alcoholics Anonymous. He wrote articles for the Grapevine, and traveled to speak at AA events, including the Convention at St. Louis in July, 1955.

On October 31, 1963, he moved on to whatever lies beyond.

SECTION III THE PROFESSIONALS

Chapter 15 William James

For better or worse, whether real or imagined, drug-induced, or brought about by the most desperate need, Bill Wilson's spiritual experience at Towns Hospital is perhaps the foundation point of Alcoholics Anonymous.

Shortly before the famous "hot flash," Bill's old friend Ebby had laid out the Oxford Group's plan of recovery which had been successful for him. This included the instruction to "pray to whatever God you think there is, *even as an experiment.*" (Alcoholics Anonymous Comes Of Age, p. 63)

There is some interesting phrasing that was used to describe the event. In Bill's Story – "I *felt* lifted up, *as though* the great clean wind of a mountaintop blew through and through." (AA Big Book, p. 14) Two decades later, the role of imagination is even more strongly insinuated – "*It seemed to me, in the mind's eye*, that I was on a mountain..." (AACOA, p. 63)

The italics are supplied by this author, but the words themselves were generously provided by AA's founder.

Bill's recounted experience bears an astonishing resemblance to that of his paternal grandfather who, almost sixty years earlier, climbed nearby Mount Aeolus, and was relieved of his alcohol obsession. We do not know Grandpa Willie's blood alcohol content on the day in question, nor do we know how long he may have stared at the "bright light" of the sun in his search for God, but we do know that Mt. Aeolus was quite Aeolian (windy).

The Varieties of Religious Experience

"The next day more light dawned. Bill could never remember exactly but was inclined to think that Ebby, visiting again, brought him a copy of William James' The *Varieties of Religious Experience*. What Wilson got - or thought he got - from the book was to prove significant to the history of Alcoholics Anonymous." (Not-God, Ernest Kurtz, p. 20)

"Here in a book written by the country's most eminent psychologist was confirmation of the efficacy of what he had experienced." (Bill W., Francis Hartigan, p. 62)

"The book was not easy reading, but I kept at it all day. By nightfall, this Harvard professor, long in his grave, had, without anyone knowing it, become a founder of Alcoholics Anonymous." (My First Forty Years, Bill W., p. 151)

"Spiritual experiences could have objective reality... they could transform people. Some flowed out of religious channels; others did not... Complete hopelessness and deflation at depth were almost always required to make the recipient ready. The significance of it all burst upon me. *Deflation at depth* (Mr. Wilson's own italics this time) - yes, that was it." (AACOA, p. 64)

It's, of course, somewhat of a shame that the "deflation at depth" phrase is nowhere to be found in Mr. James' book!

> *Neither this expression nor the bare word deflation appears anywhere in Varieties. On the other hand, Wilson apparently did not note and certainly did not cite what was in James: the openness to explicit religion... the only cure for "dipsomania" is "religiomania".*
>
> *...Second, if there is one key word as well as concept in Varieties, it is not "deflation" but "conversion".* (Not-God, p. 23)

Mr. Kurtz italicized "deflation", the "nots", and "was" in the above quotation.

There was a "utility" in Wilson's attaching AA to William James. "This underlined linkage with a major figure in American intellectual history was therefore eminently useful to him. He made pragmatic use of the pragmatic James - with all the helpful connotations of this to those looking for 'results,' for the 'cash-value' of the idea of Alcoholics Anonymous." (Not-God, pp. 23-24)

The pluralism of William James was also valuable as AA moved forward selling itself as a spiritual "big tent."

Jamesian ABC's

The varied stories of religious conversion in Varieties have a commonality of precipitating conditions, leading to an appeal to a higher power for help. Describing his initial reaction to James' book, Wilson writes:

> *...I began to see that all the experiences cited, or at least nearly all of them, had certain common denominators...The first was calamity. Nearly every recipient described had met utter defeat in some controlling area of his life...Each had been in despair and seen no way over, under, or around...The next condition was the admission from the very depths of being that defeat was utter and absolute. (My First Forty Years, p. 151)*

The influence on the Big Book's ABC's is patently obvious:

> *Our description of the alcoholic, the chapter to the agnostic, and our personal adventure before and after make clear three pertinent ideas:*
>
> *(a) That we were alcoholic and could not manage our own lives.*
>
> *(b) That probably no human power could have relieved our alcoholism.*
>
> *(c) That God could and would if He were sought." (AA Big Book, p. 60)*

William James:

> *(a) calamity;*
>
> *(b) admission of absolute defeat;*
>
> *(c) appeal to a higher power for help.*

It is worth noting that in Bill Wilson's analysis of Varieties, God is optional. Sort of.

> *This appeal could take innumerable forms. It might be accompanied by a faith in God or it might not, but an appeal it had to be. The cry for help could course through religious channels, or a despairing agnostic could look at a growing tree*

and, reflecting on how the tree could respond to the law of its own nature and he, the human, could not, he might raise his voice to the god (sic) of nature. (My First Forty Years, pp. 151-152)

The Calamity of William James

William James was no alcoholic, but he had issues. The evidence indicates that clinical depression was endemic in the James family. His father, Henry James Sr. was a nineteenth century intellectual who consorted with Ralph Waldo Emerson, Thomas Carlyle, William Makepeace Thackery and Walt Whitman. The elder James was a liberal, an opponent of slavery, a proponent of radical ideas regarding education, and a supporter of the utopian socialism of French philosopher, Charles Fourier, who is credited with having originated the term "feminism" in 1837.

A substantial inheritance from an entrepreneurial father provided the freedom to live and philosophize as a "man of leisure." Henry Sr. married Mary Robertson Walsh in New York City, in 1840, and in time, they had five children.

William (b. 1842), and Henry James Jr. (b. 1843) followed in their father's footsteps as "men of letters." Henry was the author of "The Ambassadors," "Daisy Miller," "Turn of The Screw," "Portrait Of A Lady," and other works that were both critically acclaimed and popularly received.

Two younger brothers served in the Civil War. Garth Wilkinson (b. 1845) died in his thirties of combat injuries, while Robertson (b. 1846) was a writer of minimal achievement, remembered by history as a "ne'er-do-well" and an alcoholic. Alice (b. 1848) was a diarist whose achievements were deep in the shadows of her two oldest brothers.

Henry Sr., William, Henry Jr., and Alice all suffered from severe bouts of depression that reduced them to "invalidism." Henry Sr. seems to have mitigated the effects of his depression with a religious conversion to, and a passionate enthusiasm for Swedenborgianism, following the severest of breakdowns. Coincidentally, this was the religion of Lois Wilson and her forebears. Notwithstanding the newfound sense of purpose, Henry Sr. remained a somewhat dark and erratic character. The descriptions of various biographers indicate that he was possibly bi-polar.

Alice James died at 43, ending a lifetime of severe emotional breakdowns and confinements, having never found any significant relief from her physical and psychological problems. Her brother, Robertson seems to have done better with his own self-medicating practice, as he managed a well-lubricated survival into his sixties.

Thus, the writings of William James concerning debilitating difficulties were not of a "theoretical" or "hypothetical" nature, but bred of personal, and familial experience. It is not a fluke that he one day authored a book offering a solution for "calamity."

Young William James

The eldest child of Henry James and Mary Robertson Walsh was born on January 11, 1842. William benefitted from the family's views on cosmopolitan education and took many trips to Europe. He acquired a fluency in both French and German.

In early adulthood, William James suffered from a variety of physical ailments, psychological symptoms and neurasthenia. There were periods of enervating depression and suicidal ideation. More than once, his education was interrupted by "rest cures," but he completed an MD degree in 1869.

"I originally studied medicine in order to be a physiologist, but I drifted into psychology and philosophy from a sort of fatality. I never had any philosophic instruction, the first lecture on psychology I had ever heard being the first one I gave." (The Thought and Character of William James, Vol. 1, Ralph Borton Perry, 1996 Edition, p. 228)

James spent almost his entire academic career at Harvard, beginning as an instructor in physiology, then anatomy, and later rotating between psychology and philosophy until he retired in 1907.

His "soul sickness" seems to have been resolved in 1872, from a combination of extensive philosophical searching, and enthusiasm for his nascent academic career. His later philosophy points toward the acceptance of spiritual beliefs that ran counter to his intellectual leanings, but proved useful. In some very real sense, he copied the "spiritual experience" of his own father, having witnessed its worth.

A very practical decision.

Pragmatism and The Will To Believe

William James was a prolific writer and ventured into several fields - epistemology, education, metaphysics, psychology, religion and mysticism. The mammoth Principles of Psychology (1890) was a groundbreaking work in American psychology and a prominent text for decades.

His connection to Alcoholics Anonymous is most evident in his philosophy of pragmatism, "The Will To Believe" essay, and of course, The Varieties of Religious Experience.

"Beliefs were ways of acting with reference to a precarious environment, and to say that they were true was to say they (were efficacious) in this environment." (Pragmatism, Bruce Kuklick, p. xiv) James defined true beliefs as those that prove useful to the believer.

A commonly heard AA bromide comes to mind: "Would you rather be right, or would you rather be happy?"

Plainly, "all of the above" is NOT a conference-approved response.

The Will To Believe doctrine allows one to assume belief in a god, and prove its existence by what the belief brings to one's life. James sought to ground justified belief in an unwavering principle that would prove more beneficial. For Bill Wilson, facing a future of death or alcoholic insanity, the belief that supernatural force could and would rescue him had great utility, pragmatic value, "cash value."

Pragmatists contend that most philosophical topics are best viewed in terms of their practical uses and successes, rather than in terms of representative accuracy. Essentially we have a recycling of Pascal's Wager.

Two Williams

William James and William Griffith Wilson had many things in common. Both suffered from depression that was at times incapacitating, likely genetically acquired, and exacerbated by unconventional child-rearing of self-absorbed parents. Both made practical decisions to seek transformation through spiritual conversion experiences, and to some very real extent were successful in this.

Both men were fascinated by mysticism, psychic phenomena and the occult. Wilson's interest in producing spiritual experiences led to experimentation with LSD, while James' investigation of mysticism led to the sampling of chloral hydrate, amyl nitrate, nitrous oxide and peyote.

Bill Wilson came to an incredible understanding of alcoholism, and William James was not without insight. "The sway of alcohol over mankind is unquestionably due to its power to stimulate the mystical faculties of human nature, usually crushed to earth by the cold facts and dry criticisms of the sober hour. Sobriety diminishes, discriminates, and says no; drunkenness expands, unites, and says yes. It is in fact the great exciter of the yes function in man." (Varieties, p. 282)

William James abandoned a career in medicine to become, in the eyes of many, the "Father of American Psychology." William G. Wilson was abandoned by a career in the stock market but went on to become, in the eyes of many, the "Father of American Recovery." Both men are spoken of by millions, decades after their deaths. Mr. James died of heart failure on August 26th, 1910.

Both thought that the best solution to the most serious of life's problems was to abandon them to the care of a higher power.

That certainly seems to work for some. We continue to debate the exact nature of the "how."

Chapter 16 Carl Jung

In 1961, Bill Wilson, reached out, rather belatedly, to the famous psychoanalyst, Carl Jung, in order to express some gratitude to him, on AA's behalf, for "… the conversation between you (and Rowland) that was to become the first in the chain of events that led to the founding of Alcoholics Anonymous." (Not-God, Ernest Kurtz, p. 8) Rowland Hazard's visit to the famous psychiatrist, now believed to have taken place in 1926, and not 1931, is recounted in the Big Book story of a "certain American businessman" on pages 26-27.

Fairly recent access to previously unavailable Hazard family and business records has led historians to conclude that AA's account of Jung's treatment of "a certain American businessman" is somewhat inaccurate. The duration of Rowland's therapy under Jung was perhaps two months. This all could have been the result of entirely innocent misremembering of a collection of drunks, or, the tale may have been intentionally aggrandized.

"Like his father before him, Bill W. was a spellbinding storyteller: and, as Robertson observes, he had a 'lifelong penchant for embroidering the facts while accurately summarizing the gist of an event.' Thus his factual liberties may be regarded as acts of poetic license." (Bill W. and Mr. Wilson, Matthew Raphael, p. 12. The "Robertson" referred to in Mr. Raphael's quotation is Pulitzer Prize winning Nan Robertson, author of "Getting Better - Inside Alcoholics Anonymous.")

Emotional Displacements and Rearrangements

The alcoholic's need for a "spiritual experience" comes from this Jung-Hazard encounter, an event historian Ernie Kurtz calls one of the four "founding moments in the history of the idea and the fellowship of Alcoholics Anonymous." (Not-God, p. 33) It comes as well, from the work of William James. But what IS that exactly?

"To me (Jung) these occurrences are phenomena. They appear to be in the nature of huge emotional displacements and rearrangements. Ideas, emotions, and attitudes which were once guiding forces of the lives of these men are suddenly cast to one side, and a completely new set of conceptions and motives begin to dominate them." (BB, p. 27)

Of course, such change is often associated with religious conversion, but Jung's language is evocative of the "personality change" of APPENDIX II. Jung had attempted to produce such a personality change, or "emotional rearrangement," in Rowland, through therapeutic methods. Even James includes an "atheist" recovery. The very term "mind-cure" points directly at what needs to be "cured."

Carl Jung was a world-renowned psychiatrist, psychologist, therapist, researcher and writer. He is seen by many as "a superstitious genius." A review of his work is beyond the abilities of this writer and outside of the scope of this essay. Such information is easily accessible elsewhere for those who seek it.

For someone who so profoundly influenced the course of events leading to what would become AA, there is remarkably little about him in our histories, and that's a shame as he is quite a fascinating fellow.

The Unconscious

"My life is a story of the self-realization of the unconscious. Everything in the unconscious seeks outward manifestation... I can only understand myself in the light of inner happenings. It is these that make up the singularity of my life... " (Memories, Dreams, Reflections, Carl Jung, p. 5)

Psychology as a science is divided into two distinct branches, normal and abnormal, each of these, of course, further segmenting into schools and substrata. Freud, Jung, Adler and others treated and studied the mentally ill, and in doing so, came to understandings regarding the brain function, emotionality, and maturation processes of "normal" people. This was a grand era of psychology where all-encompassing theories of personality were postulated. The field grew and progressed through the examination, and eventual debunking, of the majority of these ambitious hypotheses.

Modern psychology is a far less exciting world of statistical analysis, control groups, random samples, and elaborate examination of minutiae, all reflecting the desire to be scientific, and to be seen as being scientific. The era of Jung, Freud, and Adler was quite different. Before the "Behaviorist Manifesto" of John B. Watson brought real science and measurement to psychology, the discipline was much more of an offshoot of philosophy.

Wilhelm Wundt, seen by many as the father of modern psychology, employed as his main technique, "introspection," looking inward, self-examination. Edward Titchener introduced a modified version of this to America. Although this method is fraught with perils, most especially perhaps for alcoholics who "cannot after a time differentiate the true from the false" (Doctor's Opinion, BB, p. xxviii), these 19th century techniques lie at the heart of the theorizing of Carl Jung.

Early Years

Jung was born in Switzerland on June 26, 1875. He was the son of a Protestant parson who suffered from hypochondria, and a developing crisis of faith. His mother had ongoing psychiatric problems. By age three, young Carl developed some seemingly emotionally induced physical problems, as the result of tension in his parents' marriage.

"My illness, in 1878, must have been connected with a temporary separation of my parents. My mother spent several months in a hospital in Basel, and presumably her illness had something to do with the difficulty in the marriage... I was deeply troubled by my mother's being away. From then on, I always felt mistrustful when 'love' was spoken. The feeling I associated with 'woman' was for a long time that of innate unreliability." (MDR, p. 8)

Those familiar with the life of Bill Wilson will recognize similarities to the rapid unraveling of Emily Wilson's marriage to Gilman, and her various "rest cures" away from the family. Later on, there was to be a further similarity to Wilson's feelings of inferiority. As a "townie" from the unsophisticated mining town of East Dorset, Wilson was cowed by the wealthy "summer people," and their grand Manchester residences. At ten, Carl Jung was sent to the Gymnasium in Basel.

"I was taken away from my rustic playmates, and truly entered the 'great world,' where powerful personages... lived in big, splendid houses, drove about in expensive carriages drawn by magnificent horses, and talked a refined German and French. Their sons, well dressed, equipped with fine manners and plenty of pocket money, were now my classmates." (MDR, p. 24) This is much like a young Bill Wilson at Burr & Burton Academy. The ten year old, poor parson's son became intensely aware of the holes in his own shoes.

Vivid Memories and Dreams

Jung's course in life seems to have been profoundly influenced by some childhood experiences and dreams which remained indelibly etched in his mind for the rest of his life. He confesses some morbid fascination with death, from the very early age of about four. That dead folks were said to have "gone to Jesus," made the youngster greatly wary of Jesus. This was compounded by seeing a frightening looking man whom others called a "Jesuit." The black cassock was a dress to a small child, and an unusual garb for a man.

"For days afterward the hellish fright clung to my limbs and kept me in the house. Later I realized, of course, that the black figure was a harmless Catholic priest. At about the same time... I had the earliest dream I can remember, a dream which was to pre-occupy me all of my life... I discovered a dark, rectangular, stone-lined hole in the ground... (Descending, he finds a platform on which) stood a wonderfully rich gold throne... a real king's throne in a fairy tale." (MDR, p. 12) Standing on the throne was an enormous, fleshy, one-eyed, tree trunk-like object, which he later realized was a phallus, and still later, a "ritual phallus".

In the dream, his mother says, "That is the man-eater". Introspection, the study of Freudian dream interpretation, and the study of myth lead to an interpretation of these dark, dreamed events, the phallus of this dream being "a subterranean God, 'not to be named,' and such it remained throughout my youth, reappearing whenever anyone spoke too emphatically about Lord Jesus". (MDR, p. 13) Somehow, the giant phallus, and the feared "black man" are linked, and Christianity is well on the way to being abandoned by Jung, in favor of a very AA-like, mystical "experience of God".

Yes. Really.

Memories of a tumble downstairs, another blood-letting fall against a stove leg, and a near toppling into the Rhine river, for Jung, pointed to "an unconscious suicidal urge or, it may be, to a fatal resistance to life in this world". (MDR, p. 9)

Sigmund Freud

Jung found Freud's "The Interpretation of Dreams" to be a brilliantly insightful tome which "cast a valuable light on schizophrenic forms of expression... it all linked up with my own ideas". (MDR, pp. 146-147) At the time, the early twentieth century, Sigmund Freud was "persona non grata" in the academic world. When, in 1906, Jung wrote a paper supporting Freud's theory of neuroses, he put at peril his own professional reputation.

When Jung met personally with Freud, in 1907, he was greatly honored. Although Jung did not agree with the universality of Freud's sexual theory, he was too intimidated to debate the issue. Ultimately, Freud's dogmatic adherence to his own theories, and differences in views on the role of spirit, led to a breakdown in their friendship.

Freud was seen as "emotionally involved in his sexual theory to an extraordinary degree" (MDR, p. 150), and militant in his battle against all things smacking of "occultism." Writing his autobiography some fifty years later, Jung remembers Freud as both bitter and one-sided, "a man in the grip of his daimon". (MDR, p. 150)

A Flourishing Career

No lasting harm appears to have been forthcoming to Jung as the result of his estrangement from Dr. Freud. As the years have passed, Jung's position in the history of psychiatry has even, in the eyes of many, surpassed his old mentor. Jung was a prolific writer, and he had a wide variety of interests which included astrology, mysticism, alchemy, and the occult.

Although he had a compelling desire to be viewed as a "man of science," his eccentric passions pushed him toward the fringe of the academic community.

Within his field, he is remembered as the founder of a new school of psychotherapy, "analytical" or "Jungian" psychology. He is the creator of the idea of two distinct personality types, "introverts" and "extroverts," and of the concept of a "complex". He wrote volumes on dream analysis.

His interactions with women, including patients, marred his reputation, and provided fodder for critics.

Individuation

At the core of Jungian theory is his concept of the tripartite human psyche. The conscious mind he called the "ego." The two other elements were the personal unconscious and the collective unconscious. "Individuation" was his term for the integration of these components necessary for a healthy person.

His intense exploration of a multiplicity of world religions led him to conclude that a "journey of transformation" is at the mystical heart of all religions.

Rowland Hazard and AA

"Rowland Hazard's prominence could not hide the ravages of his alcoholism…. In desperation, the investment banker went to Zurich in 1926 and placed himself under the care of Carl Jung… When Hazard later relapsed (late 1927 or early 1928), he returned to Jung, only to be told… that there was nothing left medical or psychiatric treatment could do for him." (Slaying The Dragon, 2nd edition, William L. White, p. 170)

Jung's first gift to AA highlighted the hopelessness of the condition.

"Bill Wilson linked James's portrayal of 'conversion' with what he had learned directly from Dr. Silkworth and indirectly via Rowland and Ebby from Dr. Jung, of the necessity and role of hopelessness." (Not-God, Ernest Kurtz, p. 23) Jung also pointed to the solution that was found in greater depth in the ideas of William James's.

"Jung went on to say to say that Rowland's only hope was a 'spiritual awakening' or religious experience. Jung also told him that such transformative experiences were quite rare. Jung understood that alcoholism created a spiritual void… a spiritual experience seemed to fill that void and stem the alcoholic's voracious appetite for the instrument of his or her own self-destruction." (Dragon, p. 170)

Rowland's treatment under the renowned psychoanalyst was no more than a couple of months. He did bring home, if not sobriety, the notion of the need to seek a spiritual experience, and he seems to have found it some seven or eight years later with the Oxford Group. Jung's disparagement of the "human power" of medicine did not stop Hazard from pursuing other therapy. It is known that he was being treated by Courtenay Baylor in 1933-34.

Synchronicity

Henrietta Seiberling thought that there were just too many elements of happenstance leading up to the fateful meeting of AA's cofounders. She saw powerful evidence, to no one's enormous surprise, that "the hand of God" had written the script. "Or as Carl Jung might have said, the uncanny concatenation of circumstances surrounding the seemingly fated meeting of Wilson and Smith exemplified synchronicity, Jung's term for 'a meaningful coincidence of two or more events, where something other than the probability of chance is involved.'" (Raphael, p. 102)

In our very large world, each day there are trillions upon trillions of daily events. Some of these occurrences are unusual, and mathematical probability teaches us that a series of anomalous happenings is consistently among the expected results. Those seeking evidence of divine intervention will find it. God bless them. Jung's synchronicity idea is somewhat more convoluted, and beyond the scope of this essay.

Religiomania

"In Varieties James repeats an adage... 'The only radical remedy I know for dipsomania is religiomania'. (VRE, 268n) This is the same advice Carl Jung gave Rowland H., and that Ebby T. in turn passed on to Bill W. : that getting religion was the key to getting sober." (Raphael, p. 84)

This is essentially the message of AA's Big Book, written as it was against the background of Protestant pietism of 1930's America. That non-believers were able to achieve sobriety as well, by transformations that were less religious, or less THAN religious, prompted the somewhat "Jungian" Appendix II, added in 1941. Moving forward, Western society is opening itself both to ancient Eastern philosophies, and ultramodern notions of "spirituality" that is unattached to all things supernatural.

Some truth remains in the view of the "hopelessness" of the alcoholic condition. Jung did not lie to Rowland. There are few credible reports of real alcoholics returning to social drinking, and merely quitting drinking without other changes is generally remarkably unsatisfying. Although the AA process brings "God" to some, along with the AA fellowship, it can bring to ALL a new and rewarding connection to the "human network".

Helping others brings purpose. Having purpose is both gratifying and esteem-building. Reverend Rick was right, in part, about a "purpose driven life", but people in our diverse world are finding fulfilling objectives within the physical world, especially if they are led to a "personality change sufficient to bring about recovery from alcoholism". (BB, p. 567)

Such a change "has manifested itself among us in many different forms". (BB, p. 567)

Indeed!

Addendum - Liber Novus

There is inadequate space to deal in detail with a very recent event that has sparked renewed interest in Carl Jung, some fifty years after his passing, but it must be mentioned.

In 1913, at the age of thirty-eight, Jung experienced a horrible "confrontation with the unconscious". He saw visions and heard voices. He worried at times that he was "menaced by a psychosis" or was "doing a schizophrenia". He decided that it was valuable experience and, in private, he induced hallucinations or, in his words, "active imaginations". He recorded everything he felt in small journals. Jung began to transcribe his notes into a large red leather-bound book, on which he worked intermittently for sixteen years. The bulk of the experience spanned 1913 to 1917.

His own talk of "psychosis" may reflect an exaggerated self-deprecation, as he continued to see patients during this era, and also served in the Swiss army. Jung left no posthumous instructions about the final disposition of what he called the Red Book. The family finally allowed the book to be published in late 2009, with a Reader's Edition made available in 2012.

In 1957, near the end of his life, Jung spoke to Aniela Jaffe about the Red Book and the process which yielded it. In that interview he stated:

"The years... when I pursued the inner images, were the most important time of my life. Everything else is to be derived from this. It began at that time, and the later details hardly matter anymore. My entire life consisted in elaborating what had burst forth from the unconscious and flooded me like an enigmatic stream and threatened to break me. That was the stuff and material for more than only one life. Everything later was merely the outer classification, scientific elaboration, and the integration into life. But the numinous beginning, which contained everything, was then." (Liber Novus, p. vii)

The strangeness continues.

Chapter 17 William D. Silkworth

The "Roaring Twenties" ended not with a bang, but a whimper, as the stock market crash of 1929 plunged America into the darkness of the Great Depression. Throughout the twenties, and into the thirties, the "noble experiment" of national Prohibition was failing miserably.

The fundamental intention had been to curb drunkenness by outlawing liquor, but the very opposite was being realized. Drinking had achieved a certain "cachet," as otherwise respectable citizens visited speakeasies, and made bathtub gin at home. "In many circles, it was chic to drink and get drunk and outwit the authorities." (Getting Better - Inside Alcoholics Anonymous, Nan Robertson, p. 43)

Gangsters amassed huge fortunes through bootlegging and smuggling. It was the heyday of organized crime. The base support for the forces of temperance fell away from beneath them, and in late 1933, the Eighteenth Amendment was repealed.

Drinking was accepted, and again legitimized in American culture. Drunkards were not. "Chronic alcoholism was considered to be a moral weakness, or a sin. Seemingly hopeless alcoholics like Bill Wilson received little understanding and compassion." (Getting Better, p. 43) The idea of alcoholism as an illness, so ubiquitous in the twenty-first century, had little support in the pre-AA era in spite of being proposed by eminent physicians such as Scotland's Thomas Trotter, and American Founding Father, Benjamin Rush.

Another significant event occurred towards the end of 1933. The future founder of Alcoholics Anonymous was admitted to a detox center for the well-heeled. "Charles B. Towns Hospital, 293 Central Park West... founded in 1901, was well known then as a rich man's drying-out place; a rehab for the wealthy, and it served a worldwide clientele. American millionaires, European royalty and oil sheiks from the middle east walked its halls, side by side: brothers in humiliation in bathrobes and slippers." (The Round Table of AA History by Mike O., Silkworth.net)

The fees would have been well beyond the means of a struggling Lois Wilson and her husband, but the visit was "sponsored" by Leonard Strong, a New York physician married to Bill's sister, Dorothy. There would be three more "Towns cures" in 1934, and mother Emily was also canvassed to contribute. The chief physician at Towns was William Duncan Silkworth.

Neurology and Psychiatry

Regarding the history of "the little doctor who loved drunks," there is some disagreement, even as to the year of his birth, which most likely was 1873. It is known that he attended Princeton, achieving an AB degree in 1896. He graduated from NYU - Bellevue Medical School in 1899. During his internship at Bellevue, he discovered a flair for working with drunks.

Called simply a "medical doctor" in the Big Book, "Pass It On" says he "became a specialist in neurology, a domain that sometimes overlaps psychiatry" (p. 101), and that he entered private practice in the 1920s. Ernest Kurtz calls him a "neuro-psychiatrist."

"Silkworth's entire career had a psychiatric emphasis. He was a member of the psychiatric staff at the US. Army Hospital in Plattsburgh, New York, for two years (1917-1919) during World War I." (Mike O., Silkworth.net)

It is most likely that he "served as associate physician at the Neurological Institute of Presbyterian Hospital in Manhattan from 1919 to 1929. He had also been connected with Broad Street Hospital". (Mike O., Silkworth. net)

His start date at Towns Hospital is inconsistently reported as 1924 (Kurtz), 1930 (Pass It On), or 1932 (various sources). It seems most credible that Silkworth was laid off by Presbyterian after the market crash of 1929, an event which also vaporized his savings, and that he came to Towns in, or after, 1930.

"The pay was pitiful, something like $40. a week and board." (Pass It On, p. 101) Lois Wilson was making half that as a store clerk.

Total Abstinence

In the twenty-first century, most people know that alcoholics need to maintain total abstinence to prevail over their drinking problem. Not so, eighty years ago. The ideas that alcoholism was a "disease entity", and that complete sobriety was necessary, had been proffered much earlier in America by onetime Surgeon General, Benjamin Rush, but such hypotheses gained very little acceptance. "As far as the temperance movement was concerned, alcoholism was a moral failing, and it vigorously opposed the disease concept of alcoholism." (Bill W., Francis Hartigan, p. 51) It was not commonly known at the time that the standard advice "Buck up, man, and drink like a gentleman," was an impossible prescription for a certain element of the population to follow.

Illness Not Sin

Wilson, much later, would write of Silkworth, "From him we learned the nature of our illness: the obsession of the mind that compels us to drink and the allergy of the body that condemns us to go mad or die". (Alcoholics Anonymous Comes Of Age, p. 13) "For the first time in his life, Bill was hearing about alcoholism not as a lack of willpower, not as a moral defect, but as a legitimate illness." (Pass It On, p. 102)

"The gentle little man explained (to Lois) that my drinking, once habit, had become an obsession, a true insanity that condemned me to drink against my will." (AACOA, p. 52) This new information provoked a period of sobriety that Bill reported as two to four months, but Lois remembered as about a month."

The examples in "More About Alcoholism" reinforce the notion that awareness alone is insufficient. "But the actual or potential alcoholic, with hardly any exception, will be absolutely unable to stop drinking on the basis of self-knowledge. This is a point we wish to emphasize and re-emphasize, to smash home upon our alcoholic readers as it has been revealed to us out of bitter experience." (AA Big Book, p. 39)

So Bill Wilson had some additional benders, doozies by all accounts, but his drinking would end before Christmas of 1934.

Validating the "Hot Flash"

By the time of Bill Wilson's fourth confinement at Towns Hospital, he had been approached by Ebby, and been presented with the "I've got religion" message. As abhorrent as these ideas were to him, there was no denying that his one-time schoolmate was sober, that "he was on a different footing. His roots grasped a new soil." (BB, p. 12)

The most extreme desperation opened Bill to what William James would call "the pragmatic theory of truth". If a religious experience could save him as it had his old friend, it had "utility", and thus, was worth having.

Cue the bright light, the newfound confidence, and the cool wind a blowin.' One of the delicious ironies, so entertaining to the cynical, is that in an earlier draught of "Bill's Story", the "hot flash" is reported as happening in Bill's kitchen, immediately after Ebby's first visit. The amended version better fits the "as the result of these steps" storyline. It is also a superior timeline in that the original telling has Bill getting drunk several more times AFTER divine salvation! "He drank now as he never had." (Bill W., Robert Thomsen, p. 196)

At the hospital, he was administered a drug cure concocted by Charles B. Towns, which included hallucinogens. "There is the possibility that his 'hot flash' may have been delusions and hallucinations characteristic of momentary alcoholic toxic psychosis." (The Roots of Alcoholics Anonymous, Bill Pittman, p. 169)

Silkworth's second great gift to AA, from Bill Wilson's perspective was that the kindly doctor, a man of science, did not mock his debatable apparition. "'Whatever you've got now, you'd better hold onto. It's so much better that what you had only a couple of hours ago.' Coming from Silkworth, now a central figure in Bill's life, this evaluation meant everything." (Pass It On, pp. 123-124)

"Stop Preaching!"

Intuitively, Bill Wilson knew that in and of itself, his "awakening" would be insufficient to maintain his sobriety. Wilson's great insight was in recognizing the value of helping others, the principle which was to turn out to be the very core of AA, and its success.

Four years later, he described his early struggles - "I was not too well at the time, and was plagued with waves of self-pity and resentment. This sometimes nearly drove me back to drink, but I soon found that when all other measures failed, work with another alcoholic would save the day." (BB, p. 15) And - "Practical experience shows that nothing will so much insure immunity from drinking as intensive work with other alcoholics." (BB, p. 89)

Bill's early evangelism of his newfound solution for a drinking problem was successful only in that it was keeping himself sober.

In the Spring of 1935, Dr. Silkworth stepped up with his third major contribution to what would become AA. "Stop preaching at them... and give them the hard medical facts first...Tell about the hopeless condition, a matter of life or death." (AACOA, p. 13)

Dr. Bob Smith

Thus, it was a modified approach, directed by Silkworth's counsel, that got Bob Smith's attention, where a two and a half year exposure to the Oxford Group's religious mumbo-jumbo had accomplished nothing for the Akron surgeon.

"Dr. Silkworth's advice to Bill about talking with, rather that at, his prospects was important to the success of his encounter with Robert Smith... One thing Bob heard from Bill was the notion that alcoholism was not a sin, but an illness. This wasn't what he was hearing from the Oxford Group." (Hartigan, p. 82)

"He gave me information about the subject of alcoholism that was undoubtedly helpful. Of far more importance was the fact that he was the first living human with whom I had ever talked, who knew what he was talking about in regard to alcoholism from actual experience. In other words, he talked my language." (Doctor Bob's Nightmare, BB, p. 180)

Access to Prospects

Vital to Bill Wilson's developing method of staying sober was the intensive effort to assist others. In Akron, this had come easily through Smith's position as a physician with hospital privileges. Back in New York, Bill found some drunks with which to work, but a virtually unlimited supply was provided as Dr. Silkworth risked his professional reputation, in allowing Bill to approach the Towns clientele.

Through these auspices, Hank P. and Fitz M. were the earliest converts to the nascent movement. A couple of years later, Towns client, Jim B. would become a somewhat recalcitrant, but notable recruit.

Financing the Book Project

Bill Wilson and Hank Parkhurst developed some spectacular visions for expansion of their new methods of "curing" drunks. Dreams of Rockefeller millions danced in their heads, and yet the two sales dynamos were having enormous difficulty in raising the funds necessary to support the writing and publication of the book.

Again William Silkworth had a hand in overcoming this obstacle. That Charles B. Towns supplied $2,500, later increased to $4,000, was undoubtedly due in part to the urging of his chief physician.

Medical Endorsement

As a salesman, Bill Wilson understood the value of "third party testimonials". In spite of some undeniable successes, that a pack of drunks would seek to publish a book at such an early stage was at best ambitious, and possibly laughable.

An endorsement, at the very opening of their text, from "a well known doctor, chief physician at a nationally prominent hospital specializing in alcoholic and drug addiction." (BB, 1st Edition, p. 1) contributed some desperately needed credibility.

The brevity of the initial letter provided is suggestive of a man who was both humble and diffident, antithetical to so many of his patients.

Allergy

In the modern world, the good doctor's use of the term "allergy" is under attack, as is the notion of alcoholism as a disease. In both cases, these are rather technical debates. We are given perspective in the wise words of Bill White - "Science is unlikely to destroy the popularity of the disease concept, but a better metaphor could". (Slaying The Dragon, Second Edition, William L. White, p. 512)

Similarly, "allergy" when seen as an abnormal reaction, has explanatory value, even if alcoholism differs from other allergies in a strict diligence of science.

When one listens to psychiatrist, Nora Volkow, Director of the National Institute on Drug Abuse (NIDA) at the National Institutes of Health since May 2003, one very much hears twenty-first century talk of alcoholism and addiction that is consistent with the speculations of Dr. Silkworth, many decades earlier. Modern brain imaging has proven that alcoholics are physically different from their peers. What Silkworth saw as a "mental obsession" is confirmed, as are its physical causes.

Human Power

It has been variously estimated that "the little doctor who loved drunks" consulted with from 40,000 to 50,000 alcoholics. By his own modest admission, before AA, he saw his success rate as about two percent. This speaks to the insidiousness of alcoholism, and of the need for some sort of ongoing therapy, beyond the rehabilitation possible in a month, or a week.

For the starry-eyed fundamentalist there is an additional problem of accounting for the 400, 600, or 800 people who were successfully treated, with mere human power. The stock answer, of course, is that they weren't "real" alcoholics, and thus without any qualm, the legacy of a selfless man, one of AA's most substantial contributors, is tarnished.

Last Years

William D. Silkworth remained a friend of AA, and he took joy in watching alcoholics helping each other at a rate his most diligent efforts had been unable to match. "Dr. Silkworth was a major influence in persuading the management of Knickerbocker Hospital in upper Manhattan to set aside a small ward, beginning in 1945, for the treatment of alcoholics. Knickerbocker was the first general hospital in New York to do so. (This is significant because many general hospitals at that time would not admit alcoholics as alcoholics. Their doctors had to admit them under false diagnoses.)... At Knickerbocker, drunks off the street with no financial resources were de-toxified." (Mike O., Silkworth. net)

In 1950 and '51, Bill Wilson and some associates were raising funds so that "Silkie" and wife, Marie, could retire in New Hampshire, but, on March 22, 1951, AA's "medical saint" died before that could happen. His most famous patient rounded up $25,000 to assist the widow through her remaining years.

Legacy

"Silkworth had explained the mechanisms of the lock that held the alcoholic in prison." (Thomsen, p. 204)

William Silkworth was at the forefront of those who effected a reversal in the prevalent view of alcoholism in America, and the world. We may argue the esoterica of "disease," "disease entity," "illness" and the like, but the views of alcoholism as a "moral failing," a "willpower issue," or a "sin", are all but gone among the informed. Modern science continues to hammer nails into the "moral failing" coffin.

Only the religious ultra-right still talks of "sin."

Thank God! ... Er... I mean... whatevah!!

SECTION IV NOTABLE DRUNKS

Chapter 18 Rowland Hazard

A certain American businessman had ability, good sense, and high character. For years he had floundered from one sanitarium to another. He had consulted the best known American psychiatrists. Then he had gone to Europe, placing himself in the care of a celebrated physician (the psychiatrist, Dr. Jung) who prescribed for him. Though experience had made him skeptical, he finished his treatment with unusual confidence. His physical and mental condition were unusually good. Above all he believed he had acquired such a profound knowledge of the inner workings of his mind and its hidden springs that relapse was unthinkable. Nevertheless, he was drunk in a short time...
(Alcoholics Anonymous, p. 26)

The "certain American businessman" was Rowland Hazard. These events, thought at one time to have occurred in 1930, or 1931, are now believed to have taken place in 1926. This story is intended to demonstrate the total inefficacy of "human power", including the rising tide of psychiatry, and psychoanalysis, relatively new, but highly respected disciplines, at that time. Of course, religion was failing at about an equal rate in attempts to rehabilitate problem drinkers. The rise of AA was to prove, as had earlier groups like the Washingtonians, the Jacoby Club, and others, that drunks will listen to others drunks and that "identification" is one of the most critical tools in addressing the alcohol problem.

Dr. Bob Smith confirms this theory in his description of his initial meeting with Bill Wilson on Mother's Day, 1935;

> *He gave me information about the subject of alcoholism which was undoubtedly helpful. Of far more importance was the fact that he was the first living human with whom I had ever talked, who knew what he was talking about in regard to alcoholism from actual experience. In other words, he talked my language. He knew all the answers, and certainly not because he had picked them up in his reading. (BB, p. 180)*

Of course, before all of this, came Rowland Hazard.

The Hazards of Rhode Island

> *Members of the Hazard family were among the first settlers of the State of Rhode Island. Descendants have been known for military achievement, business success, philanthropy, and broad social activism spanning such causes as abolition of slavery, treatment of the insane and alcoholics, family planning, and innovative employee programs.*
>
> *The family fortune derived largely from its textile manufacturing business at Peace Dale, Rhode Island, mining, railroad, and chemical interests, including the Solvay Process Company. (Wikipedia)*

Succeeding generations of Hazards built and occupied the finest homes and estates in Rhode Island.

"X" Marks the Spot

Family patriarch, Thomas Hazard (1610 - circa 1680) emigrated from Britain in the mid 1630s. The young ship's carpenter came first to Boston, then Portsmouth, on Rhode Island. In 1639, he became one of nine founding settlers of Newport on Aquineck Island, in the colony of Rhode Island. The entire nine were followers of their spiritual leader, the Baptist, Anne Hutchinson.

Property acquired very inexpensively from the natives was divided among the founders. Hazard made his beginnings in America as a plantation owner and a town administrator. The progenitor of what was to become a family of "eminence", signed his name with a mark. Succeeding generations would have available to them the very best in educational opportunities, and two of Thomas Hazard's great grandsons rose to the position of Deputy Governor of Rhode Island, George from 1734-38, and his brother Robert from 1750-51. A third Hazard rose to the same heights in the 1830's.

Wool Mills

Generations of Hazards owned and operated many businesses. Much of the family fortune was made in textile manufacturing. The Peace Dale Manufacturing Co., which was started in 1802 and was in family ownership for over one hundred years, was the principal supplier of blankets to the Union Army in the Civil War. Rowland's grandfather, also a Rowland "had great respect for the dignity of his employees... (and) introduced the first employee profit-sharing in America... He shortened the work week, built decent housing, and started a school". (Rowland, The Messenger, Silkworth.net)

He was the very antithesis of the "robber barons" ruthlessly operating other companies in the post Civil War era.

Religious Roots

"Rowland's father, Rowland Gibson H., was superintendent of the Congregational Sabbath School for twenty-five years... Belief in God was an ingrained value in Rowland's life. His mother's father was a man of the cloth." (Rowland, The Messenger).

Taft, Yale, a Wife and a War

Rowland Hazard III was among the tenth generation of Hazards in Rhode Island. He added the numerical suffix "III" to distinguish himself from a succession of "Rowlands" dating back to the middle of the Eighteenth Century. Born on October 29, 1881, the eldest of five children, Rowland was thus about two years younger than Dr. Bob Smith. Born "into privilege", the young Hazard was sent to the elite Taft School in Connecticut, and then broke a family tradition of attending Brown University by choosing instead the alma mater of his maternal grandfather, Yale. Among his classmates, he was called "Ike", "Rowley", or "Roy", his nickname within the family.

We do not know if Rowland became a champion drinker at Yale, as did Bob Smith at Dartmouth, but he graduated in 1903, and was put to work in the family business. By 1906, he was Secretary/Treasurer of one of the family's concerns, advancement opportunities being readily available to all named "Hazard." He spent some time in Chicago, and it was there that he met Helen Hamilton Campbell, a graduate of Briar Cliff and the daughter of a banker. They were married in 1910. The couple divorced in 1929, but remarried in 1931.

From 1914-16, Rowland served in the Rhode Island State Senate. As America's entry to the Great War grew imminent, Rowland surrendered a civilian supply position to become a Captain in the Army's Chemical Warfare Service. By this time, the Hazards had substantial interests in chemical manufacturing.

The Code of Silence

Whatever drinking was being done up until this point had led to no embarrassing firings or material disadvantage. The family would have gone to great lengths to minimize any sort of public scrutiny of what at the time was considered to be a "moral failing". Perhaps "Roy" was seen as wild, but alcoholism would not have been seen as something that rears its head in "the best families". "There is corporate denial." (Rowland, The Messenger) Nonetheless, there is some powerful evidence that his affliction was known within the family.

In 1918, Rowland Gibson Hazard, Rowland III's father, died. At that time, Rowland III held a number of positions within the family's network of companies. This was an era where the right of primogeniture was ubiquitously honored, but the thirty-seven year old eldest son was bypassed as the reins of power were entrusted to his twenty-six year old brother, Thomas, only three years out of college.

Rowland was given a consolation prize, the presidency of one of the lesser companies, Solway Securities. A few years later, he moved outside the family circle to Lee Higginson & Co., a New York investment banker. His years with them were 1920-27. As modern research has the trip to Switzerland as occurring in 1926, his time at Higginson would have been a period of serious bingeing and interruptions for treatment (or detoxes) at various sanitariums. His employment was likely beyond jeopardy because of his access to investment by the numerous Hazard enterprises.

Rowland The Messenger

The inimitable Ernest Kurtz enumerates

> *the four "founding moments" in the history of Alcoholics Anonymous:*

1. Dr. Carl Jung's 1931 conversation with Rowland H. (now believed to have taken place in 1926);

2. Ebby T.'s late November 1934 visit with Bill Wilson;

3. Wilson's "spiritual experience" and discovery of William James in Towns Hospital in mid-December 1934;

4. and the interaction between Wilson and Dr. Bob Smith through May and June 1935... (Not-God, Ernest Kurtz, p. 33)

Rowland was present at, and involved in, the first of these, and instrumental in the second.

Geographical Tourism "Curism"

"Officially", Rowland Hazard resigned his position with Lee Higginson & Co. to go on safari in Africa, an excursion that had become popular among the very rich. His wife may have been attempting to get him away from his drinking friends and environments. "Officially", while in Africa, Rowland contracted some sort of tropical disease. Whether true or not, the tale provided a very useful explanation for his subsequent increasing need for hospitalization, and his disappearance from the world of Wall Street.

Hazard's activities during the period of 1927-35 have been described as "vague and sketchy, a time of 'health problems' and private ventures". (The First Links in the Chain, Barefoot World) In 1929, he purchased a New Mexico ranch. Ever entrepreneurial, "upon discovery of high grade clay on the ranch, he organized in 1931-32 the La Luz Clay Products to produce floor and roof tile". (First Links)

In 1932, he took up residence in Shaftsbury, Vermont, about fifteen miles south of Manchester. From 1932-36, his time was divided between Vermont and New Mexico. It was about this time that Hazard took up with the Oxford Group, and was able to get sober, a sobriety he was able to maintain, for the most part, for the rest of his life. There are some tales of some "slipping", and he may not have died sober as he became terribly distraught over the loss of two of his four children in World War II.

Fish Stories

The story of Rowland's visit to Switzerland to seek aid from the pinnacle of human power, Dr. Jung, is much ballyhooed. "He was treated by Dr. Jung for about a year, but when he left Jung, he soon got drunk. He returned to Jung for further treatment, but he was told it would be useless. In Jung's opinion, the only thing that could now help free Rowland from his addiction was a 'spiritual awakening.'" (Pass It On, p. 114) Much of this is likely true, at least, in a general way.

The error regarding the timing of the visit to Jung may have been inadvertent, but the timing of 1931 "works better", as he would then soon after recover through "supernatural power" via the Oxford Group. Relatively recent research by historians into records and letters of Jung, Hazard, and Hazard family businesses provide significant contradiction of AA's official version of the story.

"The fact is that there was at the very least a considerable exaggeration of the length and depth of Rowland Hazard's contact with Carl Jung in Switzerland. Part of the Hazard-Jung story, as recounted in later AA sources, was clearly more legend than historical reality." (The Road to Fellowship, Richard Dubiel, (2004) p. 71) The therapy sessions with Jung were nothing approaching a year.

Of course, the Bill Wilson of "no real infidelity" fame, has been acknowledged to have skills in the crafting of tales. "Like his father before him, Bill W. was a spellbinding storyteller; and, as Robertson observes, he had 'a lifelong penchant for embroidering the facts while accurately summarizing the gist of an event.' Thus his factual liberties may be regarded as poetic license." (Bill W. and Mr. Wilson, Matthew J. Raphael, p. 12)

("Robertson" above refers to Pulitzer Prize winning, New York Times journalist and author of Getting Better, Inside Alcoholics Anonymous, Nan Robertson. The quote is from p. 78)

There is another omission from AA's official version of Rowland's salvation at the hands of the Christian group, subsequent to the complete inefficacy of "human power" being proven by the failure of the great psychiatrist to effect a cure. (This tale is often further enhanced by referring to Jung as "the world's foremost expert on alcoholism!" Surely the old bearded adulterer would spin in his grave, should he hear that one.) In the early 1930s, Rowland Hazard was attending Oxford Group gatherings AND being treated on a regular basis by the highly effective lay therapist, Courtenay Baylor. (see Twentieth Century Influences on AA) The sessions with Baylor, a recovered alcoholic himself, may well have made a significant contribution to Hazard gaining sobriety. Of course, this "human power" boost would muddle an otherwise very clear, black and white message.

Rowland to Ebby

AA's second great "founding moment", Ebby's message to Bill, would not have been possible had not the message been passed to Ebby. In July of 1934, he was visited by some Oxford Groupers. Cebra Graves and Shep Cornell "had once done considerable drinking with Ebby. But this time, they 'told me that they had run into the Oxford Group and had gotten some pretty sensible thing out of it based on the life of Christ... ' Ebby said". (Pass It On, p. 113)

Ebby was even more wooed by his third visitor, Rowland. "I was very much impressed by his drinking career, which consisted of prolonged sprees, where he traveled all over the country. And I was also very impressed by the fact that he was a good guy. The first day he came to see me, he helped me clean up the place. Things were a mess, and he helped me straighten it up, and he stuck by me from beginning to end." (Pass It On, p. 113) Rowland continued working to help Ebby, but Ebby returned to the bottle after a period of sobriety, and ran afoul of the law.

Facing some dire consequences at court, "Rowland H. interceded and told the judge that he, Rowland would be responsible for Ebby... For a while he was a guest at Rowland's home... and then came to New York City, where he stayed with Shep for a while and then went to live with one of the 'brotherhood' who ran Calvary Episcopal Mission on 23rd Street. It was while he was staying there and working with the Oxford Group that he heard of Bill's desperate situation". (Pass It On, p. 115) It hadn't hurt that the presiding magistrate was Cebra Graves' father.

Ebby to Bill

As with AA, in the Oxford Group, you kept it by giving it away, and Ebby was sent to bring the message to Bill who began a historical chain of one alcoholic talking to another. It was the alcoholic Oxforders who helped Ebby, and his message to Bill had weight because Bill knew Ebby to be a drinker "of his type". Dr. Bob's two and a half year exposure to the religious cure produced no cessation of drinking. The effect of Bill's first conversation with him was profound.

Identification. First and foremost.

"But the ex-problem drinker who has found this solution, who is properly armed with facts about himself, can generally win the entire confidence of another alcoholic in a few hours. Until such an understanding is reached, little or nothing can be accomplished." (Big Book, p. 18).

Park Avenue

In 1935, Rowland Hazard returned to Wall Street as a general partner in Tailer (sic) and Robinson, a brokerage firm, and later moved to Lockwood Engineers Inc. There were two years as an independent consultant, "often a resume explanation of periods of unemployment" (First Links), before becoming a VP at Bristol Manufacturing, in 1941. It is not known if these changes of employment had anything to do with drinking, or were merely indicative of a rich guy pursuing what he found interesting.

World War II brought tragedy for Rowland and Helen Hazard as they lost one son in 1941, and a second in 1945. The death of the second son was devastating, and provoked a period of isolation.

"While at his office desk on Thursday, December 20, 1945, Rowland suddenly died of a coronary occlusion." (First Links) At the time of Hazard's death, at sixty-four, he and Helen were living on Park Avenue. Although eight years younger, Helen was gone less than a year later.

Rowland Hazard never joined AA, although he played a role in its coming into existence. Perhaps he had no compelling reason to, as he was (barring a rumored relapse in 1936) several years sober at the time the Big Book was published. He continued on with the Oxford Group through the difficult times in the late 30s, with the founder's problems and the name change to Moral Rearmament. Lois Wilson said he was an ardent Oxford Grouper until his death, and a vestryman in New York City's Calvary Episcopal Church.

It is unlikely that he would have been a big fan of the AA Agnostica website.

Chapter 19 Ebby Thacher

The story of Ebby Thacher is one of large privilege and poor performance, the tale of a classic underachiever. Iconic television character, Al Bundy, peaked at seventeen years of age by scoring four touchdowns in one game - all downhill after that! By seventeen, Ebby Thacher was already mired in mediocrity, a problem exacerbated by his being surrounded by a family of achievers. Generations of Thachers experienced successes in business, politics, society and church. Ebby, an archetypal black sheep, was a slacker, a floater, who never quite embraced adulthood. His journey through Alcoholics Anonymous is essentially an illustration of what not to do.

> *Near the end of that bleak November, I sat drinking in my kitchen. With a certain satisfaction I reflected there was enough gin concealed about the house to carry me through that night and the next day. My wife was at work. I wondered whether I dared hide a full bottle of gin near the head of our bed. I would need it before daylight.*
>
> *My musing was interrupted by the telephone. The cheery voice of an old school friend asked if he might come over. He was sober. It was years since he had come to New York in that condition. I was amazed. Rumor had it that he had been committed for alcoholic insanity. I wondered how he had*

escaped. Of course he would have dinner, and then I could drink openly with him. Unmindful of his welfare, I thought only of recapturing the spirit of other days.

Bill Wilson

That "bleak November" was in 1934. The old school friend was Edwin Throckmorton Thacher, known better then and since, as Ebby. "Fresh-skinned and glowing", sober a mere seven weeks, "he was inexplicably different". Although he did not at the time realize it, Bill Wilson was only a few short (but well-lubricated) weeks away from his very last drink. More importantly, this simple reunion of old chums, though it did not, in fact, recapture the spirit of other days, would set in motion a series of events that would dramatically affect the lives of millions of alcoholics, and change the world of addiction treatment.

The Thachers of Albany, New York

The Thacher family had a history in America dating back to pre-revolution times. Family prominence took a sharp upward rise when Ebby's paternal grandfather started a railroad wheel manufacturing business in 1852. A great fortune was rapidly amassed as the entrepreneur became the principal supplier of wheels for the New York Central Railroad. Social recognition that was greater still came with his election to the Albany mayoralty, around the time of the American Civil War. The Thachers were to provide Albany with two more mayors, including Ebby's older brother Jack.

Edwin Throckmorton Thacher, Ebby, was born into fortunate circumstances, on the 29th of April, 1896. The youngest of five brothers, Ebby's sense of entitlement, so much in evidence throughout his life, was probably formed very early on. The best of everything, servants galore, and the instant recognition and respect that the Thacher name produced outside of the home may have fore-ordained some future difficulties. Father and the brothers appear to have had their own issues, but fared better in the business and working world than the baby of the family, all managing to be "self-supporting through their own contributions".

The well-to-do Thachers spent their summers in the resort town of Manchester, Vermount about six miles from Bill Wilson's family home in East Dorset. Ebby's father was a founding member of the Ewanok Golf & Country Club where he frequently partnered with wealthy industrialist Robert Todd Lincoln, son of the Great Emancipator. Within the social circle of the "summer people" were the Burnhams, whose daughter Lois would one day marry Bill Wilson.

Meeting Bill Wilson

After a humiliating, inauspicious debut into the world of baseball, Bill Wilson, through relentless determination and hours of practice had become a local hero as a star ballplayer. It is likely that he and Ebby first met through baseball, in either 1910 or 1911. Ebby, who had been attending the Albany Academy as had his older brothers, disappointed his parents with his lackluster academic performance. In 1912, they placed him in residence at Burr and Burton Seminary, a onetime training school for ministers which was by then a co-educational institution for general education. This was Bill Wilson's school, and had been since 1909. The developing friendship of the two teenaged boys brought Bill some access to the society of the rich and famous, the very group he aspired to rub elbows with.

Only one school year was spent at Burr and Burton before Ebby was returned to his former school. Students at the Albany Academy were expected to graduate and go on to college. Ebby Thacher did neither. He was, by all accounts, a slacker. Frustrated at the failure of all efforts to motivate their youngest son to any acceptable level of scholastic diligence, Ebby was given a low-level job in the family foundry. Based on the history which was to unfold, the senior Thacher's dramatic attempt to fracture his son's "sense of entitlement" seems to have come too late. Manhood, in the form of his new full-time employment, opened the door to Saturday night drinking. By his own description, Ebby was "not a successful drinker from the start". From the outset, results of drinking were unpredictable.

Progression

World War I was a godsend for drinkers, as patriotic citizens were delighted to stand one for the boys in uniform. Weekday drinking became more acceptable than ever before, owing to the great uncertainty of what was to come in a world embroiled in conflict. Throughout the war, Ebby never had to leave the States, but as indulgence increased dramatically, so did consequences. Armistice brought a cessation of fighting but not drinking, and the distinguished Thacher family was repeatedly embarrassed by the escapades of the youngest son. Ebby was pretty cut up in an incident involving a wrecked taxi-cab, and was kicked out of the house.

By 1922, the family business folded. In the late twenties, both of Ebby's parents died, and half of a significant inheritance was lost instantly in the stock market crash. The other half, he frittered away. Ebby held a succession of jobs, including one with a brokerage firm's Albany office, but he wasn't much of a producer. From time to time he ran into his childhood friend, Bill Wilson. The very first time that they drank together resulted in a spectacular 1929 binge which gets a brief mention in Bill's Story - "There was that time we had chartered an airplane to complete a jag". This one involved Bill and Ebby being the first to land at Manchester's new airport. Before a band and a receiving delegation led by Mrs. Orvis, "a rather stately and dignified lady", and owner of Equinox House, the tiny resort town's most elite hotel, the two inebriates and their tipsy pilot followed up the historic landing, with a face plant onto the tarmac.

Older brother, John Boyd Thacher II (Jack) had become Albany mayor in 1926, and Ebby's drunken escapades had become an increasing embarrassment to his distinguished family. In Ebby's own words, "My brother was a prominent man in town and I wasn't doing him any good. So in the fall of 1932, I took off for Manchester and lived in the Battenkill Inn for about two years. And of course, the drinking went on up there just the same". A trip into the mountains, and some physical labour led to a period of sobriety of some months, but in his own terms he "fell off the wagon".

He then moved in to the once spectacular, but now dilapidated family summer home. This led to two iconic drunken Ebby stories. In the first, a very intoxicated Ebby drove his father's Packard through the side of a neighbor's dwelling smashing into the kitchen. With the panache of a true drunk, he asked his "hostess" for a cup of coffee. The second incident involved another brief period of "being on the wagon", during which time he and a local handyman repainted the house. The completion of the project led to a protracted celebration which was ruined by some inconsiderate roosting pigeons spoiling the paint job. Ebby unleashed some gunfire, bringing him once more to the attention of the local constabulary.

The cavalry rides in

Between the two episodes above, in July or August, Ebby had been visited by Oxford Groupers, Cebra Graves and Shep Cornell. The house painting incident that followed not long thereafter indicates that the mission was not an immediate success, but they had planted the seed. Facing some very serious consequences from this latest fiasco, the Oxford Groupers got a remorseful Mr. Thacher off the hook as the judge released him to the care and supervision of the eminent and newly sober businessman, Rowland Hazard. Ebby spent some time with Hazard, and a few weeks at the home of Shep Cornell, and he spoke at two Oxford Group meetings. Pushed to evangelise, he contacted Bill Wilson. It was November, 1934. At this point, the two men had not seen each other for about a year.

A telephone call to Lois gave him the opportunity to briefly tell his story and arrange the now historical get together which took place two nights later. The fresh-skinned and glowing Ebby was particularly impactful for Bill because he knew Ebby was his "type of drinker" - the chartered airplane debacle had created a special bond. Bill's current state of desperation opened his mind somewhat to the "I've got religion" solution. Wilson, who is sometimes portrayed as atheist, was not. "I had always believed in a Power greater than myself. I had often pondered these things. I was not an atheist." The author of "We Agnostics" also seems, from his own story, to have not been an agnostic as well, instead believing in "a Spirit of the Universe, who knew neither time nor limitation". He shared his maternal grandfather's "contempt of some church folk and their doings... his denial of the preacher's right to tell him how he must listen (to the 'music of the spheres')".

Why don't you choose your own conception of God?

This is a phrase that, without doubt, "widened the gateway" for hundreds and hundreds of thousands of AA's yet to come, and it is attributed to Ebby. It's right there in BILL'S STORY - "My friend suggested what then seemed a novel idea. He said, '*Why don't you choose your own conception of God?*'" But did Ebby actually say this? Probably not.

Bill Wilson was a salesman and a promoter. In the early days, prospects were called "pigeons", and an open meeting talk was known as a "pitch". The entire book *Alcoholics Anonymous* was carefully crafted to sell certain ideas. There exists, of course, a cult of book worshippers who think Bill's Story is a documentary. Some are quick to point to all twelve steps in the narrative, the very twelve steps which did not exist until four years later! Interviewed years later, Ebby had no recollection of having made the "choose your own conception of God" suggestion. Such a proposal would have represented a MAJOR deviation from the Oxford Group message, a philosophy into which Ebby had been staunchly indoctrinated during the previous seven weeks. As to Bill's own recollection of the evening's events, he was not only quite drunk, but teetering on the very edge of alcoholic insanity.

Regarding the comprehension of alcoholism, and even more so, the understanding of the mind and emotions of drunks, Bill Wilson likely remains without peer. Between Ebby's first visit, and the time the book was written, our founder had formulated some clear-cut ideas of what alcoholics would and would not sign onto. The Akronites were having tremendous success with a very Christian approach and seemed content to maintain their ties with the Oxford Fellowship. Wilson, the visionary, knew better, and was committed to a non-Christian book and a more open-ended, "choose for yourself" spirituality. His quest to sell these ideas was aided by the burgeoning membership in Cleveland, a city with many Roman Catholics. Catholics of the time were prohibited from participating in non-Catholic religious services, and thus Cleveland sobriety csar Clarence Snyder strongly supported the split from the Protestant Oxford Group.

The gate-widening suggestion - *"Why don't you choose your own conception of God"* - almost certainly came from the mind of Bill Wilson, and not the mouth of Ebby Thacher.

Sporadic sobriety, resentment, freeloading, and a lack of Steps

At various times during the thirty years that Ebby survived past his initial carrying the message to Bill, he was deeply resentful about not being granted a co-founder status in AA. He held bitterness toward the "usurper" Bob Smith, and he was aggrieved by Hank Parkhurst's partnership in the book publication. All evidence indicates that Ebby as an Oxford Grouper did as little as he could get away with, and showed virtually no interest in working AA's 12 Step program. Mrs. Wilson was NOT in the Ebby Fan Club, writing in "Lois Remembers" that "Bill wanted sobriety with his whole soul - Ebby wanted enough to stay out of trouble".

In AA's formative years, Ebby often lived with the Wilson's for months at a time, nourished by Lois' modest pay cheque and some handouts from his older brothers. A return to Albany and some modest success in the work world led, at 31 months, to the first of many slips. The best period of Ebby's adult life occurred in the 1950s when he was taken under the wing of Searcy W. who ran a Texas hospital for alcoholics. After a brief relapse in 1954, he was able to accumulate seven years of continuous sobriety.

About four years into his Texas sobriety, Ebby was asked to speak at an AA convention in Memphis. It is fascinating to hear the voice of the man who played a small but critical role in what eventually evolved into Alcoholics Anonymous. He is quite articulate, and his memory of the events of 1934 differs from Bill's in more ways than one. Of course, Ebby was sober and Bill was not, at the time of the fateful meeting. He talks a lot about "falling off the wagon", and seems to justify several of the relapses as being attributable to the actions of others. Twenty-five years after the fact, he is arguing that the behaviour leading to one of the three arrests for drunkenness which propelled him into the Oxford group and sobriety, was "not that bad". He is astonished that the arresting officer, an old Burr and Burton school chum, did not let him off on another. At four years sober, it is evident that he still was very much missing the glory days of drinking and maintained a strong fantasy of re-capturing old times.

At the core of the AA recovery process, alcoholics must at some point take personal responsibility, let go of old resentments, and move from some form of arrested adolescence into adulthood. Edwin Throckmorton Thacher never accomplished those things, and his periods of abstinence were prompted more from necessity than any "real" desire to immerse himself in a new lifestyle. In 1961 his girlfriend died and he got drunk the next day. He moved back to New York, living in several places. The twin scourges of alcoholism and emphysema dropped his weight from 170 to 122 pounds. His last two years were spent sober at Margaret and Micky McPike's farm outside Ballston Spa in New York state. He did not attend AA during this time. His expenses were covered by a small government pension and by his old pal, Bill Wilson.

On March 21st of 1966, the sad tale concluded.

Chapter 20 Henry Parkhurst

Throughout the second half of 1938, the Honor Dealers' little office was abuzz with activity. The hubbub involved neither the sale of auto polish, nor the organization of a buying co-op, but the production of the text Alcoholics Anonymous. Two fallen, forty-something entrepreneurs viewed their new venture as an opportunity to help potentially hundreds of thousands, or more, alcoholics who were suffering as they once had. And in doing so, they dreamed of solving their own economic woes.

Earlier in the year, visions of paid missionaries and alcoholic hospitals, financed by Rockefeller millions, had vaporized when John. D. agreed with subordinate Albert Scott's cautioning query, "Won't money spoil this thing?" Fancied top management positions for the two men vanished. The book was their remaining hope of large profits, and social significance.

The would-be publishing magnates were William Griffith Wilson and Henry Giffen Parkhurst. Their secretary Ruth Hock, later famously reported that AA's Big Book "wouldn't have been written without Bill, and it wouldn't have been published without Hank". (Pass It On, p. 195)

Loyalty to her memory of these two men may have been what prompted her to add that she did not "believe that either man 'expected to make a fortune.' The motive, always, was to help the Fellowship; their original idea was to begin giving the books away as soon as possible". (Pass It On, p. 195)

Ruth's ingenuous remarks are somewhat countered by the history of the events.

Summer in Akron

As the summer of 1935 drew to a close, Bill Wilson was reluctant to return to New York. He and Dr. Bob had established a small core of sober alcoholics, and had "planted the seed" with others. His proxy battle had not gone well. As the dreams of a management position that would resuscitate his business career collapsed, there was safety and strength among his new friends.

He had taken constructive action in May, in the Mayflower Hotel lobby, when he was panicked by a temptation to drink. The seeking out of another drunk to "work with" had led to the sobriety of Akron proctologist, Dr. Bob Smith. In turning his focus to the needs of the problem-laden physician, Bill had saved himself.

It was with sadness, and some trepidation that Bill Wilson returned to New York, on August 26, 1935.

Back in New York

In New York, Bill had a support base in the Oxford folk, but "it was clear almost from the beginning that Bill Wilson was not well-suited to be an Oxford Group member... He never shared in, or had much sympathy for, the Oxford Group's goals". (Bill W., Francis Hartigan, p. 65) Back when he had been approached by Ebby with the news of his salvation through the evangelicals, Bill "vaguely remembered having heard of them, but it was his impression that they were a bunch of Christers, rich folks mostly, all very chic and high-minded". (Bill W., Robert Thomsen, p. 188)

He was less than impressed with the Oxford's "reformed drunks". He saw Shep Cornell as a socialite. "As a drunk he was sure Cornell was a pantywaist, a man who had probably gone wild one night on too many sherries at a Junior League cotillion." (Thomsen, p. 189)

The Big Book promises that God "will show you how to create the fellowship you crave". (BB, p. 164) Wilson seems to have chosen to get help instead from his old friend Dr. Silkworth who "was risking his medical reputation and career in allowing Bill to roam the corridor of Towns". (Not-God, Ernest Kurtz, p. 43) Two of these clients, Henry Parkhurst and John Fitzhugh Mayo, got sober and joined Bill in his efforts.

Although it as yet had no name, AA now had a group in New York City.

Standard Oil of New Jersey

Very little is known about the early life of Henry Giffen Parkhurst beyond his being born in Marion, Iowa on March 13, 1895. He is frequently described as an ex-athlete, a former football player, but whether he played college ball, semi-pro, or just high school, we are left to wonder. We do know that the handsome redhead is said to have been "able to produce a good idea a minute for business. He had been a Standard Oil of New Jersey executive who was fired because of his drinking". (Henry G. Parkhurst, Mike O.) At one point, Parkhurst and Jim Burwell had worked together in Louisiana.

There are conflicting opinions as to whether Hank actually wrote "To Employers", but he definitely is the "one time assistant manager of a corporation department employing sixty-six hundred men". (BB, p. 136) He is also, most likely, the "case of pathological mental deterioration" (BB, p. xxxi) who was almost unrecognizable a year later.

It is known that when Bill talked to Hank at Towns Hospital, it was Hank's tenth time there, the first several sponsored by Standard Oil, in attempts to rehabilitate their otherwise valuable employee. By the time of the last trip, there was no employer.

Hank is variously described as being an agnostic, or an "avowed atheist". His First Edition story was "The Unbeliever", and though he seemed willing to cooperate in prayer, and the like, it is clear that he never accepted the notion of a personal God. "He and Jim B. led the fight against too much talk of God in the 12 steps." (Biography: The Unbeliever, silkworth.net)

The "unbeliever" did embrace sobriety, unquestionably. "Fitz, Hank and Bill were three extraordinarily healthy males… whose ambitions had been derailed. Now they had a new outlet and they brought to it a wonderful young exuberance." (Thomsen, p. 236)

Honor Dealers

Honor Dealers seems to have been started for the purpose of extracting revenge on his former employer, Standard Oil of New Jersey. Hank's small New Jersey office soon became the operating base of what would become Alcoholics Anonymous. Bill joined Hank at Honor Dealers, but not much work was done, as they were too consumed with "the work".

"Before long, Bill and Hank began to have difficulty paying both Ruth's salary and the rent on the office. Ruth went without pay for a while, but the landlord... eventually forced them out, and they moved to a smaller office... Until 1939, Bill's major headquarters was in Newark." (Pass it On, pp. 192-193)

In the autumn of 1937, Hank and Bill decided that rich people should finance their grand schemes of bringing a solution to America's alcohol problem. "The two of them immediately set to work approaching every rich man and every charitable foundation in Manhattan... After six weeks... not one cent (was) raised." (Thomsen, p. 245)

The rich folk had disagreed.

An introduction to "Rockefeller's people" spawned great dreams of literature, paid missionaries, and alcoholic hospitals, but the "world's richest man" thought the group should be self-supporting, and a mere pittance was granted.

The Book

"Bill began work on the book in March or April of 1938.... Bill soon completed his personal story and the chapter called 'There Is a Solution.' These... were Multilithed immediately to be used in a money-raising campaign in the summer of 1938." (Pass It On, p. 193) An offer from Eugene Exman of Harper & Brothers prompted the idea in the two entrepreneurs that self-publishing would be more advantageous.

"Hank, whom Bill described as 'one of the most terrific power-drivers' he had ever met, convinced him they should bypass the trustees and sell shares in their own company to publish the book themselves...Finally, even the trustees could not keep Bill and Hank from charging ahead on the new venture." (Pass It On, p. 194)

Years later, AA history has an innocent Bill Wilson being "dragged along" in Hank's whirlwind schemes, but Bill Wilson had not fallen off a turnip truck in Nebraska - he was a Wall Street wheeler-dealer. His own "authorized" biographer wrote, "Bill had a thousand ideas. The stalled motor of his imagination had started to turn again; the old power drive was coming back full force". (Thomsen, pp. 240-241)

Works Publishing Inc.

If there is anything more embarrassing to Bill Wilson than LSD experimentation, Ouija boards, séances, marital infidelity and possible sex addiction, it is his role in Works Publishing Inc. By the original deal, Bill owned a third of the book as did Hank.

Eugene Exman, of Harper & Brothers, had "agreed, quite contrary to his own interest, that a society like ours ought to control and publish its own literature". (Alcoholics Anonymous Comes of Age, p. 155) What transpired was substantially different. Bill and Hank formed a publishing company, and 67% of the book that Exman thought should be owned by the Fellowship, was owned by two men, two men insistently trying to sell the remaining 33% to supply working capital for the completion of the writing project.

AA would not own its own book at all, but the Alcoholic Foundation would receive the same royalties from Works Publishing that would have been paid by Harper & Brothers.

The histories describe Hank as the uber-aggressor in this project, Bill Wilson later regretting "this early haste, as ownership of the Works Publishing shares eventually became a sharply controversial issue". (Pass It On, p. 195) Well - DUH!!! Bill was "convinced by Hank," in the later retelling, to bypass the trustees who wanted the Harper book deal. The reluctance of the others alcoholics to purchase stock in a book not yet written, was overcome in large part by a story of interest by the then enormously popular Reader's Digest. The words of historian Ernie Kurtz are somewhat cynical - "A *presumably promised* (my italics)... supportive article in The Reader's Digest did not come to be." (Not-God, Ernest Kurtz, p. 76)

Stock was sold ($5,000 worth) and a loan from Charles Towns, initially for $2,500, then $1,500 more, provided the funding for Hank and Bill to finish the book. All of these funds were dissipated in advances to Hank and Bill, salary to Ruth Hock, rent for the Honor Dealers' office space and other poorly accounted-for miscellaneous expenditures. Once the book had been written and edited, there remained only enough to pay Cornwall Press a small deposit towards the first printing order of 5,000.

Let's Save Everybody Who Has $60

Bill Wilson detaches himself somewhat from the decision to retail the book at the ridiculously high 1939 price of $3.50 (about $60 in 2014 dollars). "Some members had insisted on a $1.00 book... They had turned deaf ears to Henry's plea that we must make something on the deal or else we could never operate a headquarters office, much less pay off the shareholders. But Henry finally won through..." (AACOA, p. 170) Kurtz says, "Stockholders Wilson and Hank P. argued for a price of $3.50". (Not-God, p. 76)

Of course, Hank hadn't sold dreams of paying office expenses to the investors. His charts delineated the "per share" profits, based on various sales projections, up to the million that might occur in the first few years. The million sales number was reached, but some thirty years beyond his optimistic forecasts.

Today, in spite of copyright issues and the onslaught of paperless technologies, AA's Big Book sells at a rate of one million copies per year. Thirty-five million copies have been sold; total revenues have reached approximately 200 million dollars. Holders of 33% of that enterprise, and their heirs, would have fared extremely well.

One can be forgiven for thinking with all of Hank's aggressiveness and ambition, that poor Bill Wilson, owner of a 33.3% interest, was just being dragged along in the slipstream of the determined "power driver." Of course, Wilson had swum with the big fishes of New York's financial center, and he had been through law school. He was not some "Candide-esque" naif.

"Hank's son said... that his father and Bill both expected to make a million dollars from the project." (Pass It On, p. 195) Bill "did hope that income from the book would enable him and a few others to become full-time workers for the Fellowship". (Pass It On, p. 194)

In the end, Hank, fueled by a variety of resentments, started drinking again, most likely around Labor Day of 1939. "Part of Hank's unhappiness, Ruth added, involved her; 'Hank and I were interested in each other. I had at one time seriously considered marrying him.' When Ruth finally decided not to, Hank blamed Bill." (Pass It On, p. 228)

Only a few months earlier, Hank and his wife, Kathleen, had taken in the homeless Wilsons when they were finally evicted from Clinton St. in April.

Does Not Play Well With Others

"Throughout his life Bill Wilson provoked passionate feelings in men and women. Sometimes men who had been close to him turned on him; sometimes there were women involved. Hank... began to rail against Bill, accusing him of all kinds of things, including seducing Ruth Hock and keeping her from marrying him. Soon Hank started to drink again." (My Name Is Bill, Susan Cheever, pp. 163-164)

"Male friends and colleagues like Hank Parkhurst and Tom Powers stormed off after working with him." (Cheever, p. 206)

A New Deal

At the time of the "self-publishing" deal, Hank sold the New York members on the idea, and Bill convinced Dr. Bob to go along, but in his fear of the reaction of the Akronites, Smith left the Ohioans in the dark as to the details of the Works ownership. As the financials came to light, there was outrage, and in early 1940, Bill accepted a new deal from the Alcoholic Foundation.

He and Hank were to surrender their shares to the Alcoholic Foundation. The other share buyers were to be reimbursed what they had invested. When a Rockefeller loan financed this buyout, most were delighted to be "breaking even", as the book was not selling well. "But Hank resisted all their pleas to turn over his one-third ownership in Works Publishing to the foundation." (Pass It On, pp. 235-236)

One day, Hank turned up at the new Vesey St. office. Whether he was drunk, and taken advantage of, as his son claimed later, or just "completely broke and very shaky", Hank was persuaded to sign a release in exchange for being paid $200 for some office furniture that had previously been his.

"Hank's son said that Hank always felt he had been treated badly. He thought Bill had made a deal with the foundation that excluded Hank from any future share of the book's profits." (Pass It On, p. 236)

Bill's royalty on the Big Book "eventually became substantial and provided Bill and Lois a lifetime income". (Pass It On, p. 236) By the time of Lois's death in 1989, royalties paid to the Wilsons totaled 10 million dollars, and Lois's legatees have received an additional 9 million.

Once more, Bill's partner had received $200.

Resentment

Hank's life continued to be one of bitterness, and with no happy ending. In Cleveland, he found a sympathetic ear in Clarence Snyder, who was no fan of Bill Wilson. They supported themselves with some small business-type, marketing ventures. Nothing productive came of their rabble-rousing against the founder. Hank

> *never recovered completely, although there were some occasional, brief periods of sobriety...*
>
> *Hank and Kathleen divorced in 1939, and Hank married at least two other women. One of the women he married and divorced*

was a sister-in-law of Cleveland AA pioneer, Clarence Snyder. He later married an oil heiress from a wealthy Houston family...

(He) died on January 18, 1954 at Mercy Hospital in Pennington, New Jersey, within two months of his 59th birthday. (Mike O.)

There is much wisdom in AA's Big Book, not the least of which is - "It is plain that a life which includes deep resentment leads only to futility and unhappiness. To the precise extent that we permit these, do we squander the hours that might have been worth while." (BB, p. 66)

That these resentments are warranted seems not to reduce their destructive power. To some extent, our friend Hank was poorly treated, but relentless clinging to his bitterness, and a return to the bottle, is "on him". He forgot the lessons of a book he had a great deal to do with creating.

Chapter 21 Clarence Snyder

> **THE CLEVELAND PLAIN DEALER, SATURDAY, OCTOBER 21, 1939**
>
> ## Alcoholics Anonymous Makes Its Stand Here
>
> **By ELRICK B. DAVIS**
>
> Much has been written about Alcoholics Anonymous, an organization doing major work in reclaiming the habitual drinker. This is the first of a series describing the work the group is doing in Cleveland.
>
> **Success**
>
> By now it is a rare Clevelander who does not know, or know of, at least one man or woman of high talent whose drinking had become a public scandal, and who suddenly has straightened out "over night," of their families who all that time had been emotionally distraught, social and economic victims of another's addiction.
>
> These ex-rummies, as they call themselves, suddenly salvaged from the most socially noisome of fates, are the members of the Cleveland Fellowship of an informal society called "Alcoholics Anonymous." Who they are cannot be told, because the name means exactly what it says. But any incurable alcoholic who really wants to be cured will find the members of the Cleveland to. He drinks because he can't help drinking.
>
> He will drink when he had rather die than take a drink. That is why so many alcoholics die as suicides. He will get drunk on the way home from the hospital or sanitarium that has just discharged him as "cured." He will get drunk in the wake of a friend who died of drink. He will swear off for a year, and suddenly find himself half-seas over, well into another "bust." He will get drunk at the gates of an insane asylum where h

From time to time, various names are suggested as being worthy of "co-founder" status, for contributions leading AA to be what it is today. People such as Dr. Silkworth, William James, and Carl Jung are among the "outsiders" who, directly or indirectly influenced our society. Many Christians among us would like to see more acknowledgement of the Oxford role, Sam Shoemaker and Frank Buchman specifically. That Lois Wilson and Anne Smith were among the chief protagonists of the early AA "drama" is undeniable. Sylvia K. and Mrs. Marty Mann fought for the place of women in AA (now forming 35% of our membership). Ebby Thacher was not shy in nominating himself in spite of his inconsistent sobriety.

That Jim Burwell receives mention is particularly pleasing to agnostics and atheists, and other non-Christians. His role in "widening the gateway" by pushing for the modifying phrase "as we understood him," and the more inclusive phrase "higher power", was HUGE. It is undeniable that hundreds of thousands of AA members would not have stayed in AA, had it been one iota more "religious". For some, he is the most significant of our predecessors.

Perhaps the strongest case for "co-founder" status can be made on behalf of Clarence Snyder, under whose management Cleveland forged the template for developing and handling explosive growth in AA. Historian Ernie Kurtz tells us that "Cleveland became the testing ground for what Alcoholics Anonymous was to be". (Not-God: A History of Alcoholics Anonymous, p. 83)

One-on-one sponsorship, so ubiquitous today as to be "*de rigueur*", was popularized by Snyder, and he got new members quickly sponsoring others, not the original modus operandi of Akron or New York AA. Additionally, Snyder aggressively pursued getting publicity for the nascent society, the success of these efforts evident in the following:

> *Clarence seemed to be a visionary. But Clarence was his own worst enemy. His personality got in the way of his being recognized for these accomplishments. Many felt Clarence was arrogant and antagonistic. But he was steadfast in his ideology and principles. Principles he carried with him until his death.*
>
> *Clarence was never one to be publicity shy, nor was he one to shun any offer of help. No matter what the source. No matter what the consequence. He was open to anybody if he felt it was for the betterment of A.A. and for the betterment of the quality of life that this way afforded the alcoholic and their families. (How It Worked, Mitchell K., Ch. 5.3, Silkworth. Net)*

I Was Born At A Very Early Age

(This is the title of Chapter 1 of the biography by Mitchell K., How It Worked – The Story Of Clarence H. Snyder and the Early Days of Alcoholics Anonymous in Cleveland, Ohio. The complete version is available at Silkworth.net)

Born on December 26th, 1902, Clarence "was the ugly duckling, the scapegoat, the black sheep of the family for the rest of his time at home". (How It Worked, Ch. 1) His mother wanted a girl as she already had two sons. At the age of two, Clarence, left unattended, unwrapped a tool box, a gift for his older brother, found a hammer, and smashed every Christmas ornament on the tree. His mother wailed on him with a hairbrush, a disciplinary technique she was to use with some frequency.

Bright, and possessing a "logical mind," Clarence did well at school, at least until his beloved older brother, Dick, contracted a disease, and died. "His studies went downhill in a rapid, steady spiral. He became withdrawn, extremely depressed, and lost most of his former self-image and confidence." (HIW, Ch. 1)

As a teenager, he discovered the magical, transformative powers of liquor, which "made him more at ease, less self-conscious, and eventually invincible". (HIW, Ch. 1) "Hitting on" his date's mother somewhat flattered the woman, but her daughter and husband were not impressed. The very first drinking experience brought a "profound personality change". (HIW, Ch. 1)

Dorothy

Young Clarence met and married Dorothy in three months. "Clarence became and remained a 'periodic' drunk for a number of years." (HIW, Ch. 2) Problems were minimal until Dorothy became pregnant, and was affected "psychologically" by the pregnancy - her "sanity was fading rapidly." (HIW, Ch. 2) The doctor prescribed "Porter Ale," leading the caring husband to become a "Home Brewmeister". "Somehow or other, I must have misunderstood the instructions, for I not only made beer for my wife, but I drank it for her." (Big Book, 3rd Edition, p.297)

In his own eyes, rapidly escalating drinking was justified by his "wife and her meddlesome family". (HIW, Ch. 2) Aided by talent, and a friend on the board, he was able to keep his job at the Morris Plan Bank through three and a half years during which he was constantly intoxicated. Clarence was a "system guy", and his debt collection practices made him "the best manager they ever had". (HIW, Ch. 2) Finally fired for being a drunk, there came a series of jobs where he could scarcely last a few weeks. Then Clarence became "between jobs" for several years, until a "last chance" truck-driving job with his brother-in-law. In spite of virtual round the clock security, he managed to violate the "no-drinking" rule, and got dumped in New York City where his wits enabled him to survive as a street hustler. Fifty cents a night for "guarding" trucks gave him both a place to sleep, and excellent purchasing power for the seven cent pints of swill sold at the hardware store.

Incredibly, during a year of homelessness in New York City, Clarence was able to save up some money. He decided to go home to Ohio, and did, getting rides from truckers. He tried to beg his way back into Dorothy's home, but she stood her ground. Virginia, sister of Dorothy (who later would become Hank Parkhurst's sister-in-law) had learned something of a new plan for "curing" alcoholics from her physician, Dr. Leonard Strong, whose brother-in-law was Bill Wilson. Clarence was carted off to the bus depot, where a ticket to Akron was purchased, and his boarding was supervised. Dorothy even trailed the bus for a few miles to be sure that her husband did not evacuate the bus at the first sight of a bar.

Meeting Dr. Bob

"Young feller, you must be Clarence. You can call me Doc." (HIW, Ch. 3.3) Six feet tall and one hundred and thirty pounds, the thirty-five year old was "cold, wet, sick, and most devastating of all – hopeless". (HIW, Ch. 3.3) Suffering some form of alcoholic delirium, Clarence fled Smith's office in terror, thinking that Dr. Bob was the "mad bomber," and plotting to kill him. Clarence had read a news story on the bus ride to Akron about a fugitive killer named Smith. After talking to the good doctor several times on the telephone, Clarence finally turned up at the hospital where, once partially detoxed, he began to be visited by the fifteen sober men who were all aged 45 to 60. This went on for a week.

Clarence was stunned that his first meeting at T. Henry Williams' home was "holy rollerish". Bill V.H. gave him a card inscribed, "Therefore if any man be in Christ, he is a new creature; old things are passed away; behold, all things are become as new". He was introduced to the Four Standards - aka "Absolutes" - honesty, unselfishness, love and purity. Although none too keen on all of this, Clarence was desperate to be sober and to keep Dorothy happy. Back in Cleveland, "Clarence had little to show other than himself. There was no AA Big Book. There were no AA pamphlets, no AA history, nor AA groups". (HIW, Ch. 3.9) Our protagonist went on a vigorous recruiting mission, all to no avail. His first success was transformational - Bill H. stayed sober two years, but his surrender was "forced," he was not really "into it".

Those Darned Catholics

By April, 1939, the Cleveland squad had grown to about a dozen rummies who drove down each Wednesday to what was still the "alcoholic contingent" of the Oxford Group. The Catholics had problems generally with participation in these Protestant services, and specifically with the requirement of "open confession". Clarence, the Clevelanders' leader, faced a dilemma. His sponsor, Bob Smith, was loyal to the Oxfords, and refused to separate from them. Under increasing pressure from their pastors, the Catholics couldn't keep going.

On May 10, 1939, Clarence announced that the Cleveland folks would no longer be coming down to Akron for the gathering at the Williams. Abby G., a patent attorney who was still in the hospital, and his wife Grace offered their very large house to host the new Cleveland meeting.

On May 11, this Cleveland group met for the first time, calling itself AA, after the book.

According to a letter to Hank P. in New York, there was "not too much emphasis on the 'spiritual business' at meetings". (HIW, Ch. 3.10) Clarence believed that prayer and bible reading were better left to be done at home. Overt spirituality was a private issue, between "baby" and sponsor.

Although far from a non-believer himself, Clarence Snyder played a crucial role in moving AA away from its religious roots, ironically on behalf of a religious "minority," the Catholics.

The Era Of Publicity

Historian Ernie Kurtz refers to the period from October, 1939 to March, 1941, as "the era of publicity". (Not-God, p. 83) "The Clevelanders were missionary-minded." (Not-God, p. 84) A series of articles by Elrick B. Davis, in October and November, 1939, led to a growth explosion in Cleveland. These reports were hugely favorable to AA, but several members were furious that Clarence had snuck the reporter into meetings, by representing him as an alcoholic. (The strong evidence is that he was NOT.) Members' fears of seeing their names in the newspaper went unrealized, but fury over Snyder's willfulness led to a schism.

Another complaint was that Clarence was suspected of having been compensated for the Plain Dealer articles, and of having kept the money rather than putting it "in the basket". Those with anonymity concerns were further disturbed by the Jack Alexander article in the Saturday Evening Post in March of 1941. this piece took Alcoholics Anonymous "national", and sparked a period of exponential growth not seen before or since. AA was "on the move", and especially in Cleveland.

Six new Cleveland groups were added in April and May, fourteen for the year. Sponsors could not handle the flood of new recruits.

AA Theatre School

A twelve step call led Clarence to Walter B., an eccentric tippler who had constructed a theater on his property – "a couple of hundred seats, a stage, and props". (HIW, Ch. 6.2) The drunken thespian was known for putting on free performances for the neighbors, but attendance had dwindled as his drinking had become more out-of-control. The Post article on AA caught his attention.

A resourceful Clarence Snyder instantly saw the possibilities. They would teach AA to classes full of "pigeons" roosting in the seats. "All these men, who were just wandering around with no place to go anyway, were told to go to this place. They came to be taught this program. By the end of the first year, the Crawford Road Men's Group had one hundred and thirty-five members. This was from a core group of only ten." (HIW, Ch. 6.2) The meeting moved a short time later to a new venue with better parking, but Clarence had created another innovative way of growing AA.

AA "Founder" Flounders

Clarence came up with the idea of rotation, a Cleveland Central Committee, and an AA bulletin. He travelled around the country speaking at AA gatherings. "He occasionally stated that he was the one who had started AA." In his defence, his Cleveland home group was the first to call itself Alcoholics Anonymous, after the name of the book.

His abrasiveness was also evident in his criticism of "New York-style" AA, which he regarded as a diluted, "Don't Drink & Go To Meetings" bastardization of the more stringent Ohio system learned from Bob Smith. In the sixties, Clarence moved to Florida, where he continued to push "hard-line" AA. He continued to work, mostly in sales, but he founded a group home in St. Petersburg. Clarence joined the Masons, was active in church affairs, and continued to be an AA stalwart. Possibly this resume did not include "good husband", as he and second wife Selma were divorced.

Clarence had never believed in the "tradition of anonymity", and he granted TV, radio, and newspaper interviews, and even had his photo taken in connection with AA.

Amazing Grace, Serenity, And Howard Cosell

If there is such a thing as "the one", Clarence found her in the summer of 1969. Grace Snipes Moore was a fellow alcoholic, an AA member, and by 1971, Mrs. Clarence Snyder. Grace was religious and it must have been contagious, as Clarence started speaking of Jesus at both meetings and retreats. (This continues to be more common in Florida, and others parts of the South, according to interviews with on-line folks in these areas.)

The seventies were a wonderful time for Clarence, his relationship with Grace bringing a serenity previously unfamiliar. His "later Florida years were filled with joy and contentment". (HIW, Ch. 9) Not merely an elder statesman, he had the longest sobriety of any living AA member. He continued taking people through the steps and led two retreats each year. He was much in demand as an AA speaker in the U.S., Canada, and beyond.

Nonetheless he spawned mixed reactions.

His biographer, sponsee, and likely number one fan, Mitchell K. states "He was respected by many, but disliked by just as many". This instantly brought to mind comedian Buddy Hackett's line about bombastic sportscaster, Howard Cosell: "There have always been mixed emotions about Howard Cosell: Some people hate him like poison, and other people just hate him regular".

Denouement

"In November of 1983, Clarence was off on one of his many speaking engagements. This particular one was in British Columbia, Canada." (HIW, Ch. 10) Ill and worsening as the week went on, he remained determined to fulfil his commitment. Both "he and Grace prayed for a healing. Other Christians... 'laid hands' upon him and anointed him with oil". (HIW, Ch. 10) He made it only halfway through his talk before being rushed off to a physician, who diagnosed laryngitis and a bronchial infection.

They eventually got back to Florida where he rallied temporarily, but "Clarence had developed a malignancy on his left lung... the doctors decided not to operate (he was 82)... It would be too dangerous". (HIW, Ch. 10) Clarence Snyder lived to see his 46 year sobriety anniversary, but on March 22, 1984, "Clarence has gone home to be with the Lord". (HIW, Ch. 10)

Would that it were so!

Chapter 22 Jim Burwell

Bill Wilson wrote the Twelve Steps in 1938, "one night, late in December. He was frankly pleased with what he had written and was in no way prepared for the violent reaction when he read his steps to the group a few nights later... The 'liberals' were appalled and said so". (Bill W., Robert Thomsen, p. 263)

"The 'radicals,' led by Hank P. and Jim B., became adamant in pressing their concerns that there was 'too much God' in the Twelve Steps." (Not-God, Ernest Kurtz, p. 75)

The Christian "conservatives" loved it all, exactly as written. The radicals found allies among the moderates who feared the aggressive evangelism would be off-putting for drunks. Later on, the voice of psychiatrist Dr. Howard, joined the push for Bill to tone down the preachy nature of the manuscript, which Howard opined was "pure Oxford Group".

"The fights raged on - and these arguments lasted much longer than the first night; some were still at it weeks later." (Thomsen, p. 254) Even the somewhat sanitized Pass It On concedes that "there were heated discussions. Jimmy B. opposed the strong references to God". (p. 199) The clear evidence of history was reiterated - "the missions did the 'God bit' and everyone knew they always failed with alcoholics". (Thomsen, p. 253)

Bill resisted at first, but the cry for change was insistent. In the end there were concessions. "The felicitous phrase 'God as we understand Him' was suggested by Jimmy B., a New York member. Weasel wording the 'God stuff' made it possible for people of widely varying beliefs - even nonbelievers - to embrace AA's process of spiritual transformation." (Bill W., Francis Hartigan, p. 124) The radicals might not have been fully satisfied, but given their minority position, their achievement was reasonable.

At the center of the battling was the truculent relative newcomer and unapologetic atheist, Jim Burwell. Many years later, Susan Cheever, in a piece for The Fix, "The Angry Atheist Who Made AA Great," wrote of her title character - "Without this nonbeliever, AA would never have thrived". (The Fix, July 13, 2013)

Burwell's influence on modern Alcoholics Anonymous has been far more profound than could have been realized at the time. As the world has become increasingly secular, and for so many, religion replaced by all manner of "spirituality", a more Christian AA would be unpalatable to a huge percentage of the current membership. It is not only the atheists of today's AA who owe thanks to this intractable advocate of "freethinking".

Prosperity, Church Overdose, AND AWOL

On March 23, 1898, Jim Burwell was born into prosperous circumstances. He spent his early life "in Baltimore where his father was a physician and a grain merchant". (silkworth.net) His parents were drinkers, occasionally overindulging, but they were not alcoholics. "Father was a well-integrated person, and while mother was high-strung and a bit selfish and demanding, our home life was reasonably harmonious." (The Vicious Cycle, BB, p. 21) However, of four children, all three sons became alcoholics. Jim's sister never drank.

At age 13, Jimmy was sent off to Virginia, to an Episcopal boarding school for boys where he stayed for four years. It was there that he developed his powerful aversion to all churches and established religion. At the academy, there was Bible reading before every meal, and church services to be endured four times on every Sunday. Over time he became contemptuous of the "mindlessness of faith".

To please his father who hoped he would become a physician, at 17, he started university. Shortly thereafter he had his introductory experience with alcohol, blacking out the very first time he drank. His academic performance was inconsistent at best, and he feared he was on the brink of being expelled. In 1917, he rushed to join the Army, pre-empting an ineluctable embarrassment. Having done some OTC in college, he entered the military as a sergeant, and exited as a private, and narrowly avoided serious consequences when he went on a drunken celebratory escapade a week before the armistice was signed.

Job Loss, Memory Loss

During his military service, Burwell had become a "periodic" alcoholic. A similar pattern was continued in the civilian world, his drinking confined for the most part to weekends. He had some early career success. Employed in sales by a new national finance company, after three years, he opened and operated their Philadelphia office and was earning an exceptional income for a twenty-five year old, "but two years later I was blacklisted as an irresponsible drunk. It doesn't take long". (BB, p. 223) Jimmy next worked in sales promotion for an oil company in Mississippi, and for a while did well and got "lots of pats on the back". Then he cracked up two company cars, and was fired by Hank Parkhurst, of "To Employers" fame. They would meet again in New Jersey, ten or eleven years later.

One more good job was lost over drinking. To that point, most of Burwell's drinking had been confined to weekends, but at about the age of 30, that changed. A dry period of working "like mad" would be followed by a "rewarding" binge. He sometimes had trouble shutting down the sprees on Sunday. In the eight years before he stopped drinking in 1938, he had and lost, or quit, forty jobs. Every time he drank, he blacked out, and he would awaken with a "gnawing fear".

> *January 8, 1938 - that was my D-Day; the place, Washington, D.C. This last real merry-go-round had started the day before Christmas, and I had really accomplished a lot in those fourteen days. First, my new wife had walked out, bag, baggage, and furniture; then the apartment landlord had thrown me out of the empty apartment; and the finish was the loss of another job... I finally landed at my mother's doorstep - shaking apart, with several days' beard, and, of course, broke as usual...*

> *Here I was, thirty-nine years old and a complete washout. Nothing had worked. Mother would take me in only if I stayed locked in a small storeroom and gave her my clothes and shoes. We had played this game before. That is the way Jackie found me, lying on a cot in my skivvies, with hot and cold sweats, pounding heart, and that awful scratchiness all over. (BB, p. 219)*

Jimmy's old school friend, Fitz Mayo, had gotten sober in October, 1935, and he had his traveling salesman sponsee, Jackie, call in on the Burwell home. They talked for eight straight hours. "I don't remember much of what he said, but I did realize that here was another guy exactly like me… Jackie told me about a group of fellows in New York… who, by working together to help each other, were now not drinking and were happy like himself. He said something about God or a Higher Power, but I brushed that off - that was for the birds, not for me." (BB, p. 220)

Good God, There's a lot of God!

After being dry two weeks, Jackie got drunk, and Jimmy became "the sponsor of his sponsor". They were both summoned to New York, where they checked in at Hank's. "All they talked about that first weekend was God." (BB, p. 226) Burwell was conflicted. He loved having new friends who were like him, but the "God" palaver was more than he could take. When he was dry two weeks, no shrinking violet, Burwell spoke out against the pious pontificating. Vociferously. Repeatedly.

"At our weekly meeting, I was a menace to serenity those first few months, for I took every opportunity to lambaste that 'spiritual angle,' as we called it, or anything else that had any tinge of theology." (BB, p. 227-228) "I became a problem to that early group with my constant haranguing… I did love the understanding fellowship." (Sober For Thirty Years, AA Grapevine, May 1968)

Tradition Three

Now it had become the turn of the godly to be conflicted, as "the elders held many prayer meetings hoping to find a way to give me the heave-ho, but at the same time stay tolerant and spiritual". (BB, p. 228) Burwell's involvement in these events made its way, years later, into the 12 + 12, as antireligious "Ed", whose disruption of the group's harmony provided an early test of the inclusionary principle of the third Tradition - "The only requirement for AA membership is a desire to stop drinking".

Years later, when Bill Wilson wrote the Traditions essays, he included a line that ranks among the most unforgettable in AA history, ranking beside "There was no real infidelity", and, "Why don't you choose your own conception of God? We'll now close with the Lord's Prayer". Making fun of the early society's exclusionary attitude and quest for respectability, "pure alcoholics" were sought, he reported. "They could have no other complications. So beggars, tramps, asylum inmates, prisoners, queers (sic), plain crackpots, and fallen women were definitely out." (Twelve Steps and Twelve Traditions, p. 140)

Burwell was out on the road selling auto polish for Honor Dealers, making nice profits for Hank and Bill. In early June, the dilemma of the bombastic blasphemer seemed to have solved itself as the polish salesman relapsed while working out-of-town. The paragons of "love and tolerance" ignored his pleas for help, by telegram and telephone. Somehow, after two weeks, Jimmy made it back to Hank's. He was meek and chastened. That part is likely true - he was doubtlessly less denigrating of the faith of his sober cohorts. But Wilson shows his creativity by adding a mysterious confrontation with a bible in a lonely hotel room.

All other accounts of Burwell's continuing "disbelief" provide a debunking of the Wilson fable. The implied conversion is a fiction.

The Big Book

Jim Burwell returned to New York, sobriety, and the as-yet unnamed fellowship at the time when efforts to finance and produce a book were underway, and about to become all-consuming. Ernie Kurtz has Jimmy at the forefront of those favoring a book. Perhaps, he thought a book would provide a further separation from the overt religiosity still lingering from the Oxford Group association, and thriving among the Akronites. Possibly, he was among the several unemployed, and under-employed New York alcoholics who envisioned career opportunities in the grand schemes being conjured by Bill and Hank. It is also reasonable to presume that the secularist may have been convinced by his former boss, the great "power-driver", that Bill would be persuaded to write a book that was primarily "psychological".

Thus we have returned to the beginning of the tale, and Bill's hyper-religious first draft. The vehement arguments of the agnostic and atheistic element resulted in these changes: "In Step Two we decided to describe God as a 'Power greater than ourselves.' In Step Three and Eleven we inserted the words 'God as we understood Him.' From Step Seven we deleted the expression 'on our knees.' And, as a lead-in sentence to all the steps we wrote these words: 'Here are the steps we took which are suggested as a Program of Recovery.' AA's Twelve Steps were to be suggestions only." (Alcoholics Anonymous Comes of Age, p. 167)

Much of the credit for these changes goes to Jimmy B., but there were others in the camp, albeit somewhat less militant. Robert Thomsen, who, of all the biographers, had by far the greatest direct access to Bill Wilson, wrote,

"There were agnostics in the Tuesday night group, and several hardcore atheists". (Bill W., Robert Thomsen, p. 230) These men essentially accepted the "strength of the group" as a higher power. Years later, Bill Wilson was obliged to acknowledge that the troublesome heathen horde had "widened the gateway".

In today's multicultural world where, in most urban regions, various shades of latitudinarian spirituality have supplanted the canon and dogma of religion, the AA of the original manuscript would be unattractive, even to substantial segments of the fundamentalist population. There are many who would argue that had every "God reference" in AA's Big Book been changed to an uncapitalized "higher power," the gateway would be far wider still.

Further Contributions

"Jimmy B... had moved to Philadelphia in February 1940 to take a new job. Philadelphia soon had its own AA group... (which) came to the attention of Dr. A. Weise Hammer." (Hartigan, p. 140) Hammer was a prominent surgeon with even more prominent friends. He shared his abundant enthusiasm for AA with Judge Curtis Bok, one of the owners of the parent company of the Saturday Evening Post.

Bok commissioned the Jack Alexander article which led to an incredible growth of AA from 2,000 to 8,000 members in the last ten months of 1941.

Later on, Burwell penned AA's first ever history piece, "The Evolution of Alcoholics Anonymous". The essay, viewable on barefootsworld.net, carries the disclaimer: "His recollection of some of the specific facts are inconsistent with other reliable versions of the same story". The less kind may perhaps speculate on possible brain damage resulting from his many blackouts. Burwell's recounting of AA's early history is woefully inaccurate.

Jim B. was not invited to contribute his story to the First Edition of the book. He may have simply not been long enough sober. "The Vicious Cycle" did appear in 1955's Second Edition, and has survived into the third and fourth. It is understandable that this proud member wanted the recognition of having his narrative in a book he helped to create. He may well have consented to some editing, or soft-selling of his stance as a nonbeliever.

In Philadelphia, he was in a leadership position as the longest sober member, and his concession to "increased spirituality", was to finally do a fourth step, thus surrendering some of his self-sufficiency. He opened himself to the "personality change" promised by the process, and gained serenity.

Sober Thirty Years

In 1968, he contributed the article Sober Thirty Years to the Grapevine magazine. Burwell documents the evolution of his chosen higher powers;

1. John Barleycorn
2. The AA Fellowship
3. The forces of "good"
4. His own better self

None of these are supernatural, although Barleycorn in his best moments could be divine. His softened attitude allowed him to use the phrase "God, as we understood Him" to refer to an understanding of higher powers that he clearly did not consider as "God" within ANY conventional meaning of the term. He took on the tone of secular humanism.

Burwell did love being sober, and he loved AA. It's also fairly evident that he was enamored of the role of "AA celebrity". But, as noted by his contemporary, the longtime sober Cleveland honcho, Clarence Snyder, "Jimmy remained steadfast, throughout his life and 'preached' his particular [non-God] brand of AA wherever he went". (How It Worked, Mitchell K., P. 107)

In 1946, Jimmy married a woman he had 12th stepped a year earlier. In the 1950's he moved to San Diego, where he passed into nothingness on September 8, 1974, sober 36 years, and 76 years of age.

Jim B. is buried in the Christ Episcopal Church cemetery in Owensville, Maryland near his boyhood friend, Fitz M. (Our Southern Friend), the son of a minister.

Chapter 23 Richmond Walker

TWENTY-FOUR HOURS A DAY
365 DAILY MEDITATIONS FOR THE RECOVERING ALCOHOLIC

The *Twenty-Four Hours a Day* book is pocket-sized, designed for both portability, and discretion. An editor's note tells us only that, "This book was compiled by a member of the Group at Daytona Beach, Fla". The author, Richmond Walker, sought neither profit, nor recognition, for his efforts. He assembled his devotional reader in keeping with the best of the spirit of Alcoholics Anonymous, the desire to help others.

Each of the reader's 365 pages is composed of an AA Thought for the Day, a Meditation for the Day, and a Prayer for the Day. The first portion "typically put forward a set of rhetorical questions designed to emphasize the difference between the alcoholic past and the sober present". (Language of the Heart, Trysh Travis, p. 146) "These daily readings contain most of the material used in the booklet "For Drunks Only" and other AA literature; also some passages from the 'Big Book' Alcoholics Anonymous." (Foreword, Twenty-Four Hours a Day)

For the meditations, "Rich drew heavily on a book he had discovered, *God Calling* by Two Listeners, which had been edited and published by A.J. Russell, one of the most famous Oxford Group authors. Several years earlier, Rich had been moved by Russell's book *For Sinners Only*". *God Calling* was taken from Protestant pietism to a more generic spirituality, at least in the eyes of Rich Walker. References to Jesus and the Christ were excised, replaced with his own concepts of a higher power. The well-educated Walker fancied himself as something of a Platonist, albeit substantially more Christian.

Short prayers supplemented what Walker saw as a dearth of devotions specific to AA members seeking to increase their "conscious contact" via the eleventh step.

Oxford Roots and Pocket Notes

After being sober in the Oxford Group for more than two years, from 1939 to 1941, Richmond Walker returned to drinking. Although he had achieved neither permanent sobriety, nor contentment, "Walker retained a great respect for the Group's teachings; he practiced Quiet Time, reading and meditation with the Bible and the Group's daily reader God Calling". (Travis, p. 146)

In May, 1942, he joined the newly formed Boston Group of Alcoholics Anonymous, "never to drink again for the rest of his life". (barefootsworld.net) Early Boston AA had absorbed a number of sober alcoholics from the disintegrating Jacoby Club. Therefore, it is not unreasonable to assume that the Boston AA of that era had an "Emmanuel Movement" flavor.

When Walker began spending winters in Florida, he had the notes on his person that eventually became the Twenty-Four Hours a Day book. "He originally wrote the material on small cards which he carried in his pocket, to aid him in his own sobriety."(barefootsworld.net) "In 1948, members of the AA groups in Daytona Beach, Fla., persuaded him to have his material printed in book form... Rich distributed them from his basement." (Richmond Walker's Twenty-Four Hours a Day, Glenn C.)

As demand for the immensely popular book spread across the country, the author/publisher was inundated with orders, to the point of being overwhelmed. Walker was shipping about 600 volumes per month, from his home publishing operation. When his book was offered to AA headquarters in New York, they refused. Whether this was a right choice or a wrong one, it has proven to have been an expensive one for AA. Mr. Walker's book has sold approximately 9 million copies.

Richmond Walker is the second most popular AA author in total sales, second only to Bill Wilson.

The venerable AA historian, Ernest Kurtz in describing the AA of the 1950s, writes of Mr. Walker's fashionable reader: "Twenty-Four Hours a Day is a black-bound, prayerbook sized manual in perhaps greater use among members of AA than Alcoholics Anonymous itself". (Not-God, Ernest Kurtz, p. 347, n. 13)

Friends of Presidents

At the time of his birth on August 2, 1892, his parents lived in a new house in Brookline, a fashionable Boston suburb. "Rich's family were personal friends with presidents of the United States, like William Howard Taft and Theodore Roosevelt." (Glenn C.) His grandfather had made his fortune in shoe manufacturing in Worcester, about 40 miles from Boston, and then had got elected to Congress.

Growing up, Rich played second fiddle to his older brother, Joe. As a result, "he misbehaved and rebelled to try to make his parents notice him". (Glenn C.) When his younger sister, Dorothy died, his grieving parents became even more distant from the older boys. Rich "became convinced his parents neither loved nor cared for him at all". (Glenn C.)

He was close only to Joe, whom he at the same time resented. His family he perceived as unloving, highly skilled in business and politics, but more concerned with status and acquisitions than with their children. Rich was sent off to St. George's, an elite boarding school in Newport, R.I. In one of life's ironies, it is likely that Sam Shoemaker, 16 months his junior, was at some point, a fellow student.

A Cloak of Reserve

Moving on to Williams College, a prestigious university in Williamstown, Mass., Rich was an outstanding student, class president, captain of the football team, and president of his fraternity. Nevertheless, he felt like a failure, his achievements paling in comparison to Joe's degree from Yale. As well, he was not close to anyone.

"Although well-respected, I did not make class friends. I was wrapped in a cloak of reserve; there was a wall between myself and other people… True love has always been a mystery to me. As a child I was not loved, and as a result, have never learned to truly love others. I was poorly adjusted to life, being self-contained, egocentric, immature, easily hurt, and overly sensitive." (Open Meeting Lead, Rutland, Vt., 1958)

The Twenty-Four Hours a Day book for March 28th describes his typically alcoholic attitude - "I wanted my own way in everything."

At first, Rich Walker's drinking was controlled and moderate. In fact, he took a dim view of those who drank a lot. When his consumption escalated, "he was the son of the wealthy and prominent, and if he seemed to be drinking a tremendous amount, he and everyone else just put it down to youth".

(Glenn C.) In World War I, he was once more outdone by his brother, who was in the glamorous Marine Flying Corps, while Rich served honorably, but unspectacularly, in the Medical Corps.

The Corporate World

After the war, Joe persuaded him to join him in founding the Walker Top Company. Although Rich was not much interested in business, the young brothers had spectacular success while still in their twenties. Rich purchased an expensive home on Beacon Hill, and at 29, married Agnes. Not only had Rich's drinking increased by this time, there is evidence of "very serious psychological problems of some sort by this point". Although there was nothing about Agnes of which to be ashamed, he told none of his family members that they had gotten married until their first child was born. This was possibly the playing out of his deep-seated resentments regarding his childhood.

The young couple had three more children, but the father spend little time with either his offspring, or with his spouse. It was now the era of Prohibition, and Rich took many trips to the Caribbean, where nightclubbing was celebrated and open, rather than discreditable and clandestine. "I craved an artificial life of continuous excitement and a hyper kind of 'good times' filling every waking hour." (Rutland Lead)

Deterioration

The Great Depression sufficiently affected the Walker Top Company that Rich and Agnes sold their Beacon Hill property, and moved, in 1932, to a more modest home. However, the belt-tightening brought on by tough economic times resulted in no de-escalation of drinking, and in 1935, when his 12 year-old daughter died of spinal meningitis, Rich plummeted to a new level of drinking and debilitation. He resigned his partnership, later returning to the company as an accounting clerk.

There was a drunk driving charge and several hospitalizations. His haunts were no longer the playgrounds of thirsty executives where smiling bartenders served premium brands, on polished oak bars. It was a new era of cheap dives and lower companions. Joining the Oxford Group in 1939 resulted in over two years of sobriety, albeit of the less than contented variety. The white-knuckling ended in an extended relapse in 1941.

Separated from his wife, and living in a small rented room, the onetime corporate golden boy lived a 9 month nightmare of frequent trips to the hospital when he drank, and DT's when he didn't. In May of 1942, when he was almost 50, Rich Walker found the newish Boston AA group of Paddy K. and some others. This led to a sobriety that lasted for all of his remaining years.

Self-Publishing

The earliest copies of Twenty-Four Hours were run off "on the printing press at the county courthouse". (barefootsworld.net) As awareness of the book spread, requests began coming in from all around the country. Thousands of copies were being sold annually, and the task of distribution rapidly became a daunting one for a man operating from his basement.

In 1953, Rich Walker very generously offered his book, gratis, to Alcoholics Anonymous, thinking they had a far greater capability of handling distribution and printing. "At the 1954 meeting the General Service Conference declined to adopt Walker's book as a piece of Conference Approved Literature." AA historian Glenn C. pointed to the demands on the Literature Committee involved in bringing the 12 + 12 to print. Kurtz mentions that the conference report expressed a fear of being flooded with similar requests, that acceptance of Walker's offer might have "set a precedent".

"An additional sticking point, however was the book's explicit religiosity." (Travis, p. 148)

Don't Give Me That Old Time Religion

"Although the conference report of 1954 did not comment on the issue, Walker apparently received a personal letter stating as much. In an angry response to the chair of the Literature Committee, he expressed his indignation at New York's squeamish secularism... For Walker, as for other AA traditionalists, the GSO's denial of the importance of surrender was akin to the individual alcoholic's denial of alcoholism..." (Travis, pp. 148-149)

Glenn C. has made the observation that there are flashes of the Emmanuel Movement's New Thought mysticism scattered throughout the book. Walker's supposedly nominal spirituality "is betrayed not only by regular paraphrases and quotes from the Bible, but also by its commitment to the pietist vision of surrendered masculinity that characterized Midwestern AA". (Travis, p. 147)

It is interesting to note that those who sound the various alarms warning of a potential "watering down", or secularization of AA, in the twenty-first century, bring us nothing new with their hysterical shrieking. After all, some substantial proportion of the venerated "First Hundred" had already been forced to tolerate the "weak tea" of "as we understood Him".

Hazelden

A mere two weeks after the "official" turn-down by General Service, the newish Hazelden organization agreed to print and distribute Walker's book. It is not unreasonable to assume that talks with Hazelden had begun somewhat earlier. This was Hazelden's first major foray into publishing, and it was a decision they would not regret.

AA rushed into publication its own countering volume, Daily Reflections, a mere 36 years later. This has diminished the sale of Walker's more religious effort, as Daily Reflections has the additional enormous advantage of being Conference Approved Literature.

AA Thought for the Day

An appropriate closing lies in Walker's own words, his January 1 - AA Thought for the Day.

> *When I came into AA, was I a desperate person? Did I have soul-sickness? Was I so sick of my way of living that I couldn't stand looking at myself in the mirror? Was I ready to try AA? Was I ready to try anything that would help to get me sober and to get over my soul-sickness? Should I forever forget the condition I was in?*

Some of us would alter the wording somewhat, perhaps replacing "soul-sickness" with "existential angst", but the feeling of demoralization is familiar, spanning a broad diversity of worldviews.

SECTION V WOMEN PIONEERS

Chapter 24 Lois Wilson

There are few people who better epitomize the sentiments of the Tammy Wynette country classic "Stand By Your Man", than Lois Wilson. As the founder of Al-Anon, she is lovingly remembered by hundreds of thousands, or more, who have seen loved ones recover, or have, at least, been comforted, and guided, in their times of struggle. The preponderance of the afore-mentioned see her as heroic, but an equally compelling case can be made by others who view her as the pathetic quintessence of a female subservience that is, thankfully, a distant memory.

Had Lois enjoyed the strength and independent spirit of her mother-in-law, Emily, she well might have, in saving herself, adversely affected millions to come. Without her persistence and seemingly limitless devotion, it is unlikely that her husband would have gotten and stayed sober. Devoid of her financial and moral support, he would surely have been unable to dedicate himself to the cause of saving others, and to pursue with single-minded dedication his far-reaching dreams.

Although certainly more saint than sinner, it is difficult to overlook an underlying desperation and codependence in Lois Wilson that is the antithesis of what is counselled in the Al-Anon brochures.

In fairness to Lois, it was a very different time. Born in 1891, Lois would not have been able to vote until she was nearly thirty. It's entirely possible that she may have consulted her drunken spouse as to whom she should vote for.

The Burnhams

Lois's "father, Clark, was a prominent physician in Brooklyn Heights, New York, and her father's father had been a physician, a lawyer, and a minister in the Swedenborgian Church... Her mother, Matilda Hoyt Spelman was from an old aristocratic family... The Burnhams had a cook, a maid, and a man to tend to the fires, make the repairs, and take care of the horses and carriage. In the spring, the whole household would follow his patients to Manchester, Vermont". (Bill W., Francis Hartigan, p. 13)

The Robert Todd Lincoln family lived in Manchester, and were social acquaintances of the Burnhams. "Bill loved Manchester Village, which seemed as far from East Dorset as Mars with its wide-open greens and two golf courses... Manchester Village was 'old' money." (My Name Is Bill, Susan Cheever, pp. 39-40) "Lois' father was a champion golfer and a founder of the exclusive Ekwanok Country Club." (Hartigan, p. 13) Lois went to Packer Collegiate, a prestigious girls' school in Brooklyn. Her siblings also attended private schools, and her brothers went on to become physicians like their father.

> *It was all quite grand, but their life had a marginal quality, as well. The Brooklyn Heights house was on Clinton Street, which marked the easternmost boundary of the exclusive Heights neighborhood... Throughout Lois's childhood, it was rented, not owned. Some of the family furnishings were other people's discards... Lois's childhood was marked by steadily diminishing expectations... During the six months a year the family spent in Vermont, her father's income seems to have been meager, at best. (Hartigan, pp. 13-14)*

In the struggle to keep up appearances, and to make ends meet, the family began to rent out the grand Spelman home in Manchester, and a few years later they sold it. A more modest camp was acquired on Emerald Lake, very near the East Dorset home of Bill Wilson.

Romance

"In her memoirs, Lois Burnham Wilson recalls how a nodding acquaintance with Bill Wilson, who was four years her junior, blossomed into love during the summer of 1914." (Bill W. And Mr. Wilson, Matthew Raphael, p. 36) Lois was one of the "summer people".

"She had social graces of which I knew nothing... so her encouragement of me and her interest in me did a tremendous amount to back me up." (Pass It On, p. 39) There may have been various elements at play in sparking Bill's interest in the older woman. "Winning the hand of the rich doctor's daughter would be one more way to prove himself a Number One man." (Raphael, p. 37) There was also the lure of "the nurturing family he was lacking... not a brilliant prospect as a son-in-law... But they liked him." (Lois Remembers, Lois Wilson, p. 16) His competitive juices may have been fired by a competing suitor, Norman Schneider, of the Canadian meat-packing entrepreneurs, who wanted Lois to marry him and move to Kitchener, Ontario. Perhaps the effectively parentless Bill couldn't stand another desertion so recently after losing the love-of-his-life, Bertha Bamford, to a minor surgery gone tragically wrong.

So, the "boating buddies" of 1914 became secretly engaged in 1915.

There was a complication. Bill had had a "flirtation" with Lois's seventeen year old sister, Barb, that seems to have overlapped his romance with Lois. In a series of rueful letters, he confessed his full sexual history, presumably to attach credibility to his story that "he had been continuing to flirt with Barb... so that she wouldn't guess that he was secretly engaged to Lois". (Cheever, p. 68) Lois's forgiveness and comforting set a pattern for their long marriage.

"Bill later suggested... that a maternal element lay at the heart of his relationship with Lois." (Raphael, p. 42) "At the unconscious level, I have no doubt she was already becoming my mother... I think Lois came along and picked me up as tenderly as a mother does a child." (PIO, p. 40)

An odd comment to pass regarding one's wife or lover.

War fever ran high

Bill was soon at Plattsburgh training for the Great War and discovering the wealthy patriots who feted the boys in uniform and were quick to excuse any over-indulgence by the brave lads.

"Here was love, applause, war; moments sublime with intervals hilarious. I was part of life at last, and in the midst of the excitement I discovered liquor. I forgot the strong warnings of my people concerning drink. In time we sailed for 'Over There.' I was very lonely and again turned to alcohol." (AA

Big Book, p. 1) Before going off to an uncertain fate, Bill married Lois in Brooklyn Heights on January 24, 1918.

Newlyweds

The conquering hero remained in Europe for an extended victory celebration, returning to the States in May, 1919, a full six months after the cessation of hostilities. He then "moved with Lois to her parent's brick row house at 184 Clinton St." By the fall of the same year, his bride was taking him on a "geographical cure", a hiking trip from Maine to Vermont, a month in the woods. Preceding this trip, Bill and Rogers Burnham had gotten very drunk together and caused some havoc, but the returned servicemen were readily forgiven.

Back in New York, it was time to get jobs, and Bill began a pattern of inconsistent employment. "Wilson got a job decoding cablegrams for an export company. He then worked for a time for... the insurance department of the New York Central Railroad. At another point, he again worked for the New York Central, this time driving spikes on one of its piers. No matter what the job, he either quit or got fired... Many of these jobs were acquired through the good graces of his wife's family and friends." (Hartigan, p. 29)

The young couple moved out to a furnished room, a humble dwelling, and upgraded to a three room flat only "when Lois found a better-paying job in the women's psychiatric ward at Bellevue Hospital". (Raphael, p. 44)

There were three ectopic pregnancies between 1921 and 1923 which led, ultimately, to radical surgery. "It seemed that after all hope of having children had died, his bouts with alcohol became more frequent... He never hit me, but I hit him." (Lois Remembers, p. 35) The bride was becoming increasingly frustrated with her recalcitrant husband. As 1923 neared its close, "his Christmas present to Lois that year was a pledge – 'no liquor will pass my lips for one year'". (Bill W., Robert Thomsen) This was to be the first of several oaths.

The motorcycle maintenance program

"Sometimes it's a little better to travel than to arrive." (Zen and the Art of Motorcycle Maintenance, Robert M. Pirsig)

Bill had a theory about the value of investigating companies as a worthwhile tool for investors, and Lois had a theory that removed from temptation her husband would drink less.

We gave up our positions and off we roared on a motorcycle, the sidecar stuffed with tent, blankets, a change of clothes, and three huge volumes of a financial reference service. Our friends thought a lunacy commission should be appointed. Perhaps they were right. I had had some success at speculation, so we had a little money, but we once worked on a farm for a month to avoid drawing on our small capital. That was the last honest manual labor on my part for many a day. We covered the whole eastern United States in a year. At the end of it, my reports to Wall Street procured me a position there and the use of a large expense account. The exercise of an option brought in more money, leaving us with a profit of several thousand dollars for that year. (BB, pp. 2-3)

The trip in 1925 ignited Wilson's career in the stock market, but it also marked the further attempt of a frustrated wife to "fix" her husband by separating him from his unsavory New York haunts and associates. This was somewhat successful, until they returned. "The great boom of the late twenties was seething and swelling." (BB, p. 3) These were conditions in which a clever drunk could thrive. The American stock market was on a steady upward climb. "For the next few years fortune threw money and applause my way. I had arrived." (BB, p. 3)

His home life was not as successful, as his drinking had further escalated. Bill did not respond well to the "remonstrances of my friends… I became a lone wolf. There were many unhappy scenes in our sumptuous apartment". (BB, p. 3)

The crash

Notwithstanding a dissatisfied spouse, "he believed he was winning and during this time it never occurred to him that success and happiness were not the same… In fact, at the start of 1929, Bill Wilson was living in what many would call an alcoholic's paradise". (Thomsen, p. 150)

By Halloween, it would all be very different.

The stock market crash of late October, 1929, abruptly ended any lingering pretense that Bill Wilson was managing, that he "had it together". When "Black Tuesday" closed, Bill's prized stock, Pennick and Ford, had fallen from $52 a share to $32. This was a loss of 40%, but owing to margin-buying, he and his associates had lost everything, and more. Bill W. went from prosperous drunk to a $60,000 debtor in a matter of hours. The ruin of his clients was devastating to his "guru" status, and all of his attempted comebacks were short-lived.

Lois Wilson revived her earlier role as principal breadwinner, a role that was to continue for more than an additional decade. "Lois got a job at Macy's... in the furniture department demonstrating folding card tables, and she brought home $19 a week." They were back living with her parents.

Lois's mother was battling cancer. She was a woman who had treated Bill like a son, "yet when she died on Christmas Day, Bill had been drunk for days, and on the day of her funeral, he was too drunk to attend". (Hartigan, p. 46)

There were periods of sobriety for Bill that sparked hope for Lois, particularly following the Towns Hospital treatments that began in 1933. Each ended in "insane" returns to drinking. The bleakest of prognoses offered by Dr. Silkworth produced a sobering terror, but no lasting abstinence.

In 1934, Lois moved from Macy's to Loeser's department store "in order to be closer to home and deal with any emergencies that might arise there". (Raphael, p. 94)

Pioneering times

The events of December, 1934 are well-known, and do not need to be recounted here. The Wilsons launched a consuming campaign of helping others, as a means of keeping Bill sober, that was at times tragic, at times comic. For the "alcoholic husband-focused" Lois, there were to be some moments of self-discovery.

Bill's summer in Akron provided the critical starting point of Alcoholics Anonymous, but "'I thought Bill would never come home from Akron,' his wife, Lois, said. 'I nagged and nagged him to return.'... The long-suffering Lois was losing her temper more frequently. She was resentful... that her husband didn't have time for her anymore". (Getting Better Inside Alcoholics Anonymous, Nan Robertson, p. 64)

Lois tirelessly lodged and fed the succession of drunks that her husband was trying to rescue. Hamilton lawyer and bridge hustler, Bill C., committed suicide in their home.

Bill and Lois had taken over the Clinton Street property after her father had remarried, and left New York. In April of 1939, they celebrated the new book, but were finally evicted from the old Burnham family home.

To Wives

Lois wanted to write both of the chapters in the Big Book "To Wives" and "The Family Afterward", and for decades following felt the hurt that came from her husband's refusal. After offering the task to Anne Smith, Bill decided to do it himself. Committing one of the most egregious of errors, he wrote "To Wives" while fraudulently representing that the chapter was penned by a woman.

Biographer Matthew Raphael is particularly harsh on Bill Wilson, the reputed womanizer, for his handling of sex issues in the book. "What's truly incredible in Wilson's handling of adultery is his impersonation of a woman's point of view in the chapter that he would not permit Lois to write... Later... he seems to hold women accountable if their men should stray. 'The first principle of success is that you should never be angry.'" (Raphael, p. 129)

"He will tell you he is misunderstood. This may lead to lonely evenings for you. He may seek someone else to console him – not always another man." (BB, p. 111)

> *The menacing coyness of this threat is calculated to put any uppity wife in her place, which is to be seen, perhaps, but definitely not to be heard... His preoccupation with infidelity... likely sprang from his own history of philandering, no trace of which, unsurprisingly, is to be found in official AA publications. (Raphael, pp. 129-130)*

An understanding?

There is a bio-pic on JFK, where Jacqueline goes into a rage, not about her husband's infidelity, but over his breaking of a promise to be discreet. We are left to speculate on the attitude of Lois Wilson regarding her spouse's behavior with other women. "Wilson's marriage to Lois Burnham in 1918 lasted until his death at the age of seventy-five in 1971. She believed in him fiercely and tended his flame. Yet, particularly during his sober decades... Bill Wilson was a compulsive womanizer. His flirtations filled him with guilt... but he continued to stray off the reservation. His last and most serious love affair... began when he was in his sixties." (Robertson, p. 36) That woman was Helen Wynn, who he considered marrying, and to whom he bequeathed a book royalty.

Money

For the first twenty-five years of the Wilsons' marriage, Lois was the principal wage-earner, save for Bill's "glory days" in the booming market of the late twenties. For a goodly portion of that time, they lacked even a home of their own, and shuffled about in and out of the homes of relatives and AA members.

Eventually, book revenues made them "comfortable." In one of life's ironies, Lois eventually became wealthy as her inherited royalties rose well into six figures annually, and approached a million dollars in her last year. The ambitious Bill Wilson's greatest financial triumphs came after his death.

A second irony came when the childless Lois Wilson sought to leave a substantial portion of her estate to Alcoholics Anonymous, but the Traditions precluded AA's acceptance.

On October 5th, 1988, Lois Burnham Wilson died at 97 years of age. Her limitless tolerance of her husband's peccadilloes is difficult to understand in the context of our twenty-first century culture. Perhaps, she was simply a creature of a different time.

Years after Bill's death, she continued to proclaim, "My husband was a great man", and indeed, he was.

Chapter 25 Anne Ripley Smith

> *For some reason, we alcoholics seem to have the gift of picking out the world's finest women.*
> Dr. Bob Smith

"In 1898, Anne Robinson Ripley was spending a holiday with a college friend in St. Johnsbury, Vermont, where she met Robert Holbrook Smith…. She was small in stature, reserved in temperament." (Women Pioneers of AA, Hunter, James & Zieger, pp. 2-3) She met her future husband at a dance in the gym of the St. Johnsbury Academy, where he was a senior.

Anne Ripley "had a cheerfulness, awareness and calm that were to remain with her throughout the years. She had been reared within a family of railroad people. It was a very sheltered atmosphere, although there wasn't much money at the time. Anne, who abhorred ostentation and pretense, always pointed out that she attended Wellesley College on a scholarship, because her family couldn't have afforded to send her there otherwise". (Dr. Bob and the Good Oldtimers, p. 16)

A Whirlwind Courtship

The high school dance began a "whirlwind" courtship that was to last 17 years, with the Smiths eventually getting married in 1915. We are left to speculate about the many possible reasons for the lengthy delay. "There were years of schooling, work, and internship ahead for Bob. There was also the possibility that Anne had a healthy fear of entering the state of matrimony with a drinking man. Perhaps she waited until Bob gave evidence of being sober for a time before she agreed to marry him." (Oldtimers, pp. 16-17)

Dr. Bob was about one year sober when the couple were wed in the home of Anne's mother on January 25, 1915. At that point, Anne either "believed he was sober for good, or perhaps she was just tired of waiting... The first three and a half years of this married life were ideal... Dr. Bob continued to stay sober." (Women Pioneers, p. 4)

It is worth noting that the history seems to be telling us that Dr. Bob stayed sober from early in 1914 to well into 1918. He did this without steps, of course, and without calling upon God. It's an interesting anomaly, countering the folk wisdom of AA fundamentalists.

We Are Family

Dr. Bob had brought his wife home to 855 Ardmore Ave. in Akron. "The $4,000 house was new then, a two-story clapboard structure with large airy rooms." (Oldtimers, p. 29) For a physician, it was a starter home at best, but the Smiths never moved on, although they came very close to losing the house to foreclosure.

With Bob's professional life going smoothly, and his practice growing, the Smiths became parents in 1918. The year of Robert Smith Jr.'s birth was also the year the 18th Amendment, Prohibition, was passed. "At the prospect of the whole country going dry, 'I felt quite safe,' Bob recalled. A few drinks at that point would make little difference... His thinking, if not quite logical (except by alcoholic logic), was quite typical at that time." (Oldtimers, pp. 31-32)

"Again it was the old, insidious insanity - that first drink." (BB, p. 154)

After starting out moderately, he soon drifted out of control again. In spite of the problems stemming from Bob's drinking, a second child, five-year-old Sue was adopted. Anne, then in her mid-forties, had been advised that she could not have any more children. Sue and "Smitty" were about five months apart in age.

Drunken Daddy Dearest

The children remembered their father "as irritable and cross when he was under the influence. They were ashamed of his abject slavery to booze and sympathized with their mother, who was trying to hold the penniless family together, praying that her husband would somehow find an answer to his problem". (Women Pioneers, p. 8)

Anne Smith blamed her mother-in-law for her husband's drinking. The wife of Judge Smith was "a stern, tight-lipped, churchgoing lady who busied herself with the countless social and religious activities of St. Johnsbury's towering, gray stone North Congregational Church. "'Grandma Smith was a cold woman,' said Sue." When free of his stern upbringing, Anne thought, Bob had "cut loose".

By 1933, the family of the drunken physician was in dire straits, as were most Americans in the throes of the Great Depression. More often than not, potato soup was the dinner entrée in the Smith household. Only the mortgage moratorium saved the family home.

Of course, Anne Smith tried to fix her husband in various ways such as extracting pledges that were rarely honored into a second day. "Mother always tried to frisk him when he came in... Like many another alcoholic, before, after, and yet to come, he was expert at obtaining and maintaining his supply." (Oldtimers, p. 40)

The Oxford Group

In early 1933, Anne Smith began attending Oxford Group gatherings, and was soon dragging her guilt-laden husband along with her. Dr. Bob became an OG regular, and began to read what was suggested. "I gave the matter much time and study for the next two and a half years, but I still got tight every night nevertheless." (BB, p. 178)

Anne Smith was a woman of faith, and she pressed on, but not without challenges. "Anne verged on a nervous crack-up, and their two children of course were greatly upset... Hope was a word they had come to avoid." (AA Comes of Age, p. 69) At the age of 56, Anne took up smoking, possibly to graphically demonstrate to her husband the effects of his self-indulgence.

In the spring of 1935, Henrietta Seiberling "felt guided" that the Oxford should have a special meeting for Bob Smith. They were successful in getting the physician to confess, for the first time, his difficulty with alcohol. "I am a secret drinker, and I can't stop." (Oldtimers, p. 58) Later, the Oxford folks would see Bill Wilson's role in Smith's rehabilitation as only a minor one, as they, and God, were progressing nicely.

It was Seiberling, of course, who telephoned the Smiths about the rum hound from New York, who had found an answer to his alcohol problem. Her husband was too drunk to make the trek to the Seiberling Gatehouse that Saturday, but she wrangled his reluctant promise to go the next day for the now famous "Mother's Day" meeting of 1935. Other than a final debauch a month later, Anne Smith's husband never drank again.

Put More Water in the Soup
We've Got Company

Seiberling arranged for Bill to move to the Portage Country Club, Akron's best, as the guest of her neighbor, John Gammeter. Lois was less than impressed to hear of her unemployed husband's hobnobbing with the wealthy. "'There didn't seem to be very much happening in the proxy fight... And I can't say I liked thinking about his playing golf at this fancy country club, while I was working at Loesers." (Bill W., Francis Hartigan, p. 83)

After a couple of weeks Bill moved in with the Smiths, and stayed until the end of August. The two men diligently searched for others to help, often lodging them in the already cash-strapped Smith home. "Progress in their work with alcoholics was not smooth... Once, when her husband and Bill had gone out... Anne found herself chased around her kitchen by a crazed ex-drunk brandishing her own butcher knife in his demand for alcohol." (Not-God, Ernest Kurtz, p. 40)

Grateful to have a sober husband, Anne Smith complained little. She "gathered guests in her arms, made them feel at home, served them endless pots of Eight O'clock coffee, moved her children out of their beds to put the drunks in, (and) read the Bible with them mornings". (Getting Better, Nan Robertson, p.20) Her home a hostel for would-be AA members, Anne Smith was truly the "first mother of AA." "Anne was especially effective in counselling wives... giving them hope." (Women Pioneers, p. 2)

"She herself was 'the sheltered place for people in trouble, a rod, a comforter,' in her daughter-in-law's memory." (Not-God, p. 55) "Anne Smith...was also directly involved in trying to help other alcoholics. So were the wives of many of the other early members. In fact, Lois (Wilson) considered herself a member of AA as well as Al-Anon. According to her, all the wives who joined their husbands in working with alcoholics during AA's formative years saw themselves as AA members." (Hartigan, pp. 70-71)

The Drunks Are Wrecking the Furniture

By the autumn of 1939, only the Akronites remained under the umbrella of the Oxford Group. The Groupers were not impressed with the alcoholics' book, which they viewed as commercialization. Clarace Williams who, with her husband, had been hosting a Wednesday night meeting, was upset about what was happening to Oxford Group principles, and her home. She shared these concerns with Henrietta Seiberling. In October of 1939, the alcoholics pulled out suddenly, and the alcoholics moved temporarily to the Smith home. In January, the location moved to King's School.

"There were some hot conversations on the telephone; it was a 3-way thing... the women decided it." (Not-God, p. 81)

Legacy

The book of James was a favorite of the mother of AA.

> *14 What does it profit, my brethren, if someone says he has faith but does not have works? Can faith save him? 15 If a brother or sister is naked and destitute of daily food, 16 and one of you says to them, "Depart in peace, be warmed and filled," but you do not give them the things which are needed for the body, what does it profit? 17 Thus also faith by itself, if it does not have works, is dead. 18 But someone will say, "You have faith, and I have works." Show me your faith without your [a] works, and I will show you my faith by my [b] works.*

Anne Smith was no hypocrite as she continued to support her husband. Both were dedicated to helping both drunkards and their spouses to recover from the horrible affliction that is active alcoholism. Emma K., who brought her husband to the Smiths for help with his drinking reported - "They were always doing things... for you. They couldn't do enough for you." (Oldtimers, p. 318) Emma, a nurse, spent a lot of time with Anne Smith. Vision was a problem for the co-founder's spouse, and a cataract operation failed. Toward the end, Anne Smith could barely see, hardly walk, and her hands were crippled with arthritis.

A selfless woman, and not a complainer, Mrs. Smith did express disappointment at her husband's lack of acknowledgement in New York. Dr. Bob was barely recognized - it was "all Bill". Of course, in Ohio, the situation was reversed.

There can be little doubt that a plethora of tears were shed on June 1st, 1949, over the passing of Anne Smith. She had provided tremendous comfort to hundreds and hundreds of people. Henrietta Seiberling may not have over-reached in calling her a founder of AA.

People like her give religious people a good name.

Chapter 26 Florence R.

> A FEMININE VICTORY
> FLORENCE RANKIN KALHOUN
> DEC. 17, 1895   APRIL 19, 1943

Florence was the first woman to get sober in AA, even for a short time. She came to AA in New York, in March 1937. She had several slips, but was sober over a year when she wrote her story for the Big Book.

(Silkworth.net, Biographies, "A Feminine Victory")

A Feminine Victory

"I am praying for inspiration to tell my story in a manner that may give other women who have this problem the courage to see it in its true light and seek the help that has given me a new lease on life." (BB, 1st Edition, p. 217) This is the noble sentiment expressed in the very first paragraph of A Feminine Victory, the only story of a woman alcoholic in the 1st Edition of Alcoholics Anonymous.

Florence would not believe she was an alcoholic - "my mind simply refused to accept it. Horrors! How disgraceful! What humiliation! How preposterous! Why, I loathed the taste of liquor - drinking was simply a means of escape when my sorrows became too great for me to endure." (BB, 1st Edition, p. 217)

Her husband was a drinker and had been "a man Bill knew on Wall Street." (Silkworth.net) "He had always been a drinker; I had never known anything about it until I was almost thirty years old and he gave me my first drink."

(BB, 1st Edition, p. 220) Florence thought the various misbehaviors of her husband were responsible for her own drinking, but when they divorced, she was the one who ended up in the alcoholic ward of a public hospital.

Progression

Florence's drinking had started with parties, "speakeasies," and cocktails after matinées. "Then came the morning when I had my first case of the jitters. Someone suggested a little of the 'hair of the dog that bit me.' A half hour after that drink I was sitting on top of the world, thinking how simple it was to cure shaky nerves. How wonderful liquor was, in only a few minutes my head had stopped aching, my spirits were back to normal and all was well in this very fine world." (BB, 1st Edition, pp. 218-219)

Morning drinking increased in frequency and amounts to where she was making excuses at afternoon bridge parties, or luncheons, for having liquor on her breath. At evening parties she found the drink service too slow. Later she was cancelling events, and still later, "simply forgetting that there were engagements at all; spending two or three days drinking, sleeping it off, and waking to start all over again." (BB, 1st Edition, p. 220)

There were periods of abstinence, that "would last anywhere from two weeks to three or four months. Once, after a very severe illness of six weeks' duration (caused by drinking), I didn't touch anything of an alcoholic nature for almost a year." (BB, 1st Edition, p. 220) Suddenly, things were worse than ever.

Bill Wilson surely was drawing on Florence's story when he wrote, "To be gravely affected, one does not necessarily have to drink a long time nor take the quantities some of us have. This is particularly true of women. Potential female alcoholics often turn into the real thing and are gone beyond recall in a few years. Certain drinkers, who would be greatly insulted if called alcoholics, are astonished at their inability to stop." (BB, 4th Edition, p. 33)

Twelfth Stepped by Lois

When she ended up in Bellevue Hospital, her husband brought Lois Wilson to visit her "hoping that she could help. She did. From the hospital I went home with her. There, her husband told me the secret of his rebirth." (BB, 1st Edition, p. 221) Bill may have been overly aggressive in selling her the "God idea," and she resisted. Bill backed off, and Florence was sent off to stay with another alcoholic and his wife. A gentler approach led her to turn to God in a sincere and earnest prayer.

Unfortunately, what she only describes as "'an incident'... put me on the toboggan again. I seemed to feel that the hurt of that incident was too great to endure without some 'release.'" (BB, p. 222) This relapse prompted an in depth examination and confession of her fears, remorse and shame. Sadly, some time later, a rainy day worked its way into her mood and she wallowed in a case of the blues.

There was liquor in the house, and Florence was alone. Feeling the temptation, she started to read from the Bible and "Victorious Living." She prayed. "In a half an hour I got up and was absolutely free of the urge to drink." (BB, 1st Edition, p. 223) It somewhat detracted from this "miracle," when she was drinking again a short time later.

On that occasion she called Lois, and ended up back at the Wilson's for three more weeks. She finally gave up the notion of doing her own "fixing," and was sober about a year when the book came out.

Ultimately, A Short-Lived Victory

"I know that my victory is none of my human doing. I know that I must keep myself worthy of Divine help. And the glorious thing is this: I am free, I am happy, and perhaps I am going to have the blessed opportunity of 'passing it on.' I say in all reverence - Amen." (BB, 1st Edition, p. 225)

Regrettably, as the Big Books were rolling off of the Cornwall Press, Florence was again drinking.

The story of the woman who had argued vociferously against "One Hundred Men," a title being considered for the book, eventually named Alcoholics Anonymous, does not have a happy ending. Florence had moved to the Washington D.C. area, where she was to have helped Fitz M. "Our Southern Friend." There she met, and married, an alcoholic who unfortunately, did not stay sober. She started drinking again and disappeared.

In April 1943, "Fitz M. identified her at the morgue". (AAHistoryLovers.com)

There is a much circulated story that Florence Rankin Kalhoun had committed suicide, but that is uncertain. The death certificate "does NOT state that her death was a result of suicide." It was possibly meningitis, in an alternative view.

Florence had been born on December 17, 1895, making her three weeks younger than Bill Wilson. At the time of her death, she was 47 years old.

Chapter 27 Sylvia K.

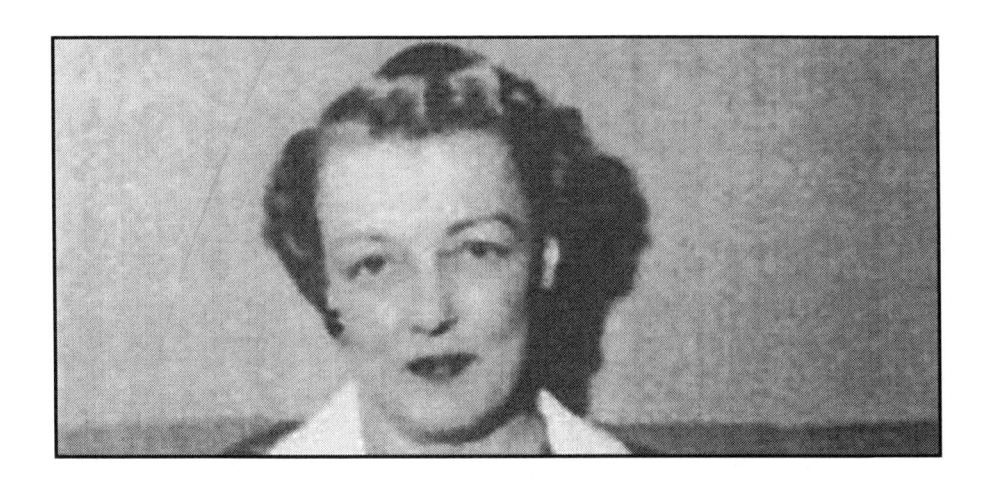

AA's earliest efforts to rehabilitate women had not gone well. The ink was barely dry on the newly printed "Big Book", when Florence Rankin, author of *A Feminine Victory* (BB, 1st Edition), returned to the bottle. Shortly thereafter, and still in the Spring of 1939, Dorothy Snyder reported to Dr. Bob that her sister in Chicago was sending a woman down to Akron for "the cure". This was done with some, not unwarranted, trepidation.

"Dr. Bob threw up his hands and said, 'We have NEVER had a woman and will NOT work on a woman.' But by that time, Caroline was on her way with Sylvia K." (Dr. Bob and the Good Oldtimers, p. 180) "Dr. Bob showed somewhat less assurance upon first confronting the most troublesome and, in some ways, the most unwelcome minority in AA's olden days - women!" (Good Oldtimers, p. 241)

The Chicago socialite needed help. "I was thirty-three years old and my life was spent. I was caught in a cycle of alcohol and sedation that was proving inescapable, and consciousness had become intolerable." (The Keys of the Kingdom, BB, 4th Edition, p. 268)

Early Advantages

Sylvia could not blame her "dilemma" on childhood environment. "I was given every advantage in a well-ordered home. I had the best schools, summer camps, resort vacations, and travel... I was strong and healthy and quite athletic." (Keys, pp. 268-269)

She drank for the first time at sixteen, and "I definitely liked everything about alcohol - the taste, the effects; and I realize now that a drink did something for me or to me that was different from the way it affected others. It wasn't long before any party without drinks was a dud for me". (Keys, p. 269)

This was the era of the Roaring Twenties - speakeasies, flappers, the Charleston, hip flasks, and bootlegged hooch. This was the time of F. Scott Fitzgerald, John Held Jr., and drugstore cowboys. The American economy was booming, and hard partying was "de rigueur." Sylvia noticed later that "most everyone else I knew had emerged from it with both feet on the ground and a fair amount of adult maturity". (Keys, p. 268)

In a 1985 interview, Earl Treat's widow, Katie, remembers Sylvia as being originally from the nation's capital.

> *Sylvia was one of the first members in the group, and a very beautiful gal. She lived in Washington, DC, and was married to one of the owners of a newspaper. She was the only one in the group that had any money. (Laugh.) She was divorced from him, and he paid her alimony. So whenever we needed coffee or cream, Sylvia would bring it, because she had the money.*
>
> *Anyway, she was an eager beaver, and a spark plug. (Katie Treat Interview, AA History Lovers)*

Her husband was very likely to have been one of the heirs of Samuel Hay Kauffmann, President, and one of three owners of the Washington (Evening) Star. At the time of his death in 1906, Kauffmann's residence housed one of the city's most impressive collections of art. For decades, the Star was DC's preeminent newspaper.

At twenty, Sylvia was married, and by twenty-three, she was a divorcee with two children.

The self-pity from a broken home and broken heart provided reasons for increased drinking. Alimony of about $700 per month (about $10,000 in 2014 dollars) may not have healed her emotional pain, but she was able to suffer "in style." (Her monthly income was approximately five times that of Towns physician, William Silkworth).

By the age of twenty-five, she had an alcohol problem, and "accumulating ailments" sufficient to seek out medical attention.

Progression

"Of course the doctors found nothing. Just an unstable woman, undisciplined, poorly adjusted, and filled with nameless fears. Most of them prescribed sedatives and advised rest and moderation. Between the ages of twenty-five and thirty, I tried everything… Nothing worked. My drinking habits increased in spite of my struggle for control. I tried the beer diet, the wine diet, timing, measuring, and spacing of drinks." (Keys, p. 269)

By thirty, Sylvia was being driven by a compulsion to drink that was beyond her control. The consequences of drinking continued to multiply.

The days of pleasurable drinking were over. Instead there were nurses, doctors, hospitals, and sanitariums. A ten-day coma nearly ended it all.

"By now I wanted to die but had lost the courage even to take my life. I was trapped, and for the life of me I did not know how or why this had happened to me… I had heartsickness, shame, and fear bordering on panic, and no complete escape any longer except in oblivion." (Keys, p. 270)

A Special Physician

For the last year, one of her doctors had a particular tenacity. He had Sylvia attending 6 a.m. mass daily, and performing "the most menial labor for his charity patients. This doctor apparently had the intuitive knowledge that spirituality and helping others might be the answer. In 1939, this doctor heard of the book Alcoholics Anonymous and wrote to New York for a copy. After reading it, he tucked it under his arm and called on Sylvia." (Sylvia K. - Barefoot's World)

The physician then gave her the cold, hard facts about alcoholism. Previously, "I had never been told I was an alcoholic… He further explained that alcohol was no respecter of sex or background". (Keys, pp. 271-272)

He then put her in touch with a man who had been experiencing success by using this plan. The man was Earl Treat, who would later author He Sold Himself Short (BB, 4th Edition, p. 258).

"I don't know what sort of person I was expecting, but I was very agreeably surprised to find Mr. T. a poised, intelligent, well-groomed, and well-mannered gentleman… He thought it would be helpful for me to visit Akron and meet many like himself... So I went to Akron... and I met more recovered alcoholics." (Keys, pp. 273-274)

Akron Chaos

Sylvia stayed two weeks at Clarence (Clarence S., "The Home Brewmeister") and Dorothy S.'s home in Cleveland. She met Dr. Bob, who brought other A.A. men to meet her. Dorothy S. said that the men "were only too willing to talk to her after they saw her". Sylvia was a glamorous divorcee, extremely good looking, and rich. But these attractions probably did not help her with the wives of the alcoholics, who were known on occasion to run women out.

"After meeting Dr. Bob she wanted to move to Akron, but this caused great consternation, since her presence threatened to disrupt the whole group. Someone told her it would mean a great deal more if she could go back and help in Chicago." (Sylvia K. - Barefoot's World)

The little white pills she was gobbling rendered her "rubber-legged," and were clearly not saccharin, as claimed.

There were exhales of relief when the very "medicated" divorcee, and her nurse, boarded the Chicago-bound train, and headed immediately for the dining car.

Sweet Home, Chicago

Back in Chicago, Sylvia got sober. "According to member list index cards kept by the Chicago group, Sylvia's date of sobriety was Sept. 13, 1939. Sylvia was probably the first woman to achieve long term permanent sobriety from then until her death." (Sylvia K. - Barefoot's World)

Marty Mann had shown up earlier in 1939, in New York, and her early relapses seem to have been ignored in order to favor her with the "first woman" accolade. Her friendship with Bill Wilson, and her later very public role as spokesperson for the National Committee for Education on Alcoholism (NCEA), may have been contributing factors in the commonly held perception that graced her with this distinction.

"On September 20, 1939, Chicago had what is known as the first group meeting. Held in Evanston in Earl's apartment, there were eight present." (The History of the Chicago Group, p. 1) These included Dick R., Ken A., Earl, Sylvia, and a non-alcoholic Grace Cultice, who was Sylvia's secretary, and went on to serve as secretary to the Chicago Intergroup, which set up its first office in Sylvia's apartment.

AA's rapid growth in the Midwest became explosive with the publication of the Jack Alexander article in the Saturday Evening Post. It is well-known that the skeptical newsman visited New York, Akron and Cleveland, but "he next visited the Chicago group and met several members who were newspaper people, and he said these guys talked my language. He then went to the group in St. Louis, where he had grown up, and met some people he had actually known who were now A.A. members. This convinced him; he wrote an excellent article, which was published March 1, 1941. This article opened the flood gates." (History of the Chicago Group, p. 3)

Reflections

Sylvia wrote a retrospective for the AA Grapevine that appeared in January, 1969.

> *The first ten years of AA in the Chicago area were years filled with much activity. During the first four or five years, the activity was at times even feverish. Early national publicity produced a "flood of requests that poured in from all over the Midwest". This tremendous activity... provided me with everything I most desperately needed to save my life - quite literally.*

> *As I look back, I realize this was the most exciting period of my life, filled with great humor, incredible thrills, and revelatory happenings.*

> *By 1955, when I wrote my story for the revised edition of Alcoholics Anonymous, our membership in the Chicago area had grown from six to six thousand.*

> *I now live in Florida with my husband (Dr. Ed S.)... He is an alky, too, and our lives have been enriched by our mutual faith and perseverance in the AA way of life. Through it we have found a quality of happiness and security that, we believe, could not have been realized any other way. Small wonder our gratitude knows no bounds.*

Remembered

AA, at least in theory, has no icons. Nonetheless, in many geographical areas, there are special people who are very fondly remembered, usually for their pioneering efforts and diligence of service to their fellows. Chicago AA retains a unique fondness for two of its earliest trusted servants, Earl T., and Sylvia K.

Sylvia passed away on October 31, 1974, thirty-five years sober, and her memory is honored by the very large number of people she was able to help.

Chapter 28 Marty Mann and the Early Women of AA

Margaret "Marty" Mann

A tremendous change has taken place over the past few generations in the way alcoholics are viewed in our society. Although it is undeniable that some level of unawareness and misunderstanding remains, substantial improvements have been effected since the 1930s. We have cause to be grateful.

The once virtually universal stigma that besieged alcoholic men was exponentially greater for women. "Nice women" didn't drink to excess. This made it extremely difficult to admit to a drinking problem in the first place. As our pioneers battled not only for their own sobriety, but for some level of "respectability," their reluctance to associate themselves with "beggars, tramps, asylum inmates, prisoners, queers (sic), plain crackpots, and fallen women," (12 & 12, p. 140), can be looked on with some degree of sympathy.

Of course, many men failed to get sober, but were able to come and go without fanfare. The women drunks seemed more disruptive. Explosions took place over "out-of-bounds" romance and the arrival of alcoholic women at the early gatherings. According to Bill Wilson, "Whole groups got into uproars, and a number of people got drunk. We trembled for AA's reputation and for its survival." (Dr. Bob & the GO, p. 241)

It did not help that AA's earliest efforts to rehabilitate women did not go well. When Caroline, also a sister-in-law of Hank Parkhurst, called her sister

Dorothy, the wife of Cleveland AA member Clarence Snyder, to tell her that she was bringing a woman to Akron from Chicago for "the cure," Dorothy was nervous about telling Dr. Bob. From Dr. Bob and the Good Oldtimers we know that her trepidation was warranted: "Dr. Bob threw up his hands and said, 'We have NEVER had a woman and will NOT work on a woman.' But by that time, Caroline was on her way with Sylvia K." (p. 180)

Sylvia K.

Sylvia arrived in the late summer of 1939, and the men of AA were immediately tripping over themselves in their efforts to talk to her. By all accounts, the drunken divorcee and heiress from Chicago was stunningly beautiful, and in an era when America was still feeling the effects of the Great Depression, Sylvia was getting alimony of $700 per month. A comparison to Dr. William Silkworth's rather paltry salary of forty dollars a week as a psychiatrist at Towns Hospital puts proportion to the enormity of this stipend.

All too soon after her arrival in Akron, Sylvia began tripping over herself. Clearly, the "little white pills" that she was taking were NOT "saccharin" as she was claiming. A nurse was flown down from Chicago to take care of her.

"After talking to Bob, Sylvia decided to live in Akron. This caused great consternation, since her presence threatened to disrupt the whole group. But someone told her it would mean a great deal more if she could go back and help in Chicago. This appealed to Sylvia, so the members put her and her nurse on the train. Sylvia headed for the dining car and got drunk." (Dr. Bob & the GO, p. 181)

This tale has a happy ending as she sobered up when she got back to Chicago and contacted Earl T. They both worked diligently to grow AA in Chicago, and to this very day remain revered and legendary figures in Illinois AA. Sylvia's personal story "The Keys of the Kingdom" appears in the 2nd, 3rd, and 4th editions of our book. Sylvia K. was the first woman to achieve long term sobriety in AA, although that distinction is often erroneously conferred on Bill Wilson's close friend, Marty Mann.

"Lil"

Dr. Bob's concerns about women in AA pre-date Sylvia's 1939 arrival. The first woman, ever, to seek help from the folks who were not yet, but would one day be, AA is identified in Dr. Bob and the Good Oldtimers only as "Lil."

There was a man we'll call "Victor," a former mayor of Akron, and a lady we'll call "Lil," who was the first woman to seek help. Together, Victor and the lady known as Lil started out to write the "thirteenth step" long before the first twelve were even thought of. What is more, they say it began in Dr. Bob's office - on his examination table - while he was at the City Club engaged in his sacrosanct Monday night bridge game. In any case, Victor decided it was time for him to go home - but Lil was loaded. (p. 97)

Lil wouldn't leave so Victor called Ernie G., (AA #4), for assistance. Lil grabbed some pills from Dr. Bob's medicine chest and was trying to gobble them while the two men chased her around the examination table in what must have appeared like a scene from "Benny Hill," or "The Keystone Cops."

Ernie recalled, "Then she made a dive for the window. I caught her halfway out. She was strong as a horse and used some profanity I have never heard before or since. I got her quieted, and Doc came. We took her out to Ardmore Avenue (the Smith home) and put her in a room in the basement. She stayed there two or three days, and then her people took her home. Of course, they were never too kind about it and thought we didn't handle her right." (Dr. Bob & the GO, p. 98)

This tale also has a happy ending, as well as a message of open-mindedness. According to Sue Windows (Dr. Bob's daughter), "Lil" straightened out after a few years - but NOT through the AA program - got married, and had kids. AA isn't the answer for everyone. "They say that Dr. Bob was leery of anything to do with women alcoholics for a long time thereafter, although he still tried to help as best he could with any who came along." (p. 98)

Florence R.

Some consideration that was being given to the name "One Hundred Men," as the title of what would become the Big Book, was squashed by the presence of Florence Rankin, whose story "A Femine Victory" appeared in the Big Book's First Edition. At the time Florence had been sober for a little more than a year. Florence's hard-drinking ex-husband, who knew Bill Wilson from Wall Street, brought Lois to talk with her. This was in March of 1937. She reports having great difficulty in seeing herself as an "alcoholic," but after some slips she got sober in early 1938.

Again, this is another tale of AA's early women that does not end well. Florence moved to Washington D.C. where she tried to assist Fitz Mayo ("Our Southern Friend") in getting AA off the ground in and around the nation's capital. One of the prospects drew her romantic interest and they married. The bridegroom was unable to stay sober and after a time, Florence got drunk as well and disappeared. When Fitz finally located her, it was at the morgue - she may have committed suicide.

Jane Sturdevant

"Women who joined the Akron group in the earliest days had adequate, if not impressive social credentials. Jane was married to the vice-president of a large steel company, and Sylvia was an attractive heiress." (Silkworth.net)

Dr. Bob's February, 1938 list of "successes" showed Jane S., 12 months. Jane was making the 35 mile trip from Cleveland to the meetings at T. Henry Williams' house from early 1937. Described as "colorful and vivacious, with a fine sense of humor, Jane was the first woman to have attained any length of sobriety - meaning a few months." (Dr. Bob & the GO, p. 122) That she has no story in the First Edition is evidence that she relapsed, AND by the time of Sylvia's arrival in the Spring of 1939, she remained only as a bad memory for Dr. Bob, prompting the previously-cited "we have never had a woman, we will not work with a woman" remark.

Others came from the opposite end of the social strata. There is brief mention of an "Indian waitress," and early member Warren C. recalled one woman who sought help but was "thrown out of AA by the wives. She was so bad that they wouldn't allow her in their homes."

Dr. LeClair Bissell

Bissell was an M.D., an addiction researcher with an "inside knowledge" of the malady, and the co-author of the 1987 book, *Ethics for Addiction Professionals*. Joining AA in 1953, at the age of twenty-five, she stayed sober until her death in 2008. William L. White, who interviewed Dr. Bissell in 1997 described her as "an unabashed atheist, a vocal lesbian, and a visible woman in addiction recovery before such openness was in vogue." Dr. Bissell's specific relevance to this essay is that she was personally acquainted with Mrs. Marty Mann, and was able to relay to us Mann's own experience of AA in 1939:

Marty shared with me that when she went to her first AA meeting at Bill and Lois' home in Brooklyn, the men were very afraid. The experience of some of the earlier women was that the men were very threatened by them, and didn't want them in the group. That is what happened with Marty Mann... It was Lois Wilson who made her welcome, and pretty much insisted the men behave themselves. (White, William, Reflections of an addiction treatment pioneer: An Interview with LeClair Bissell, MD (1928-2008), conducted January 22, 1997)

Marty Mann

Born in 1905, Margaret "Marty" Mann grew up in Chicago, where her wealthy family provided her with every advantage including the finest boarding schools and finishing school in Europe. In her Big Book story "Women Suffer Too" we are told "My family had money - I had never known denial of any material desire." An attractive and popular débutante, Marty's circle was a young, privileged and fast-moving crowd. It was the "roaring twenties," after all.

Following her own debut in 1927, at the age of twenty-one, Marty eloped with a handsome New Orleans "party boy" from a socially prominent family. Both bride and groom were considerably high on alcohol at the time. The young husband's dubious claim to fame was being his town's worst drunk. In her words, "My husband was an alcoholic, and since I had only comtempt for those without my own amazing capacity, the outcome was inevitable. My divorce coincided with my father's bankruptcy, and I went to work (1928), casting off all allegiances and responsibilities to anyone other than myself." (Women Suffer Too, p. 203)

Described by those who knew her as "favored with beauty, brains, charisma, phenomenal energy, and a powerful will," she merged these with strong social connections to forge a successful career in Public Relations. "I had my own business, successful enough for me to indulge most of my desires." She even "went abroad to live." That her life of success, hedonism, and fulfilled desires left her "increasingly miserable," is reminiscent of Oscar Wilde's insightful dictum - "There are only two tragedies in life: one is not getting what one wants, and the other is getting it." The fun and frolic of the late 20s had become something altogether different ten years later.

"Hangovers began to assume monstrous proportions, and the morning drink became an urgent necessity. 'Blanks' became more frequent... With a creeping insidiousness, drink had become more important than anything else. It no longer gave me pleasure – it merely dulled the pain – but I had to have it." (Women Suffer Too, p. 204)

A return to America and her "drinking grew worse." The one-time debutante, then PR whiz kid, found herself on the charity ward of first Bellvue Hospital and then the Blythewood Sanitarium in Greenwich, Connecticut.

Mann's psychiatrist, Harry Tiebout had been given a manuscript of the book Alcoholics Anonymous which he gave her to read.

> *"The first chapters were a revelation to me. I wasn't the only person in the world who felt and behaved like this! I wasn't mad or vicious – I was a sick person. I was suffering from an actual disease that had a name and symptoms like diabetes or cancer or TB – and a disease was respectable, not a moral stigma." (Women Suffer Too)*

Spreading the message expressed in the previous quotation would eventually take Marty Mann far beyond the rooms of AA.

Meeting Bill Wilson

In spite of not being happy with "the number of capital 'G' words" present in the manuscript, in April 11 of 1939, Marty was driven by Popsie M. to the Clinton St. meeting of Alcoholics Anonymous. The occasion must have been somewhat somber as the government-imposed moratorium on foreclosures had been recently lifted, and the Wilsons were about to lose their home. At the gathering of "this group of freaks or bums who had done this thing" a surprising thing happened: "I went trembling into a house in Brooklyn filled with strangers... and I found I had come home at last, to my own kind." (Women Suffer Too, p. 206)

In spite of this auspicious debut, and a somewhat secular "awakening" about the need to let go of anger, Ms. Mann did not go deaf to the siren call of fermented beverages. Several relapses preceded her achieving a long term sobriety well into 1940 - possibly just one more illustration of the insidious nature of the malady.

The Yale Plan for Alcohol Studies

When Dr. E.M. Jellinek, America's premier researcher into alcoholism, joined Dr. Howard Haggard (medicine) and Dr. Sheldon D. Bacon (sociology) to form "The Yale Plan for Alcohol Studies," they had a problem. In order that they not be viewed as "Ivory Tower" types with only a superficial, academic knowledge of "real" alcoholism, they needed a "real" alcoholic, "Exhibit A." Of course, this issue was not unrelated to fund-raising. Marty Mann joined these men in their noble cause of bringing change to public attitudes toward the disease and its sufferers. She felt the calling to work in the field of alcoholic education, and in particular she desired to help women alcoholics who were cursed with a "double stigma."

> *The National Committee for Education on Alcoholism, Inc., the organization Marty founded, opened its offices on October 2,*

> *1944. N.C.E.A. - eventually to become the National Council on Alcoholism - received an enthusiastic endorsement from the Grapevine, itself only four months old. It also received the support of many prominent (and some not so prominent) people, whose names, including those of Bill Wilson and Dr. Bob Smith, appeared on the committee's letterhead... The AA co-founders' names on the letterhead gave the impression that the two groups were connected. To confuse matters further, Marty, as she spoke across the country on behalf of her new organization, was breaking her own anonymity. (Pass it On, p. 320)*

Ultimately, Wilson and Smith withdrew from N.C.E.A. and became persuaded that total non-affiliation was the only answer, as they had inadvertently associated AA with the plea for public funds by Mann's organization, a solicitation that went out at some point to AA members. Additionally, Marty agreed to discontinue publicly identifying herself as an AA member. This was not entirely satisfactory, as the public was becoming aware that only AA members tended to refer to themselves as 'alcoholics' after becoming sober through the fellowship, while those who had gotten sober by any other means typically referred to themselves as "ex-alcoholics."

Anonymity issues aside, the N.C.E.A., with Mrs. Mann as spokesperson and 'Exhibit A,' was quite successful in communicating the three tenets of its core message:

1. Alcoholism is a disease, and the alcoholic is a sick person;
2. The alcoholic can be helped, and is worth helping;
3. Alcoholism is a public heath problem, and therefore a public responsibility.

These ideas are so universally accepted today, that it can be difficult to imagine that they were both revolutionary and counter-intuitive at the time.

In the 1950s, famous journalist and newscaster (he was HUGE, young people), Edward R. Murrow included Marty Mann on his list of the ten "Greatest Living Americans." (Murrow is brilliantly portrayed by Canadian David Strathairn in the 2005 film "Good Night and Good Luck," directed by George Clooney and nominated for several Academy Awards.)

Mann's breach of her own anonymity "for the sake and good of others" clearly had mostly positive outcomes. It is hard to know the causes leading to her relapse at twenty years sober. Perhaps the aggrandizement of ego that is at the core of AA's fears for members who "go public" was a factor. AA also warns of the dangers of being a "secret keeper," and Mann was an "in-the-closet" lesbian for decades. Her close friends knew the truth, but she shielded this additional "stigma" from the public to the point of retaining and using the title "Mrs." her entire life, in spite of returning to the use of her maiden name. Her volatile love affair with "the Countess" may have also been a factor - all matters of speculation.

People have also speculated that later in her life she had been drinking at times when she was representing herself as sober. Regardless, she is an iconic character in the history of AA, and at a far broader level in the worldwide treatment and understanding of alcoholism. Mrs. Marty Mann died in 1980 shortly after suffering a stroke. She was seventy-five years old.

There are few things that have changed more since these earliest days than the position of women within the fellowship of Alcoholics Anonymous. From this less than auspicious debut and a mere token presence in 1939, women now comprise fully thirty-five percent of our society. Young women, arriving new to AA in the twenty-first century, may well be surprised and even displeased with the male-dominant language of the Big Book, but it is a reflection of a different era, fully three generations in the past. Much is owed to these intrepid female pioneers, for blazing the trail for the women of today.

Chapter 29 Henrietta Seiberling

Bill Wilson was having some panicky moments in the lobby of the Mayflower Hotel, in the early afternoon of the second Saturday of May, 1935. Much has been made of his "hot flash" spiritual experience of five months earlier at the Towns Hospital, but at least equally important was his theory that attempts made to reach out and help others could KEEP him sober.

Away from home, and from his sources of struggling alcoholics - the Calvary Mission and Towns Hospital, how could he possibly find someone who might embrace his new and only partially developed ideas? He was in Akron engaged in a proxy battle that, if successful, would provide him with an executive position and the opportunity to rise up from his current indignity of being a man supported by his wife. The venture was not going as well as hoped, and when his colleagues returned to New York, Bill was left to make continued efforts on behalf of a cause that was most probably lost.

His associates gone, he was alone and felt the lure of the cocktail lounge, "'God,' he thought, 'I am going to get drunk.'" (Not-God, Ernest Kurtz, p. 27)

But, he knew already what he would write a few years later - "...when all other measures failed, work with another alcoholic would save the day." (BB, p. 15) Lest we missed the point that this one thing surpasses all others in providing protection from relapse - "Practical experience shows that nothing will so much insure immunity from drinking as intensive work with other alcoholics. It works when other activities fail." (BB, p. 89)

Better even than prayer, white lights a'flashin', or cool winds a'blowin'!

In the hotel lobby was a display with the names and phone numbers of various ministers. Bill called Reverend Tunks, an Oxford Group affiliate. The clergyman supplied a list of contacts which included Norman Sheppard who supplied the name of Henrietta Seiberling, who was desperately trying to bring a religious cure to a rapidly declining local physician.

Bill's recognition of the "Seiberling" name made him timid about calling whom he presumed to be the wife of the great Akron tire magnate, F.A. Seiberling. When he eventually telephoned, he discovered that Henrietta was the daughter-in-law of the man known as the "little Napoleon" of the rubber industry. Estranged from her husband, she was living not in the 65 room mansion, Stan Hywet Hall, but in the estate's gatehouse.

A Rum Hound and a Potted Plant

"Henrietta was bent on saving her drunken doctor friend. But she never drank much herself and did not understand his compulsion." (Getting Better - Inside Alcoholics Anonymous, Nan Robertson, p. 32) Bill spoke directly - "'I'm from the Oxford Group and I'm a rum hound from New York.' Her silent reaction, she said, was: 'This is really manna from heaven.' Aloud, she said, 'You come right out here'". (Pass It On, p. 137)

Anne Smith was forced to decline Henrietta's invitation to come over that night. Dr. Bob was as potted as the plant he had brought home as a gift for the morrow's Mother's Day. A meeting was arranged for the next day. Dr. Bob reluctant agreement to attend carried the stipulation that "'I'll give him fifteen minutes. And that's it,' he declared to his wife". (Bill W., Francis Hartigan, p. 81) They stayed six hours more than that.

Decades later, on December 6th, 1979, Henrietta's New York Times obituary called her "a key figure in the founding and development of Alcoholics Anonymous". Without her brokering of this vital encounter, history most surely would have followed a different path.

Growing Up

Henrietta McBrayer Buckler was "born in Lawrenceburg, Kentucky, on March 18, 1888. She was reared in Texas where here father, Julius Augustus Buckner, was a judge... She was well-educated, graduating from Vassar College when she was only 15. She majored in music...". (Summit County Historical Society)

"She was a well-bred Kentuckian... a lifelong seeker of things of the spirit. She had married a son of Frank A. Seiberling, the founder... of the Goodyear Tire and Rubber Company, but her husband had abandoned her and their three adolescent children." (Robertson, p. 32)

At the time of her marriage to J. Frederick Seiberling, in 1917, the Goodyear Co. had gross annual sales of one hundred million dollars. At the time of the Wilson/Smith meeting in her home in 1935, "she was forty-seven years old. Snubbed and condescended to by her rich and socially prominent relatives, she had found solace in the Oxford Group meetings". (Robertson, p. 32)

First Impressions

Henrietta was a handsome woman with captivating ways and a magnolia skin who put a brave face on her struggles to survive and raise three children. She was also a bit of a snob. Despite her estrangement from her husband, the Seiberling family had allowed her to stay on in the gatehouse...

When the tall, awkward Wilson slouched over her doorstep that Saturday and proceeded to make himself too readily at home, Henrietta was appalled. She found him both vulgar and servile, with a smarmy grin; he was loud and garrulous. She disliked him on sight... He laughed too loudly, and showed too many teeth even when talking. He had this mannerism of rubbing his hands together and a simpering smile - a regular Uriah Heep. (Robertson, pp. 32-33)

This Bud's For You, Jesus

The so-called "First Century Christian Fellowship" had been a presence in Akron since 1924. Unlike their peers at New York's Calvary Church, the Akronites had a zeal for the special task of helping alcoholics, a passion that blossomed with "the 1931 conversion of Russell 'Bud' Firestone, scion of tire tycoon Harvey Firestone. Young Firestone was a notorious sot whose drinking had exasperated and mortified his prominent family". (Bill W. and Mr. Wilson, Matthew Raphael, pp. 100-101)

The grateful paterfamilias sponsored a huge festival for the Oxford Group in January of 1933. Buchman himself appeared at the gala. Reverend Tunks was among the dignitaries who met him at the train station. Henrietta Seiberling was present at this event as was Anne Smith. Dr. Bob was not.

Though the drinking problem was not mentioned in newspaper accounts, Bud and his grateful wife were fearless in their sharing at the banquet and rally. "'I gave my life to Jesus Christ,' Firestone told some of the nearly two thousand people in Polsky's auditorium....' (New Wine, Mel B., p. 67)

Shortly after the mammoth rally, Dr. Bob Smith would be dragged to Oxford Group gatherings by his increasingly impatient spouse.

"About the time of the beer experiment I was thrown in with a crowd of people who attracted me because of their seeming poise, health, and happiness.... I sensed they had something I did not have, from which I might readily profit. I learned that it was something of a spiritual nature, which did not appeal to me very much, but I thought it could do no harm. I gave the matter much time and study over the next two and a half years, but still got tight each night nevertheless." (BB, p. 178)

On a Mission from God

"Sometime in late 1932, Delphine Webber, a friend of the Smiths, called Henrietta Seiberling... to urge that 'something has to be done about Doctor Smith - his drinking, you know.' Henrietta had not known." (Not-God, p. 31) Although Anne Smith was persuaded to bring her husband to the Oxford Group meetings, the taciturn Vermonter remained what would be called in the modern AA world "walled up."

Over time, Henrietta grew closer to the Smiths, but there was no change in the doctor's drinking. She arranged, in the spring of 1935, a small meeting where other members bared their souls by sharing something "costly" to them. The strategy worked, and Dr. Bob confessed that he was a secret drinker.

"'From then on'", said Dorothy (Henrietta's daughter), "'that was a major concern - how to help him. No one knew anything about the problem.'" (Robertson, p. 53)

The timely arrival of Bill Wilson, loutish as she may have perceived him to be, was seen as Divine Providence.

The Portage Country Club

"Henrietta Seiberling arranged for Bill to move from the Mayflower Hotel to the Portage Country Club, Akron's finest. The club was just down the road from the Seiberling estate, and it also put Bill closer to the Smiths. Officially, he was the guest of club member John Gammeter, a self-made man with whom Bill felt himself to have a lot in common. Bill golfed at this club throughout his stay in Akron." (Hartigan, p. 83)

Wife Lois was less than impressed with her unemployed husband's hobnobbing with the wealthy. "There didn't seem to be very much happening in the proxy fight... And I can't say I liked thinking about his playing golf at this fancy country club, while I was working at Loesers." (Hartigan, p. 83)

After a couple of weeks Bill moved in with the Smiths, and stayed until the end of August. "Years later, Wilson looked fondly back on the summer of 1935 as the period in which Anne and Henrietta provided him and Dr. Bob with their 'infusion of spirituality.'" (Not-God p. 40)

In addition, "they readily accepted the generous invitation of T. Henry and Clarace Williams to bring whatever alcoholics they could to a regular Wednesday Oxford Group meeting at the Williams home - a meeting which had had its origin largely in Henrietta Seiberling's much earlier effort to 'do something' for Dr. Bob". (Not-God, p. 40)

Henrietta was involved that summer on almost a daily basis, and "always counted herself, along with Anne Smith, Bob, and Bill, as one of the four co-founders. From her perspective... the true origin of AA lay not in faraway events in New York, or even in Wilson's crisis in the Mayflower lobby, but rather in the Oxford Group's prior conversion of Doctor Smith". (Raphael, p. 106)

Not Religious Enough

Many find Alcoholics Anonymous to be religious, overly religious. From Henrietta Seiberling's perspective, the greater danger came from a conflicting source, a creeping secularism. She reacted adversely to a couple of speakers who were more psychology than "grace of God".

"Bob and Bill said to me, 'Henrietta, I don't think we should talk too much about religion or God.' I said to them, 'Well, we're not out to please the alcoholics. They have been pleasing themselves all these years. We are out to please God. And if you don't talk about what God does, and your faith, and your guidance, then you might as well be the Rotary Club or something like that. Because God is your only source of power.'" (1971 Interview with John Seiberling)

In the autumn of 1939, Clarace Williams complained to Seiberling about the alcoholics' abuse of her home, and of the Oxford Group's tenets. The OG folks thought that the Big Book was "commercial", and likely were not fans of the diluted spirituality of God "as we understood Him". October, 1939 saw the final split from the Oxforders. Cleveland had seceded six months earlier.

"'Henrietta told Dr. Bob that it (the split) was the worst mistake he had ever made,'... 'How could you do this? You'll be sorry.'" (Oldtimers, p. 218) Henrietta later reunited with the AA folks, but she was not active long in Akron, as she moved to New York.

Opposing the AA Conference

Bill Wilson led a campaign in the late forties to turn over AA's leadership to the groups. Seiberling was vehemently antagonistic to this plan. "Seiberling's campaign against the conference system of representation included charging Bill with having taken complete leave of his senses." (Hartigan, p. 188) Her private communications were even more strongly stated as "HS equates Wilson with 'the devil' come to 'destroy' AA". (Not-God, p. 355)

Bill did not hold a grudge, and the two saw a great deal of each other in New York. From 1944 and on, she spent time in both New York City, and Akron. Henrietta outlived Bill Wilson, passing in 1979 at the age of 91.

SECTION VI Publicity

Chapter 30 Willard Richardson and the Rockefellers

As Bill Wilson progressed through his third year of sobriety, his personal finances remained a struggle. He was forced by the compelling arguments of the "group conscience" to refuse a very appealing offer from Charles Towns to practice as a "lay therapist" at the upscale, but declining facility. But if he couldn't work for Towns, perhaps he could BE the next Towns.

"Bill knew all about the lucrative enterprise Towns (Hospital) had been in the boom days of the twenties, when wealthy actors such as John Barrymore and equally famous playboys had been willing to pour thousands of dollars a week into Charlie's till for a little discreet drying out." (Bill W., Robert Thomsen, p. 232) It was Towns' prescient hunch "that this AA business of yours is someday going to fill Madison Square Gardens". (Not-God, Ernest Kurtz, p. 64)

Spurred on by Hank Parkhurst, "the greatest high-pressure salesman Bill had ever known… the two of them immediately set to work approaching every rich man and every charitable foundation in Manhattan… and although many professed their sympathy, they saw no real reason to help drunks, who after all had brought their problems upon themselves… After six weeks of such talk, not one cent was raised". (Thomsen, p. 245)

"Angry and depressed, Wilson vented his spleen to his brother-in-law, Dr. Leonard V. Strong, in a 'diatribe about the stinginess and short-sightedness of the rich.' Bill had chosen his listener well and perhaps craftily." (Not-God, p. 65) Leonard was acquainted with Rev. Willard Richardson, a man connected with the philanthropies of the Rockefellers.

The Baptist Pastor

Willard S. Richardson (1866—1952), was an alumni of the International YMCA Training School, now called Springfield College, graduating in 1891.

> *Richardson was born in Painesville, Ohio and attended Denison University for two years. He also studied at the University of Rochester, worked at Springfield College, worked at Columbia University, and received his B.D. from the Union Theological Seminary in 1897. From 1894-1909, he worked as the assistant pastor at a Baptist church in New York City. He later joined the advisory staff to John D. Rockefeller, Jr., and was secretary for the Laura Spelman Rockefeller Memorial in New York City. Richardson served on the Board of Trustees at Springfield College and the American Institute of Christian Philosophy.*
>
> *In 1938, Springfield College presented him the Tarbell Medallion, an award for alumni who have demonstrated varied outstanding service to their alma mater. (Springfield College Digital Collections)*

Pink Cloud # 17

Strong called Richardson, and was well-remembered and graciously received. The clergyman, at the time in his early seventies, agreed to meet with Bill the very next day. Strong, in true "old school" gentlemanly fashion, provided a letter of introduction. The date of the letter, Oct. 26, 1937, shows that Wilson and Parkhurst were seeking funding for projects at least two months before the Akron "group conscience" vote giving approval to their grand schemes.

Richardson was favorably impressed with Bill's ideas, and after consulting other colleagues, set up a luncheon meeting with himself, Leonard and Bill. Out of this meeting came Richardson's offer of a meeting in John D. Rockefeller's private boardroom.

"Getting so close to Rockefeller money was a staggering notion, and as Bill remembered it, 'We were riding high on pink cloud number 17.'" (Pass It On,

p. 184) Dr. Bob and Paul S. came to New York for the meeting. A group of reliable New York alcoholics was gathered.

"The meeting... got off to an awkward start until somebody suggested that each alcoholic in the room tell his own story. After... Albert Scott declared, 'Why this is first-century Christianity!' Then he asked 'What can we do to help?'"(Pass It On, p. 184)

Scott was "head of an engineering firm and Chairman of the Board of Trustees of the Riverside Church in New York." (AA Comes of Age, p. 15) Following Bill's presentation re: hospital chains, paid missionaries, and literature, "Mr. Scott... asked an important question: 'Won't money spoil this thing?' ...The meeting ended, however, on what Bill considered to be a favorable note: Frank Amos offered to make an investigation of the tiny Fellowship." (Pass It On, p. 185)

The Amos Report

The advertising man, and close friend of John D. Jr., was impressed with Dr. Bob and the work going on in Akron. He wrote a report on his trip for Mr. Rockefeller.

"Bill's version of Amos's recommendations varies strikingly from what the report actually said. As Bill told the story... Amos said that an initial sum of fifty thousand dollars was needed. The money was to be used in building either a hospital for alcoholics or a 'recuperating home... Amos's report, which was submitted... (and) endorsed by Richardson, Scott, and (A Leroy) Chipman, suggested that Rockefeller provide a total of $10,000., $5,000 a year for two years, and it makes no mention of hospitals or recuperating homes." (Bill W., Francis Hartigan, p. 106)

In the end, the "world's richest man" cut this in half. The reformed drunks were crushingly disappointed with the $5,000. "In AA's case he felt so strongly that the fellowship must become self-supporting that, in agreeing to provide half of the ten thousand dollars Amos was requesting, he told his associates not to ask him again for money on its behalf." (Hartigan p. 107)

The Rockefellers were strict Baptists, allowing neither drinking nor smoking in their home, and this faith had a direct bearing on the interest in AA. John D. elected to assist the budding organization, but on his own terms.

Dreams Never Die, Just the Dreamer

The most ambitious of the dreams for hospitals, and paid missionaries had vaporized, and with them Bill Wilson's dream of becoming "Recovery CEO". In the end, John D. Rockefeller may have saved AA from the ambitions of its own members.

"Uncle Dick Richardson was definitely disappointed, and so were friends Amos, Chipman, and Strong. Seeing that they were not in complete agreement with Mr. Rockefeller, we renewed our pleas for aid. Maybe they knew other men of wealth who might be solicited with more success. To our delight all four thought this possible, and we held frequent meetings to talk about it." (AACOA, p. 151)

These discussions led to the formation of the Alcoholic Foundation.

The Alcoholic Foundation

"On August 11, 1938, with the help of John Wood, a young lawyer, they established a tax-exempt, charitable entity called the Alcoholic Foundation. The foundation had little money, but it gave the movement a legally formed, New York-based center." (Getting Better, Nan Robertson, p. 68) The five members of the board of trustees were Dr. Bob, Bill R. of New York, and the nonalcoholic majority of Willard Richardson, Frank Amos, and John Wood.

"The trust agreement stipulated that an alcoholic trustee would have to resign immediately if he got drunk. (This actually happened in the case of the New York member, and he was replaced forthwith.)" (Pass It On, p. 188)

The Name "Alcoholics Anonymous"

There has been much debate, and some misinformation, regarding the first use of the name "Alcoholics Anonymous". The book thumpers like to say that the fellowship is named after the book, and came after the book.

"There is some dispute about who first thought up this title; most thought it was Joe W., a New Yorker writer who remained sober only 'on and off.' ...The first documented use of the name in the AA archives is in a letter from Bill to Willard Richardson dated July 15, 1938.... (in) an invitation to... (members of) the Rockefeller Foundation to come to any of the Clinton Street meetings, Bill wrote, 'we shall gladly waive the heavy drinking that has qualified us for Alcoholics Anonymous.' ...There, the name is used in such a way that Richardson was already familiar with it." (Pass It On, p. 202)

At this point in time, only two book chapters had been written, and the members' decision regarding the name of the book was some six months away. "'One Hundred Men' was still the working title in a letter from Frank Amos to the Rockefeller associates dated January 6, 1939. But 'Alcoholics Anonymous' headlined the letter, indicating that this had by now become an informal way, at least in New York, of identifying the movement." (Pass It On, p. 202)

The claim that the fellowship is named after the book has serious problems.

Steeee-Rike Two

"In 1940, John D. Rockefeller Jr. gave a dinner for AA. Although Rockefeller had stayed in the background, he had continued to follow AA's progress with real interest. Willard Richardson, by now 'Uncle Dick' to Bill, announced the proposed dinner at a trustee meeting. Bill was elated; he again started to think in millions...

"The dinner was held on February 8, at Manhattan's exclusive Union Club. Of the 400 prominent and influential people invited, 75 accepted." (Pass It On, p. 232) All went well until a young Nelson Rockefeller, standing in for his unwell uncle, declared to the assembled captains of industry that "it is our belief that Alcoholics Anonymous should be self-supporting so far as money is concerned. It needs only our goodwill." (Pass It On, p. 233)

"It is as marvelous as Bill told it... It has come down as a key scene in AA's oral history. But that is not quite what happened. The minutes of the after-dinner remarks show that Nelson Rockefeller did not speak at all.... The two accounts... illustrate perfectly Bill's life-long penchant for embroidering the facts while accurately summarizing the gist of an event." (Robertson, pp. 77-78)

Again, dreams of millions were quashed, and possibly also the disastrous problems that a great influx of capital may have generated. AA did get a few thousand, a mailing list, and a tremendous headline - "Rockefeller Dines Former Tosspots". The Rockefellers would again assist Richardson and the Alcoholic Foundation with a loan to redeem the outstanding Works Publishing shares. It would be the mid-40s before AA became self-supporting.

Denoument

Willard Richardson had provided the access to the Rockefeller millions that may have led to the very downfall of Alcoholics Anonymous. Wiser heads prevailed, and the great Rockefeller gift to AA was credibility. Additionally, the Rockefeller people established, and served on the Alcoholic Foundation. Legal services were provided by a Rockefeller man.

In 1951, AA lost William Silkworth, "the little doctor who loved drunks", and in 1952, they lost another treasured friend, longtime trustee and staunch supporter, "Uncle Dick" Richardson. "These two died happily confident that AA was at last secure and on its way." (AACOA, p. 219)

Indeed it was.

Chapter 31 Selling AA - Early Publicity

"The reminiscences available and those interviewed from early Akron and Cleveland all strongly testify that in the early days, at least in their area, 'selling the program' was a work of promotion rather than mere attraction." (Not-God, Ernest Kurtz, p. 100n.)

When the co-founders "counted noses" in the Fall of 1937, the forty or so now sober, previously "incurables" encouraged the idea that what they were doing was working. While Bob Smith glanced backwards with gratitude and satisfaction, the visionary Bill Wilson's focus was directed toward the future.

Dreams of alcoholic hospitals, a book, and paid missionaries were perhaps, simultaneously grand and grandiose. These schemes would require money, and lots of it. "If a world-wide movement was going to take millions of dollars to launch, no problem: they'd raise millions." (Bill W., Robert Thomsen, p. 245)

These grand schemes did not materialize, the alcoholics receiving only a pittance from the "world's wealthiest man". A small 1938 bequest was gone in a short time.

The Reader's Digest

There was no Rockefeller money remaining to proceed with the book, the most modest of the envisioned projects. Bill and Hank had decided to "self-publish", and to raise the requisite financing through the sale of shares.

"They approached everyone who'd attended a meeting, every rich man they knew, and they did not sell a single share of stock...They needed some kind of inspiration and Hank P. was the man for inspirations. Their timid customers had to believe the book would sell, and a book had to have one thing in order to sell - publicity, a huge spread in some national magazine." (Thomsen, p. 252)

Then, they reported that the Reader's Digest was interested.

The Reader's Digest tale sparked share sale funds, and full-scale work on the book writing began, the funds paying the office costs and living expenses of the two entrepreneurs. It is entirely possible that the two desperate promoters may have completely exaggerated the magazine's level of interest. When they returned, a year later, with an actual book, the "editor seemed not to remember his earlier conversation... and no article was forthcoming." (Hartigan, p. 126)

Another version of the tale has the Digest editor reporting that the editorial board had vetoed the plan for a piece on alcoholism.

The most cynical might suspect that the entire story had been concocted.

5,000 Books. Buyers?... Not so much

"The 5,000 copies of the Big Book lay idle in Edward Blackwell's warehouse. For months after their publication, it seemed, that they were a waste of the paper they were printed on." (Pass It On, p. 207)

There were some favorable book reviews, none of which led to any significant book sales. On June 25, 1939, the New York Times review said, in part, "the general thesis of Alcoholics Anonymous is more solidly based psychologically than any other treatment of the subject I have ever come upon". (Pass It On, p. 223) The fact that the book was not available in stores was unquestionably detrimental.

A paean from Dr. Harry Emerson Fosdick appeared only in religious publications. "In February, 1940, reviews in Newsweek and Time also produced some inquiries and sales, though they remained modest." (Bill W., Francis Hartigan, p. 128)

Some reviewers were less than kind.

"Alcoholics and God"

In the summer of 1939, the fellowship's very good friend, Charles Towns, "told the AA story to Morris Markey, a writer, who took it to Fulton Oursler, at the time editor of Liberty Magazine, a popular national weekly. Oursler accepted an AA piece by Markey entitled 'Alcoholics and God'". (Pass It On, pp. 223-224)

"Most members of Alcoholics Anonymous - wary of being labeled a 'religious' group - winced at both the heading and the article's content." (Not-God, p. 90) Markey's insistence that the root of the new fellowship was religion failed to fire the imagination of the American public.

Although generally presented as a success, historian Ernest Kurtz disagrees. "The Liberty treatment was the second failure of nationwide publicity. Earlier in the summer of 1939, the irrepressible Morgan R... remembered still another well-placed friend... the popular radio journalist Gabriel Heatter (who) was willing to interview him on his nationwide broadcast." (Not-God, p. 90)

On the Radio

The group was ambivalent, anonymity concerns battling an honest desire to bring the benefits they were sure would result, should their new solution be brought to the American consciousness. There were also, of course, the unsold books sitting idly in the Cornwall Press warehouse.

Further trepidation came in the reality that Morgan's sobriety was inconsistent - there had been some "unfortunate incidents". The red-headed Irishman reluctantly consented to being put under 24 hour guard, for the time leading up to the April 25th radio program.

The entrepreneurial Hank P. concocted a plan to magnify the publicity value of the "We The People" appearance. Promissory notes were issued to raise the $500.

On the fateful evening, Morgan performed brilliantly, and the expectant alcoholics waited three days before heading to their PO box, armed with suitcases, to retrieve the avalanche of reply cards. There were twelve, mostly conveying the sarcastic comments of inebriated physicians. Only two were orders for the book.

It was a crushing blow.

My Name is Elrick, and I'm an Alcoholic, Sort of

"Elrick B. Davis, a feature writer of deep understanding, was the author of a series of articles that were printed in the middle of the (Cleveland) Plain Dealer's editorial page... In effect the Plain Dealer was saying, 'Alcoholics Anonymous is good, and it works. Come and get it.' The newspaper's switchboard was deluged". (Alcoholics Anonymous Comes of Age, p. 20)

Cleveland's power-driving AA proselytizer, Clarence Snyder, told his fellow members that he had found Davis "on a barstool". But, early Cleveland member Warren C. thought otherwise. "'Clarence sneaked a Plain Dealer reporter into one of the meetings. He posed as an alcoholic. He wasn't really. He was a writer,' Warren said." (Dr. Bob and the Good Oldtimers, p. 203)

The articles appeared in the latter part of October, 1939, and were clearly one of the primary factors leading to the explosive growth of AA in Cleveland. There was an almost immediate multiplication of the city's number of groups, "but the split had less to do with greater numbers than with the Cleveland members' disagreement with Clarence S. over the publicity itself and so over the fellowship's yet uncertain understanding of anonymity". (Not-God, p. 85)

A follow-up sermon by Dilworth Lupton on November 26, 1939 - a sermon widely distributed in pamphlet form - "furnished the occasion for further favorable newspaper treatment into 1940". (Not-God, p. 85)

AA growth in Cleveland exploded.

Rocky and Friends... Revisited

On February 8th, 1940, John D. Rockefeller gave a dinner for AA at Manhattan's exclusive Union Club. "Bill was elated, he again started to think in millions. He assumed...that Mr. Rockefeller had changed his mind and had decided to give AA money." (Pass It On, p. 232)

Four hundred of New York's "prominent and wealthy" were invited. Former ad man, and star of the Gabriel Heatter broadcast, Morgan R. provided the evening's finest line. The impeccably dressed former tosspot was asked by a gray-haired banker who was his tablemate, "'Mr. R., what institution are you with?' Morgan grinned and replied, 'Well, sir, I am not with any institution at the moment. Nine months ago, however, I was a patient in the Greystone Asylum.'" (Pass It On, p. 233)

Bill was crowd-watching, and could tell that the 75 or so of New York's elite who had come were "deeply impressed with what they were hearing... It was evident we had captured their sympathetic interest. Great influence and great wealth were soon to be at our disposal." (Pass It On, p. 233)

The words of the substitute host, Nelson Rockefeller, were devastating.

"'It is our belief that Alcoholics Anonymous should be self-supporting so far as money is concerned. It needs only our goodwill.' ...after cordial handshakes and good-byes all around, the whole billion dollars of them walked out the door." (Pass It On, p. 233) There are more reliable reports that Nelson, in fact, said nothing beyond that he was not empowered to speak on behalf of his absent uncle.

In spite of a few bizarre headlines, the Rockefeller endorsement provoked some credibility-enhancing write-ups, and an increasing portion of the public came to know, at least in a general way, what Alcoholics Anonymous was.

"In the Spring of 1940... Rollie H., catcher for the Cleveland Indians, revealed that he had been sober in AA for a year. The story, when it broke, was carried in sports pages of newspapers across the country. Because his drunkenness was a matter of public record... his sobriety was very big news." (Pass It On, p. 236)

"Rollicking Rollie" was subsequently interviewed about his rehabilitation, in all the American League cities throughout the nation. "His full name and picture, as a member of AA, were seen by millions of fans. It did us plenty of good, temporarily, because alcoholics flocked in."(Grapevine, Jan., 1955)

For alcoholics, these forays into the alluring limelight can be fraught with perils to the individual, and to the society itself.

"We found that we had to rely on the principle of attraction rather than of promotion... Obviously, AA had to be publicized somehow, so we resorted to the idea that it would be far better to let our friends do this for us." (12 + 12, p. 181)

Anonymity's "deeper purpose is actually to keep those fool egos of ours from running hog wild after money and public fame at AA's expense". (AA-COA, p. 43)

Nevertheless, "through the summer of 1940, the wake of the Hemsley publicity proved not only unthreatening but uniquely beneficial... Hemsley's example contributed to the sobering of a strategically located and respected Catholic priest... Later in 1940, Wilson could and would approve the use of pictures in the Jack Alexander Saturday Evening Post story, but for which concession the story might not have been carried... (T)he foundation was laid for the later breaking of anonymity 'for the sake of the good of others' by Marty Mann". (Not-God, p. 87)

Founder Flounders

Bill Wilson himself was something of an anonymity breaker himself in the forties. He later told self-deprecating tales of ego inflation, but at the time, he justified these actions. "Bill granted interviews, complete with full name and pictures. When AA members criticized his seeming thirst for publicity, his answer was that, as AA founder he should be an exception. People responded to leaders." (Hartigan, p. 156)

He also defended his own breaches based on noble motives. "He wasn't doing it for himself, but for the greater good of the greater number. The others weren't buying it." (Hartigan, p. 135)

And, "he created another firestorm in 1945 when he endorsed Marty's decision to reveal her membership in AA in order to garner publicity for the new organization (NCEA)." (Hartigan, p. 184)

The Saturday Evening Post

In the twenty-first century, it is difficult to have a full appreciation of the magnitude of the Saturday Evening Post within the American culture, during that era. In a world of limited media, newspapers, magazines, and radio had a scope defying our imagining. The biggest and most popular of these were within the awareness of a huge segment of the population.

"On March 1, 1941, an article on AA by Jack Alexander appeared in the Saturday Evening Post. The effect of the Alexander article was stunning. AA membership opened 1941 at 2,000 and closed the year at 8,000." (Dragon, p. 178)

"Unlike the fellowship's previous media hits, this time the response exceeded anyone's wildest expectations. Within days, meeting attendance doubled. Within weeks, these newcomers were being sent out on Twelve Step calls to other prospects." (Hartigan, p. 143)

"It accomplished exactly what Bill had first hoped the Gabriel Heatter broadcast would do. It put AA irrevocably on the map of national consciousness." (Pass It On, p. 248)

At the last moment, there was a real dilemma, the editors "wanted real photographs to illustrate the article... and some of them had to be on the sensational side... We objected... Finally the Post said, 'No pictures, no article.' The choice was ours, and it was a hard one." (Pass It On, p. 247)

"'It was a crucial decision which happily turned out to be the right one - that is, for the time being.' Bill said." (Pass It On, p. 247)

AA was now a national institution.

Afterword

By the early 1950s, Bill Wilson was able to write that regarding AA's need for publicity, "it would be far better to let our friends do that for us. Precisely that has happened, to an unbelievable extent". (Twelve and Twelve, p. 181) Overall, the press has been kind to Alcoholics Anonymous, and continues to be so. Alcoholics Anonymous can well afford, if it chooses, to follow its anonymity traditions.

Some individual members, especially in the new millennium, are opting for a different approach. Following the examples of celebrities who have gone public with previously hidden issues such as depression, some recovered celebrity alcoholics are "outing themselves" regarding their own battles with alcoholism. The obvious hope is the removal of the shame attached to the admission of such "failings". Time will tell if this latest approach to publicity causes more harm, or more good.

Either way, non-anonymous publicity is not unprecedented.

Chapter 32 Anonymity in the 21st Century

Hemsley 'Through Drinking Forever'

'Alcoholics Anonymous' Given Credit For Reform

Rollicking Rollie Says He's Been On Wagon A Year

By The United Press

CHICAGO, April 18—Rollie Hemsley, Cleveland Indian catcher announced today that he was "through drinking forever."

"I'm telling all this because I'm sure I can help somebody else who can't leave the bottle alone," said the 33-year-old player. Drinking has had him in trouble since he joined the Pirates in 1928.

Hemsley gave all credit for his reform to an organization known as "Alcoholics Anonymous," to which he was introduced by two Cleveland

you might call a drinking disease, people who can't stop, no matter how hard they try."

From Pittsburgh Hemsley went to the Cubs, the Reds and the Browns before going to Cleveland. With each club it had been his drinking that prevented him from making good.

"I haven't had a drink in a year," he said today, "so that proved the thing to myself. I've been meaning to tell this for some time and I guess Feller's no-hit game put me in the right frame of mind for it."

A Nameless Group of Drunks

In the 1930s the whole concept of "anonymity" was very simple.

Bill Wilson's "nameless group of drunks", helping themselves by helping each other, were progressing into unprecedented months, and even years of sobriety. The admission of alcoholism, so vital to recovery, could, at a public level, bring career and social consequences, as devastating as those from active drinking. It was vital that "prospects" be able to come and try this new therapy with the explicit assurance that they could do so with absolute confidentiality. Wilson recounts for us the thoughts of this time period:

> *Anonymity was not born of confidence; it was the child of our early fears. Our first nameless groups of alcoholics were secret societies. New prospects could find us only through a few trusted friends. The bare hint of publicity, even for our work, shocked us. Though ex-drinkers, we still thought we had to hide from public distrust and contempt.*
>
> *When the Big Book appeared in 1939, we called it "Alcoholics Anonymous." Its foreword made this revealing statement: "It is important that we remain anonymous because we are too few, at present, to handle the overwhelming number of personal*

> *appeals which may result from this publication. Being mostly business and professional folk, we could not well carry on our occupations in such an event."* Between these lines, it is easy to read our fear that large numbers of incoming people might break our anonymity wide open. (Twelve and Twelve, pp. 184-5)

The actual impact of the book was initially stingingly disappointing, but tremendous growth did come, albeit somewhat later. The earliest anonymity concerns were the least complex, and the most important. "Clearly, every AA member's name – and story too – had to be confidential, if he wished." (Twelve and Twelve, p. 185) Though the social stigma attached to alcoholism has diminished significantly, each person's right to decide his own level of privacy remains paramount. As the new society experienced explosive growth in the early forties, lessons were learned, and the initial simple "anonymity" idea morphed into a broader "tradition", incorporating principles of humility, unity, equality, sacrifice, and responsibility.

The Yellow Card

The "Yellow Card" is read at many meetings: "Who you see here, what you hear here, when you leave here, let it stay here".

> *In the early days of AA, when more stigma was attached to the term "alcoholic" than is the case today, this reluctance to be identified – and publicised – was easy to understand. As the Fellowship grew, we came to realize also that many problem drinkers might hesitate to turn to us for help if they thought their problem might be discussed publicly, even inadvertently, by others; and that much of our relative effectiveness in working with alcoholics might be impaired if we sought or accepted public recognition. (Alcoholics Anonymous in Devon)*

The Oxford Group

Several reasons propelled the "nameless group of drunks" to disassociate themselves from the Oxford Group. One motivation involved the contradictory views of the two societies regarding publicity:

> *Because of the stigma then attached to the condition, most alcoholics wanted to be anonymous. We were afraid also of developing erratic public characters who, through broken anonymity, might get drunk in public and so destroy confidence*

in us. The Oxford Group, on the contrary, depended very much upon the use of prominent names—something that was doubtless all right for them but mighty hazardous for us. (AA Comes Of Age, p. 75)

The Cleveland Indians

The eyes of America were firmly fixed on the sport of baseball in 1940. It was a way of celebrating an economic recovery that had been such a long time coming, and it provided a distraction from the escalating problems in Europe. Baseball excitement was especially feverish in Cleveland, Ohio, where Indians' fans were electrified by the performances of future Hall of Famer, "Bullet" Bob Feller. The Iowa farm boy had pitched his first game in 1936 at the age of seventeen, and struck out an astonishing fifteen batters. To provide guidance and support to Feller, the team's manager and owner hired an experienced catcher, and an alcoholic, Rollie Hemsley.

Hemsley had talent and experience with a variety of teams. However, "wherever he had played, the catcher's bizarre behavior revealed him to be the team drunk." (Ernest Kurtz, Not-God: A History of Alcoholics Anonymous, p. 86) Rollie Hemsley's fame as personal catcher, and mentor to the young "phenom", exponentially escalated on opening day of the 1940 season when he caught Feller's no-hitter.

> *In a Chicago hotel news conference of 16 April 1940, Rollie Hemsley, erratic star catcher for the Cleveland Indians baseball team, announced that his past eccentric behavior on and off the diamond had been due to "booze," that he was an alcoholic who had been dry now for one year "with the help of and through Alcoholics Anonymous." (Not-God, p. 85) Newspaper stories about this event were sensational and they brought in many new prospects. Nevertheless this development was one of the first to arouse deep concern about our personal anonymity at the top public level. (AA Comes of Age, pp. 24-5)*

The Hemsley publicity continued, and it was nationwide. Although not always decorous, the exposure was effective in drawing problem drinkers into AA. Hemsley's status as a "spokesperson" for AA provoked a reaction in Bill Wilson: certainly jealousy, and perhaps a bit of resentment. "Soon I was on the road, happily handing out personal interviews and pictures", Bill wrote. "To my delight, I found I could hit the front pages, just as he could. Besides he couldn't hold his publicity pace, but I could hold mine... For two or three years I guess I was AA's number one anonymity breaker." In fact, Wilson may have over-sold his own misbehavior "to illustrate how baser human emotions such as competitiveness and envy can be disguised as motives of altruism and desire for the highest good." (Pass It On, pp. 237-38)

Explosive Growth in Cleveland

Cleveland had become the hot-bed of AA, six months prior to the Hemsley media hype, and that had everything to do with a series of articles in the local newspaper, the Cleveland Plain Dealer.

Clarence Snyder was the driving force behind the phenomenon that was Cleveland AA. A highly successful car salesman, Clarence had skills that were the result of hard work and very innovative marketing approaches. He brought these skills to AA, and was an aggressive recruiter and a publicity seeker. Clarence told everyone that Elrick B. Davis, a reporter from the Cleveland Plain Dealer, had been plunked off a bar stool and was attending AA meetings "as a customer". But was he?

According to early member, Warren C., "Clarence sneaked a Plain Dealer reporter into one of the meetings. He posed as an alcoholic. He wasn't really. He was a writer.... Whatever his status, the articles Davis wrote set off an unprecedented wave of growth for AA in the Cleveland area."

> *On 21 October 1939, Cleveland's most prestigious newspaper, the Plain Dealer, published the first of an editorially supported series of seven articles by reporter Elrick B. Davis. Both the articles and the editorials calmly and approvingly described Alcoholics Anonymous, emphasizing the reasonable hope this new society held out to otherwise hopeless drunks. (Not-God, p.84)*

As Bill described the series: "In effect the Plain Dealer was saying, 'Alcoholics Anonymous is good, and it works. Come and get it'". Hundreds did; by the following year, the city had 20 to 30 groups and several hundred members. Said Bill, "Their results were...so good, and AA's membership elsewhere...so small, that many a Clevelander really thought AA had started there in the first place". (Pass It On, p. 224)

Clarence, Rollie, & Marty – Beneficial Breaches

The story of Rollie Hemsley, recounted in detail above, was used as evidence of the danger of a public relations policy which employs "promotion", i.e. celebrity endorsement. Without debating its reality as a problem, there were unquestionable corresponding benefits. Hundreds of thousands of people came to know of the existence of Alcoholics Anonymous as the result of the Hemsley interviews, and it is unimaginable that this celebrity endorsement did not lead to a significant spike in membership numbers and sales of the Big Book.

The most dramatic positive outcomes EVER produced by an anonymity breach, were those that resulted from Mrs. Marty Mann going public as a person who had recovered from alcoholism through participation in AA. This tale is told in some detail in another chapter (Marty Mann and the Early Women of AA). Tremendous benefits came from disregarding AA's pro-anonymity position, a stance in the process of being codified. With the blessing of Bill Wilson himself, the opposite of our "official policy" was done to "serve the greater good." Clarence Snyder had taken it upon himself to do the same seven years earlier, with the Cleveland Plain Dealer. The explosive growth of AA in Cleveland witnesses the upside to his "wrong" actions.

The 12 Traditions

> *Everywhere there arose threatening questions of membership, money, personal relations, public relations, management of groups, clubs, and scores of other perplexities. It was out of this vast welter of explosive experience that AA's Twelve Traditions were first published in 1946 and later confirmed at AA's First International Convention, held at Cleveland in 1950. (Twelve & Twelve, p. 18)*

These then are the long form traditions developed in the early years of AA that deal with the issue of anonymity. "Our AA experience has taught us that":

> **Tradition Eleven.** *Our relations with the general public should be characterized by personal anonymity. We think AA ought to avoid sensational advertising. Our names and pictures as AA members ought not be broadcast, filmed, or publicly printed. Our public relations should be guided by the principle of attraction rather than promotion. There is never need to praise ourselves. We feel it better to let our friends recommend us.*

> **Tradition Twelve.** *And finally, we of Alcoholics Anonymous believe that the principle of anonymity has immense spiritual significance. It reminds us that we are to place principles before personalities; that we are actually to practice a genuine*

humility. This to the end that our great blessings may never spoil us; that we shall forever live in thankful contemplation of Him who presides over us all.

Anonymity in the 21st Century

The stories of Marty Mann, Clarence Snyder, and "Rollicking Rollie" Hemsley have specific relevance to the recovery world of 2013. That there has been a recent spate of anonymity breaches by celebrities is nothing new, but of late, AA's very principles of anonymity themselves have been called to question. David Colman, a writer for the New York Times, broke his own anonymity as a 15 year sober member of Alcoholics Anonymous, with the May 6, 2011 article "Challenging the Second 'A' in AA": "More and more anonymity is seeming like an anachronistic vestige of the Great Depression, when AA got started and when alcoholism was seen as not just a weakness, but a disgrace."

Colman then lists a few of the numerous memoirs of recent years from recovered/recovering 12 steppers from Eric Clapton and Nikki Sixx to Nic Scheff and Augusten Burroughs. James Frey's "A Million Little Pieces", fabricated in part though it was, took an significant segment of the North American public to the worlds of addiction, treatment, and Oprah. Ironically, Frey is not an anonymity breaker from AA's perspective as he rejected AA, and is not a member.

Eminem ("Recovery") and Pink ("Sober") have been very public about their enthusiasm for sober living which they achieved and sustain through participation in 12 Step recovery. "I think it's extremely healthy that anonymity is fading", says Clancy Martin, a philosophy professor at the University of Missouri, who had recently broke his own anonymity in "Harper's" magazine.

The violations by ordinary members of Facebook, and other social media, are legion. Maer Roshan's excitement about sobriety led to his becoming editor of The Fix, a Web magazine directed at the recovery world. "Having to deny your participation in a program that is helping your life doesn't make sense to me", he offers. Author and AA member Susan Cheever wrote an essay in "The Fix" entitled "Is It Time to Take the Anonymous Out of AA?" She writes, "We are in the midst of a public health crisis when it comes to understanding and treating addiction". She's sees AA's anonymity policies as contributing to the public's lack of insight into these problems and their solution.

Congressmen Patrick Kennedy and Jim Ramstad acknowledged their own membership in AA while actively campaigning for a bill to get insurance companies to provide better coverage for addiction treatment. "The personal identification that Jim and I brought to this issue as recovering alcoholics gave us a place from which to speak about this. Stigma here is our biggest barrier, and knowledge and understanding are the antidote to stigma."

Comedian and late night talk show host, Craig Ferguson, on the occasion of his 15th year sobriety anniversary, talked for about ten minutes about his addiction and recovery from alcoholism. Without explicitly saying that he was a member of Alcoholics Anonymous, he cleverly and clearly made the disclosure advising anyone with a problem with alcohol to seek help from an tremendous organization that is listed "at the front of the phone book, the VERY front!" Years before, a different celebrity told Johnny Carson that "he was attending a 12 Step program that dealt with alcohol".

Such word games are addressed by Cheever. "I am increasingly uncomfortable with the level of dishonesty. This dancing around and hedging, figuring out ways of saying it that aren't saying it... all the 'code words.' I am sure this is not what Bill intended."

My name is Roger, and I'm an alcoholic

Chicago Sun-Times film critic and television personality, Roger Ebert, died Thursday, April 4, 2013, ending a lengthy battle with cancer. On August 25, 2009, Ebert had gone very public in a well-read blog – *My name is Roger, and I'm an alcoholic* – about his "other" disease, alcoholism, and his 30 years of recovery as a member of Alcoholics Anonymous. (Friends from Chicago assure me that he was a real member, and a good one.) The blog, of course, is a horrendous violation of AA's eleventh tradition, but it is done magnificently – a glowing tribute to Alcoholics Anonymous. The piece is well-written, respectful, accurate, and dripping with gratitude. I see NO attempt at self-aggrandizement or attention-seeking.

This is a "good-bye letter" from a dying man.

Here are Ebert's own words in answer to the obvious question.

> *You may be wondering, in fact, why I'm violating the A.A. policy of anonymity and outing myself. AA is anonymous not because of shame but because of prudence; people who go public with their newly-found sobriety have an alarming tendency to*

relapse. Case studies: those pathetic celebrities who check into rehab and hold a press conference.

In my case, I haven't taken a drink for 30 years, and this is God's truth: Since the first AA meeting I attended, I have never wanted to. Since surgery in July of 2006 I have literally not been able to drink at all. Unless I go insane and start pouring booze into my g-tube, I believe I'm reasonably safe. So consider this blog entry what AA calls a "12th step," which means sharing the program with others. There's a chance somebody will read this and take the steps toward sobriety.

The 1,400 + comments BEFORE his death indicate that he very likely did reach some folks, and his recent passing will surely add to the numbers who will read the essay. With AA's admonition to "Keep an Open Mind", I urge you to read Ebert's blog. It is difficult to imagine any harm done by this exceeding the good.

Good or bad, right or wrong, the pathway for these anonymity breakers was forged many years ago by Mrs. Marty Mann. Time will tell if disaster is to befall us. Thus far, the sky is not falling.

Made in the USA
Middletown, DE
20 June 2017